AF322950

LANGUAGE AND STYLE SERIES

General Editor: STEPHEN ULLMANN

15

THE LITERARY TEXT: An Examination of Critical Methods

P. M. WETHERILL

OXFORD
BASIL BLACKWELL
1974

ISBN 0 631 15290 3

Library of Congress Catalog Card No.

73–86ø1ø

Printed in Great Britain by
Western Printing Services Ltd., Bristol
and bound at
The Kemp Hall Bindery, Oxford

Words move, music moves
Only in time; but that which is only living
Can only die. Words, after speech, reach
Into the silence. Only by the form, the pattern,
Can words or music reach
The stillness, as a Chinese jar still
Moves perpetually in its stillness.
Not the stillness of the violin, while the note lasts,
Not that only, but the co-existence,
Or say that the end precedes the beginning,
And the end and the beginning were always there
Before the beginning and after the end.
And all is always now. Words strain,
Crack and sometimes break, under the burden,
Under the tension, slip, slide, perish,
Decay with imprecision, will not stay in place,
Will not stay still.

T. S. Eliot: *Four Quartets*:
Burnt Norton V ll. 137–59

This world is very fair to see.
The artist will not let it be.
He fiddles with the works of God
And makes them look uncommon odd.

Sir Walter Raleigh

CONTENTS

ACKNOWLEDGEMENTS

Many people have helped me to write this book: Professor Stephen Ullmann, whose bibliographical, planning and stylistic advice was invaluable; Mrs. L. R. Harrison, of the University of Salford, who read the manuscript, part of which she also typed and who helped to correct many stylistic lapses; Miss Margaret Johnston, who typed the rest of the manuscript; my wife, who scrutinized the manuscript and made many useful suggestions; Dr. A. R. W. James, of the University of Manchester, who showed me how to make my points more clearly; Mr. R. P. Carr, Assistant Librarian in the University of Manchester, whose invaluable help enabled me to produce a precise and homogeneous bibliography and index. Mr. Carr, with Dr. James and Mr. B. Jean, also helped me to check the proofs.

My warm thanks are due to all these. The faults which my book still undoubtedly contains are my sole responsibility.

Manchester, May 1973.

AUTHOR'S NOTE

References in square brackets given in the body of the text relate to the bibliography. The first figure given indicates the number of the bibliographical entry, the second ('p. ') indicates the page number.

INTRODUCTION

Criticism, like the literature it serves and feeds upon, gets more bewildering every day. Traditionalism and advanced attitudes clash and combine to produce a vast multiplicity of approaches and methods. Thibaudet [681, p. 21] divided criticism into that of the cultivated man in the street, professional criticism and the criticism produced by writers themselves. Such a division is still valid but it hides a process of increasing fragmentation within each category—or between categories. It is startling to realize, for example, that critical methods firmly rooted in the nineteenth century are still very much alive in the age of Joyce and Proust.

This means, as one might expect, that the subject of my book only concerns one aspect of modern criticism. It also implies that even within the area I have examined a large number of different approaches are possible: although they are all anxious to base their findings on a close examination of literary texts, Jean-Pierre Richard and Jean Starobinski are very different, as are Cleanth Brooks and I. A. Richards.

There are reasonably different national trends too: French close criticism which is at times given to contorted and pretentious expression tends rather to be based on a pre-established body of theories (linguistic, psychoanalytical) and 'authorities'; it frequently aims at overall general statements. In the English-speaking world under the influence of such pioneers as I. A. Richards and W. Empson, the tendency is rather towards more detailed empirical description often in a much more relaxed style. Influences peculiar to one group of scholars play their part therefore in distinguishing them from critics working in a somewhat different tradition. The difficulty for anyone writing a book like this is therefore to maintain an adequate balance when surveying different national groups. Even where basic common influences are involved, critics tend to be cut off from their colleagues in other countries. It takes time for ideas and attitudes to filter through to them. A reading of a journal like *Modern Fiction Studies* shows how ignorant English speakers tend to be of foreign critical methods and theories. The French would seem to be even more strikingly isolated: at a colloquium recently Gérard Genette, a sensitive and gifted critic, said 'I am almost incapable of reading anything which is not in French . . . some of us here think they have invented things which in fact already exist elsewhere.' [538, p. 258] Doubrovsky's useful survey *Pourquoi la nouvelle critique* gives the impression that only French speakers go in for criticism. Elsewhere a writer is praised for 'renewing modern criticism' [130, pp. 127–8] although the structuralist notions of coherence which he is supposed to have clarified have been current in English-speaking countries for some forty years. A number of *Langue française* [373] contains a general article on the *New Critics* which would be superfluous in a specialized English language journal [263]. Such a time lag, which can be explained in terms of the French educational system (especially as far as the teaching of modern languages and of subsidiary subjects at University is concerned) is illustrated by other phenomena: Richards's two fundamental books (*Principles of Literary Criticism* and *Practical Criticism*) have, as far as I know, never been translated into French. What scant reference to them there is gives the impression that they were published some time in the 50s!; Auerbach's *Mimesis* (1946) Spitzer's *Stilstudien* (1928) and a key work like Hugo Friedrich's *Montaigne* (1949) have only just been translated . . .

On the other hand there is a community of interest over and above national differences. The importance of the subconscious is recognized generally, as is the need to bear linguistic and perhaps even Marxist-sociological attitudes in mind. The main influence (because it concerns the whole cultural context of the nineteenth and twentieth centuries) is, of course, Romanticism itself. Romanticism, which is the climate in which all western society has lived for the last 150 years, stresses what distinguishes one man from another; it also attaches great importance to the world of feeling. It therefore makes the two primary aims of textual criticism possible: *to consider a text in its individual entirety and as an imaginative phenomenon* (*rather than as a mere collection of ideas*).

This was the context which made close textual criticism possible. The initial impulse actually to put such an approach into practice may well have been the swing in taste in the 1920s towards English metaphysical poetry. Readers of Donne, Crashaw or Marvell are confronted with such compactness of language, such an exploitation of ambiguity that only close inspection and careful description will enable us to understand the mechanisms and meanings involved. Once this principle is established, the extreme usefulness of textual criticism becomes apparent (especially if, as was the case, such a tendency coincides with the growth, inter alia, of linguistics, structuralism and psychoanalysis).

Once a movement starts, it feeds on itself. The inter-action of the ingredients so far given strengthened the growing desire to examine literary texts on their own terms. Literary criticism, it was felt, should be concerned with literature and not with the extraction (or injection) of biographical, philosophical or historical ideas or even literary ones. Textual criticism helps to ensure this.

This attitude to criticism is encouraged by another factor which has assumed great importance since the early nineteenth century: the death of genres and the demise of rhetoric. External criteria are no longer really appropriate. Whether we are dealing with the England of the early Thirties or the France of the late Fifties, the same battle cries are heard: notions about technique and value cannot be referred to a higher authority—they have to be worked out according to individual cases.

As a result, the relationship between author, book and public changes radically. The latter two become much more important. The job of the critic in consequence is more and more to *read.* Indeed, Cleanth Brooks calls his criticism *readings.* He describes in detail what he sees. As a result, given the new tools the twentieth century has put at his disposal, he finds much more than earlier critics would have suspected. His attitude is radically different from that of Voltaire, who proclaimed that 'Any line of verse or any sentence which needs explanation does not deserve to be explained.' (Letter to Tressan 27 March 1775 [v. 741, vol. I, p. 266].) Now 'difficult' expression is much more widely considered to be acceptable and therefore worth scrutinizing. Moreover, the content of a given work is now considered to be very closely associated with the form in which it is expressed—poems, it is stressed, do not *mean*, they are.

In these circumstances, careful description is justified. Not merely justified, but for a twentieth-century reader, very necessary. One is therefore surprised at the extent to which close critical techniques are ignored in teaching and reading. Undergraduates in most countries are still encouraged to think that literature is largely a matter of theories, biography, ideas and historical development. Literature as linguistic expression is very widely ignored—although key passages for ideas are not necessarily significant for style. On the occasions when style is alluded to, abstract, outdated and rather meaningless criteria like *smooth*, *harmonious*, *economical* are considered to be a satisfactory basis for judgement. The tools supplied by linguistics, semantics, psychoanalysis and the like are rarely used.

The more conservative techniques clearly are not invalid: literature is the product of a culture and may therefore be studied as such. What is regrettable is that newer techniques may not be considered at all—that a text is never looked at from a more exclusively literary point of view. This reaches an extreme point in such publications as the present, definitive edition of *Pepys' Diaries* [527]. Questions of style and theme are not examined. The historical aspects of the diaries loom very large, as indeed they should, but only fragmentary information about methods of composition is given. And yet the Diaries are much more than a collection of facts—the way events and attitudes are selected and recounted is paramount for an understanding of the diarist's personality.

The tangible phenomena which go to make up a literary or

a semi-literary work are thus very often ignored. If the lazy reading habits which result from this are to be corrected it can only be by concentrating on the verbal and more widely semantic phenomena which are actually present in an individual text. Abstract ideas and 'problems' where they do arise in a text itself may thus be situated and evaluated in relation to the way they are expressed. The text (providing all editorial problems have been solved) is seen therefore as a product, a finished fact, with its own rules, and not as the result of pre-existing theories, which, even in highly conventionalized literature, are only superficially relevant. Any attempt to paraphrase it, to tell the story, becomes difficult if not impossible.

Textual criticism offers the advantage of being universally applicable—an ode by Horace may just as easily be analysed closely as a novel by Dreiser. This means that although, mercifully, textual critics are less mystical about their task than they once were, the scope for further close analysis is pretty well limitless; more and more medieval and classical literature is being analysed according to techniques which I shall be examining.

The need for really detailed analyses of individual literary texts, especially the novel, is still very great. In addition a large amount of textual criticism is rather mediocre: works already covered are often in need of more sensitive and objective study, which is, perhaps, at the same time less impressionistic and less discursive.

This last paragraph is in a sense a justification of the chapters which are to follow. The criteria I mentioned earlier are also a basis for what is to come: that it is important for anyone interested in literature to see at close quarters how a writer achieves his effects. This involves questions of sound, grammar, lexis, meaning, construction and sequence. It also includes the need to consider what the notion of style involves nowadays, as well as the value of counting elements which recur in a given work.

These categories should not be interpreted narrowly, nor should they be seen as watertight compartments: the chapters represent different angles from which a text may be approached. They are therefore *interdependent*. This is a point I shall insist upon with monotonous regularity. Sound has no value without detailed consideration of meaning in the narrow (*Meaning I*) and the broader (*Meaning II*) sense. Construction is not fully significant unless we consider the way a work develops and the order in which events arise in it. I have therefore not hesitated when the need arises to mention subjects to be dealt with more fully in a later chapter.

I should like to stress too that if many scientific or semi-scientific attitudes are referred to, and if the importance of objectivity is my constant preoccupation, this book should in no way be taken to be a scientific treatise. Broadly speaking the chapters are presented (up to *Construction* and with the exception of *Style* and *Counting*) in order of increasing importance. This order is also one of increasing complexity: the precise definitions of what is involved become more and more difficult, not to say subjective. If the phonetic transcription of a poem (*Sounds*) is a simple task, the definition of that poem's overall meaning (*Meaning II*, *Construction*, *Sequence*) is much more arduous and allows for wide variations. Scientific criticism is (fortunately) impossible because literature involves the contact of an individual human being with an experience which brings in a large measure of emotion. Any attempt to make criticism scientific will dehumanize it therefore.

This is not to say that considerable documentary and methodological backing is not most useful. One thinks of the *Dictionnaire des critiques littéraires*, the Italian series *I Critici*, Lausberg's *Handbuch der literarischen Rhetorik* and Morier's *Dictionnaire de Poétique et de Rhétorique*. An outstanding examination of the problems of modern criticism is Wellek and Warren's *Theory of Literature* with its very detailed bibliographies. Chapters of Wellek's *Concepts of Criticism*, especially the first twenty pages and pages 344 to 364, are a useful contribution to the history of criticism in the twentieth century. Hyman's *The Armed Vision* is also essential. Works which attempt to link linguistics and literature should be consulted too: an example is G. N. Leech's basic *Linguistic Guide to English Poetry*. Perhaps even non-literary studies in linguistics may be borne in mind, like Trager and Smith's *Outline of English Structure*—but I have reservations about such an approach, as will be seen.

Such bibliographical suggestions should not, however, give a false impression of what I am setting out to do. This book is neither an exhaustive study, nor a catalogue, nor a general synthesis (although I give as many references as seem useful). My aim is basically to point to the problems which I think arise when a text is examined closely. Often this means raising problems without necessarily solving them—awareness of these is frequently more important than unrealistically pat solutions. My method also leads to bittiness in places: *Meaning II* and parts of *Construction* suffer especially from this, but the subject is so vast and varied and limitations in length are such that I have preferred a rather disjointed approach which gives a large amount of detail to a rounded and deceptively simple one.

My book is incomplete in other ways too: with the exception of Shakespeare, I make few references to drama. This is perhaps cowardly but I felt that staging and acting bring in problems which cannot concern criticism centred mainly on the text.

I am also aware that whilst it was necessary to look at the value of statistical analysis, my attempt to consider the subject is not adequate. I have no mathematical training, and this is a drawback. What I do say in this chapter (*Counting*) may well nevertheless offer food for thought to people who have not come across its problems before.

This book therefore offers the main lines of thinking which relatively advanced criticism has adopted. References, the bibliography and the index should enable the reader to see or find out who is thinking what about a particular problem. I have tried to give examples wherever possible, because I believe criticism to be an essentially practical, empirical affair. It has been necessary on occasion to give some basic theoretical information first, but I have tried to keep this to a minimum. The discussion of practical examples is the central element in this study. I have tried to make these examples as international as possible (unless otherwise stated, I am responsible for their translation). Often it would not have been difficult to invent new examples or say something straightforward without quotation marks. My quotation of secondary sources might at times seem unnecessary. I feel however that it is a way of killing several birds with one stone: a practical example is accompanied by a reference which offers a lead-in to more discussion and speculation.

This further underlines the fact that my study is in no way an end in itself (as if any criticism practical or theoretical could ever be so). This point hardly needs debating. What is worthy of speculation however is the extent to which *textual criticism* is an end in itself. How far may one assume that the text is in some way an independent entity which can be described without reference to any external context: society, literary traditions, historical events, moral values?

The chapters to come may help to clarify this problem—which also relates to the ways in which traditional and more recent techniques of analysis might combine.

My remarks so far should explain my general aims. I am also anxious to stress what I am *not* trying to do. First and foremost I am not offering a manual of *explication de textes*. Although opinions differ, *explication*, as practised in France and in University departments of French, is more often than not a very broadly based discipline. Literary passages are examined not merely as an end in themselves but especially as a means to an end: they are the basis, the excuse even for describing the linguistic, cultural and biographical climate of the time in which they were written. The text, which more often than not is a fragment, is seen rather as a basis for teaching than a means of research. The guiding factor is rather the pupil's ignorance than the researcher's need to find out new things [v. 134, pp. 31 ff.]. All, in the circumstances, is grist to the cultural mill. There is no need specifically to define the text itself. The attack on *explication de textes* which has been undertaken by recent critics [v. 166, and 74, pp. xiii ff.] would seem largely to be justified where serious research is concerned,—and can be justified as far as teaching is concerned, for it very rarely makes use of modern analytical techniques.

This book then is purely about the problem of looking closely at a literary text and remaining as close to it as we can. I am concerned both with *interpretation*: establishing what the text actually achieves, its meaning and impact; and *criticism*: the evaluation of that achievement. This latter element, evaluation, is only possible at a late stage in analysis. Appropriately, I leave it to the conclusions.

By then I will have covered not only central aspects of textual criticism but fringe areas like archetypal criticism and the notion of literature as the product of a cultural group at a particular point in its development. These questions must be raised before evaluation can be attempted.

Finally, there is another aspect which I have tried to avoid, and that is any attempt at a systematic formulation of the links between linguistics and literary criticism. Such a link is as fashionable as *explication* is out of favour. Reference to linguistics will inevitably be frequent for our only key to a work of literature is the language through which it is expressed. I am, however, interested in the examination of texts as texts and not as linguistic documents. In linguistic documentation, passages can be extracted with little regard for general context. This is impossible in literature. Linguistics is therefore of interest to me as a means (see *Sounds*, *Grammar*, *Meaning I*) and never as an end. When it is of little use (v. *Construction*) it is dropped. Much textual criticism is indeed non-linguistic, e.g. that of Georges Poulet, or only linguistic as a result of rather startling gymnastics, e.g. that of Roland Barthes. French critics in general seem to be little preoccupied with basic linguistic features like grammar or sounds and tend to be mainly interested in semantics. This is their right (although one feels at times that more facts would restrain their fancy). As Mounin says of them therefore [487], I should not be surprised if linguisticians were to judge my use of linguisticians' terms to be somewhat crude. But this, as I have suggested, would be to miss the point: in criticism, linguistics, like history, philosophy, sociology or any other discipline is of use only inasmuch as it helps one to describe and understand a text *as literature.* Even nowadays, such understanding and discipline relate not only to scientific activities but, as we shall see, to critics' intuition, sensitivity and moral sense. This study will try to show how important it is not to neglect such qualities.

PART I

CHAPTER ONE

SOUNDS

A literary text, like anything which uses speech, is a collection of sounds. This is one of its most elementary aspects. Any reader of poetry will know that sound (which of course includes rhythm) can be one of its most striking aspects too. And even if it does not strike us, it is an element without which the poem does not exist: the movement and pause of strong and weak syllables, the flow of sounds and rhyme are, with imagery and the combination of all these elements, constant features of the poem. Brought together by the lines of verse, they 'poeticise' the subject matter, as we shall see [141, p. 53 and 363 passim].

In this field, recent critics have suggested [128, p. 1] that three main questions should be asked:

1: what are the significant literary arrangements of individual sounds?

2: how are they best described?

3: what is the relationship of these sounds to meanings?

These questions are fundamental and I intend to look at the ways in which they may be answered. Whatever methods are used however, it is essential to translate the text to be studied into terms of sound: a phonetic transcription (using the international phonetic alphabet) showing line endings and the position of stress marks (which determine rhythm) and even using musical notation to express the true nature of rhythm, must be undertaken. This produces an objective statement of the sounds in a poem and shows the relationship between sound, rhythm and metre. Just how much clarification can be achieved especially with a language which like English or French has somewhat aberrant spelling, can be seen from the following examples:

The beginning of a La Fontaine fable:

> Les Levantins en leur légende
> Disent qu'un certain rat, las des soins d'ici-bas,
> Dans un fromage de Hollande
> Se retira loin du tracas.
> La solitude était profonde,
> S'étendant partout à la ronde.

may be transcribed as follows:

> le ləvɑ̃tɛ̃́ ɑ̃ lœr leʒɑ̃́:d
> dízə kœ̃ sɛrtɛ̃ rá la de swɛ̃́ disi bá
> dɑ̃z œ̃ frɔmá:ʒ də ɔlɑ̃́:d
> sə rətirá lwɛ̃́ dy traká
> la sɔlitýd etɛ prɔfɔ̃́:d
> setɑ̃dɑ̃́ partút a la rɔ̃́:d

These lines from Tennyson's *Morte d'Arthur*:

> And slowly answered Arthur from the barge:
> 'The old order changeth, yielding place to new,
> And God fulfils Himself in many ways,
> Lest one good custom should corrupt the world.
> Comfort thyself: what comfort is in me?
> I have lived my life, and that which I have done
> May He within himself make pure! but thou—'

have the following phonetic transcription:

> ənd slóulɪ ánsəd á:θə frəm ðə bá:dʒ
> ðɪ óuld ɔ́:də tʃéɪndʒəθ jí:ldɪŋ plɛɪs tə nj́u:
> ənd gɔ́d ḅfulfílz hɪmsɛ́lf ɪn mɛ́nɪ wéɪz
> lɛ́st wʌ́n gúd kʌ́stəm ʃú:d kərʌ́pt ðə wə́:ld
> kʌ́mfət ðaɪsɛ́lf: wɔt kɔ́mfət íz ɪn mí:
> áɪ həv lívd maɪ láɪf ənd ðát wɪtʃ áɪ həv dʌ́n
> meɪ hí: wɪðɪn hɪmsɛ́lf meɪk pjú:ə bət ðáu

It will readily be seen that true similarities and dissimilarities in sounds are made perfectly clear in the phonetic transcriptions. The regularity and shift of stress patterns are also underlined.

Whether phonetic transcriptions should be supported by a performance of the text is more debatable. A reading produces too subjective a version (although some critics have tried to avoid this by obtaining a consensus of readings [125]). The kind of transcription I have used is much safer to my mind [v. 769] although, clearly, much poetry (Dylan Thomas's is a fine modern example) has often been written with a view to performance aloud [v. 26]. I am aware that one of the most famous studies of sound in poetry, that of Grammont [252 see too 413], does bear the question of performance in mind, but it is nevertheless prudent to avoid the confusion which comes from an attempt to account for individual intonations.

At the outset, it should be realized that the study of sound is extremely complex. So much so that major critical treatises sometimes try to sidle past the problem: Richards's *Practical Criticism* devotes its shortest chapter to poetic form, and the author claims that it is hopeless to try to understand the impact of sound in poetry. A recent collection of essays called *Directions of Criticism Today* [538] tries to pretend that phonetic considerations (with style, grammar and lexis . . .) hardly exist. Critics of individual poets adopt similar attitudes: a major postwar study of Keats ignores the problem; a recent detailed analysis of a Ronsard sonnet is excessively vague about its sound structure [v. 727; 116, p. 21]. But Dupriez is surely right to insist that even where sound does not seem to play a leading stylistic rôle, it must be taken into account, if only to ensure a correct interpretation of the work [187, p. 25]. For example, Ker [348, p. 163], commenting on Milton's line:

> Or whether thou to our moist vows denied . . .

affirms that '*vows* is mere pedantry; Milton means *prayers*; he is thinking of the Latin *vota* and uses the English *vows* . . .' And yet the word, containing sound components of *thou*, and (in preceding lines) *whelming tide*, *monstrous world* and *visit'st*, does poetic work which *prayers* could never have undertaken. Perhaps the real pedant here was Ker.

A phonetic transcription will have helped to bring out one key element: rhythm, which has been the object of many studies [v. 453 and 221]. The main need which is constantly stressed is to avoid impressionism, for impressionism prevents one from concentrating on the fact that rhythm may be more objectively related to such elements as accent, accent and syllable combined, combinations of sounds and combinations of words [352 passim esp. pp. 192 ff.].

Only by being aware of the mechanisms involved in this variety does one realize that rhythm is produced by one central phenomenon: contrast. Contrast between the rhythms of the verse and those of everyday speech. Contrast too between the stress patterns in a particular line and those set up in a piece of verse at large. Metre, actual stress and the reader's speech habits are thus constantly vying with each other and a number of questions must be asked if we are to grasp what is taking place: what rhythmic patterns are involved; what percentages of different types of feet there are; what the relations are between line ends and feet; to what degree the rhythm is irregular; to what extent the rhythm is exploited as a poetic device. This kind of analysis can lead us for example to a better understanding of the variety of impacts created by Pope's 'regular' and to a large extent 'normal' prose rhythms. One can also examine the way they contrast with Donne's, the patterns of whose verse and thought in no way coincide with line-ends and established metre [v. 123], in addition to the tension which Fowler talks about when he states that grammar and lexis normally relate not to metre but to prose rhythm and 'may or may not correspond with [the stress patterns] of the metrical matrix they are made to occupy' [217, p. 84]. If, then, one is faced with a line like:

So, if I dream I have you, I have you

one realizes that the metrical ambiguity, the inability to decide exactly where the stress should go, gives the thought expressed its complexity [666]. Grammont has studied the multiple possibilities of such flexibility in French verse [252, pp. 49 ff.]: the sudden drop in speed which can turn poetry into prose; the short line (as in La Fontaine or in Hugo's *A Villequier*) used like enjambement to stress an unexpected or important idea; the levelling out of ideas through regular metre; the extreme effects of tumult and flat calm to which changes in line length in a poem like *Les Djinns* (again by Hugo) contribute so much.

This flexibility exists, of course, within the framework of the poem and the regular patterns it has set up. This framework, this regularity is something we must constantly strive to establish. Mme Remacle, studying Ronsard's 'Comme on voit sur la branche ...' in the first volume of the *Cahiers d'analyse textuelle*, points to the fact that important lines will tend to have the same rhythm. R. de Souza claims that Ronsard's lines rarely exist as isolated rhythmic units [643, pp. 110 ff.]. Even free verse will have such unity [485, vol. I, passim].

The way such unity is achieved in different poets varies enormously: the balance of the Shakespearean sonnet contrasts radically with Verlaine's flirtation with a disintegrating verse form. By using 9 or even 11 syllable lines (as in *Crimen Amoris*) Verlaine creates extreme effects of insecurity, incompleteness and contradiction (only to be expected when the reader is faced with such decapitated, disfigured alexandrines) [498, pp. 151 ff.]:

> Dans un palais, soie et or, dans Ecbatane,
> De beaux démons, des satans adolescents,
> Au son d'une musique mahométane,
> Font litière aux Sept Péchés de leurs cinq sens.
>
> C'est la fête aux Sept Péchés: ô qu'elle est belle!
> Tous les Désirs rayonnaient en feux brutaux;
> Les Appétits, pages prompts que l'on harcèle,
> Promenaient des vins roses dans des cristaux.

Ronsard on the other hand, often creates unexpected imbalance within his framework by running over into one, two or three feet of the line following [643, pp. 95 ff.]:

> ... et fait naistre les cœurs
> Masles, cœurs de rochers dont les nobles ardeurs ...
> [*Amours* II, LX.]

Verlaine is perhaps the most useful example here, for even when using a 12 syllable line, his methods are quite unorthodox:

> Et pour sa voix, lointaine et calme, et grave elle a
> L'inflexion des voix chères qui se sont tues.

Nadal comments: 'the twin beat has disappeared. A kind of hesitation holds back, but does not stop the pendular stress of the line and almost deprives it of any regularity. The strong and weak beats, the usual and one would have thought necessary support for the lines' rhythmic structure, give way to harmonious discord.' [498, p. 121.]

Our phonetic transcription enables us to study the grouping of sounds in a poem as well as their stress patterns. The unified pattern of the poem is created, as Jakobson points out, by the reader as he perceives its phonetic and phonemic regularity [335, pp. 303 ff.]. This is not putting the cart before the horse. Nor is it a surrender to the subjectivity I was so suspicious of at the beginning of this chapter: the poem *must* be the creation of the sensibility which experiences it. This does not, however, mean that our attempt to describe the poem critically should be overburdened by one individual's experience. We can be objective by noting and even listing the ways in which the poem achieves its regularity of sound and its parallel effects. The extent to which these may be described is amply shown in the analysis of Baudelaire's *Les Chats* made by Jakobson and Lévi-Strauss [339, v. 584, p. 201], as we shall see in the course of this book. Extreme and startling though it may be however, it represents no more than an extension of procedures Grammont adopted much earlier: the desire to indicate as many possible sound parallels, however far removed. Such description offers a multiplicity of uses. It could be applied to poems like Arnold's *Dover Beach* [v. 418] or Baudelaire's *Albatros* to demonstrate lack of unity where a stanza has been added later.

It has been pointed out that there are two polar types of sound patterns in European poetry: pure sequence (the same sounds repeated in the same order) and pure chiasmus in which the order is exactly reversed [441, p. 4]. Masson, who makes this statement, supports his argument with very faulty reference to French and Spanish, but his point is correct. There is of course an infinity of combinations between the poles mentioned, and it is suggested that these may best be examined by '[dissolving] the phonemes into their constituent bundles of distinctive features (based on the opposition vowel/consonant, voiced/voiceless, nasal/oral, saturated/diluted, grave/acute, continuous/intercepted, tense/lax, strident/non strident. [The critic] will also need to note how these features, from which phonemes are built, significantly persist or disperse in the chordal progression of the poetic textures' [755, p. 416]. This is a development of Jakobson's notion of distinctive features and is clearly a refinement of the description of phonemic groups in the poem. It allows one to carry even further Stephen Booth's admirable description of the sounds in Shakespeare's sonnet 33: 'a good example of the contraction and expansion of phonemic particles operating in conjunction with other manifestations of unity and division ...': *full*→*fl*atter ... *gl*orious→*gold*en→*gild*ing→*cl*ouds→u*gl*y; *fr*om→*forl*orn→wo*rl*d etc. In parallel with this one might follow the patterning of *m* and *n* [79, pp. 88 ff.]. The shift and repetition here could indeed be described further by reference to the phoneme quality I have just mentioned, as well as by simply identifying the phonemes [v. to 516; 382, p. 91].

Other ways of analysing a poem's undeniable sound parallels and oppositions have been suggested. D. I. Masson, for example, talks of 'bond density' which relates to the 'connection between sounds in equivalent positions relative to syllable, word or rhythm and the presence of stress'. By scoring these according to their relative importance, he arrives at notions of comparative bond density in Hopkins (very high), Shakespeare and Pope (occasionally high) and Mallarmé (very high in the individual sonnets) [440].

Inevitably the precise nature of these sounds will vary not only from one poem to another but also from one language to another. Masson states that languages like Spanish, Italian, Greek or Latin will have a greater degree of assonance and that, whereas Germanic languages will have dense or reasonably concentrated consonant subpatterns, the Romance languages will have similarly concentrated consonant/vowel two-element subpatterns 'often with vowel modulation' [441, pp. 9–10]. Such statements are perhaps of little use when it comes to analysing individual poems, but they are a contribution to our understanding of style. They clarify impressions of which we are dimly aware when we read poems in different languages.

This is just one additional element which points to the phenomenal variety of techniques and descriptive principles which may be brought into play when one sets about analysing the sound element in a literary work. Some are empirical, like those Stephen Booth uses. Others are made up of pre-established categories against which the work is set. It would seem obvious that the best use can be made of all these techniques if they are used *where suitable.* They should not straight-jacket the poem. Empirical techniques are safest—however, if one bears other methods in mind, a deeper understanding of the phenomena may often be achieved.

So far we have been looking at the objective elements of sound and the ways in which they may be analysed. Their *impact* must also be considered and here I intend to examine the most intangible aspect first: the 'musicality' of verse.

This, for Valéry, was the central essence of a poem: 'a poem is that which cannot be summarized. You cannot summarize a melody' [707, vol. II, p. 638]. When one speaks of the music of verse one might tentatively suggest therefore that this is not *background* music. Whether the term is a good one or not is debatable. Wellek and Warren reject it because it is excessively metaphorical: 'poetry cannot compete with music in the variety, clarity and patterning of pure sounds'. The term 'euphony' is not quite sufficient either 'since "cacophony" needs to be considered in poets like Browning or Hopkins who aim at deliberately harsh expressive sound effects' [744, pp. 160, 159]. Music however, is not necessarily concerned with sounding nice, but rather with the organization of sound into significant patterns and impressive patterns [229, pp. xii–xiii]. Those who see the musicality of Poe's poetry as a necessary quality are confused therefore, and Nadal is right to use not only *music* and *melody* but also *major and minor modes* as well as *symphony* to describe Verlaine's poetry, although it would be wrong to see such terms as a definition rather than as a description of poetry [v. 531, p. 14].

Critics very often relate musicality to a suppression of logical structures and the stressing of connotations, to the detriment of denotations. Wellek and Warren quote the efforts of Tieck and Verlaine in this direction, but comment that 'blurred outlines, vagueness of meaning are not in a literal sense "musical" at all' [744, p. 127]. Literal or not, this blurring underlines the sound quality of the poem. The obsessive repetition of certain words (in a Sponde sonnet for example) becomes the obsessive preoccupation with a certain sound. Words *become* sounds—elements other than (or as well as) the meaning of words are foregrounded:

> Mortels, qui des mortels avez pris vostre vie,
> Qui meurt encore dans le tombeau du Corps:
> Vous qui rammoncelez vos thresors,
> De ceux dont par la mort la vie fust ravie . . . etc.
> [Sponde: *Sonnets de la Mort I.*]

The poem becomes a *continuous* body of sound and the taut impact involved needs to be described. There are objective criteria for doing this: Masson's notion of sound bonding for example or the principles of symmetry, repetition and chiasmus which we have already seen. Ruwet's analysis of Racine's 'le jour n'est pas plus pur que le fond de mon cœur' [610] shows how effective the impact of such symmetry may be.

André Spire's approach to the whole problem is worthy of careful study. Whilst suggesting that musicality is very difficult to define, Spire asserts that it relates to a physiological process and that the sequence of muscular movements involved in reading poetry (silently or out loud) tells us whether the verse is musical or not. For example, discomfort will be felt if the poem brings together vowels (consonants could be looked at in a similar way) whose points of articulation are distant from each other. The opposite ('muscular pleasure') is produced when vowels articulated close to each other are brought into contact. Hence the musicality of a line like: 'France, mère des arts, des armes et des lois': articulation passes easily from one vowel to the next [645, esp. pp. 193 ff.]. This is all close to Donald Davie's suggestion that musicality in verse is a linguistic as well as a purely sonorous process. It is a syntactical problem relating to 'tensions and resolutions of movements . . . sustained or broken' [162, pp. 24, 29–30].

Ants Oras suggests a very different but equally penetrating method in his attempt to explain the power of Milton and the mellifluousness of Spenser. These two poets would seem to produce contrasting effects not because of any difference in relative numbers of vowels and consonants but rather from the position of consonant clusters: at the beginning of words in Spenser, at the end in Milton. This, especially in Spenser, is supported by alliteration. In line endings, the frequencies of Spenser's prevocalic clusters are more than doubled. Such patterns lead to a primacy of effect over content in Spenser and the opposite in Milton. One result of this is that sound effects, alliteration and other Spenserian devices are much more noticeable when Milton indulges in them [513, pp. 19–32].

Before long, however, the critic faced with such methods must (if he is to remain a critic rather than a student of some isolated aspect of literature) ask to what extent sounds in poetry may be studied independently of sense. Valéry makes the dangerous claim that 'every word is the simultaneous bringing together of a sound and a sense, which are completely separate' [708, p. 147]. The poem on that score would tend to be two parallel but unrelated phenomena. It is perhaps safer to start from Grammont's suggestion that sound may be the support for the idea [252, pp. 236 ff.], and then go on to the suggestion that such support may vary in intensity according to the sounds and senses involved. For it does seem to be true that certain sounds are associated with certain emotional experiences or states. M. Chastaing has examined the symbolic value of the vowel [I] and has demonstrated, conclusively to my mind, that it can be associated with cries, sudden movements, sharpness and smallness. Albert Wellek has shown that there is a relationship between front vowels and quick, clear or bright objects, and that back vowels have opposite associations [122, 736 and 744, p. 295; v. 121B]. Grammont, as is well known, takes this a great deal further, associating sharp vowels with pain, anger, irony, worry, linking bright vowels with joy and dark vowels with anger, heaviness, grave or sombre ideas and languor [252]. The trouble here, of course, is that Grammont is too ambitious and ends up associating the same, over-explicit state with apparently antithetical vowels and consonants. Recent scholars have been noticeably more modest. But the link, however vague at times, does exist, and is part of the way language affects us in our everyday lives—it even helps us to decide whether someone is vulgar or distinguished! [398, pp. 76 ff.]. At the same time, as Stephen Ullmann has pointed out, we know that words expressing related notions like snip, snap or flip, flap etc. often have similar roots [703, p. 84].

But is it satisfactory to go to the extreme of suggesting that sound can work independently of sense? This is not merely a favourite undergraduate pastime; mature critics (in diminishing numbers perhaps) sometimes adopt a similar approach: 'Form emerges little by little from the text, takes on a life of its own and dispenses with the help of words' [485, vol. I, p. 138]. Another critic approaches this line of Pope:

> And ten low words oft creep in one dull line

in the following way: 'we account for the impression of slowness and weight in the first line, not by referring to the meaning of the words, or to some fictional variation in the length of syllables, but by recognizing the tension sustained from suppressing secondary stressed syllables' [125, pp. 424–5]. Is it really possible to suggest that *contributory* factors can act so independently? It would seem that no matter what may be adduced to demonstrate the innate semantic value of sounds, such propositions must remain abstract. In practice the words are there, in the text; they carry meaning and it is foolish to pretend that the sounds they make can fruitfully be considered by themselves. Signs are arbitrary and *sounds are not really suggestive in an a priori way* [252, pp. 206–32 and 165, pp. 19 ff.]. The only practical exceptions are the proper names writers sometimes invent, and pure onomatopoeia, which is very rare.

It is clear too that if emotions may be associated with specific sounds, the converse is not necessarily true. The poem, which *creates* emotional and other states, must therefore, once again, use words as a starting-point.

These points have been repeatedly stressed by critics from Grammont to Delbouille: sounds are only potentially expressive, they underline meanings which would exist nevertheless without their support [v. too 699, p. 151].

Also, sounds may be seen to set up not semantic relationships but supralogical ones. Then the sound pattern bears little relation to meaning.

Delbouille suggests, sensibly, that in the majority of cases the sound aspect of a text needs no commentary, poetry being primarily a linguistic art [165, p. 108]. Sound in this way would be studied only when it was strikingly present in the text.

Critics who have become aware of these factors have attempted to study sound as part of a wider whole. Krafft, for example, breaks down the poem into its different elements: rhythm, the interaction of vowel sounds, the 'contour of speech', the basic idea, unconscious meaning, rhyme, syntax and the sequence of ideas. He then gives a value to each of these according to the lines studied and works out what he calls their dominant voice. It is all very ingenious and as a supporting technique certainly not without value [361 passim], although Krafft himself bases his findings on isolated lines.

The techniques of Ants Oras, described above, would be valuable in establishing the precise relative importance of form and content. The sound quality of an 'intellectual' poet like Donne or Pope could thus be compared to the intellectual content of a 'harmonious' poet like Verlaine or Poe. This would allow us to test Francis Berry's highly romantic claim that 'what an Epistle of Pope loses if a piece is excised is at most a vital link in the intellectual chain of argument: but remove a passage from the *Pardoner's Tale* and . . . not only is a step in the narrative missing but much extra-intellectual or specifically poetic cross-reference with the rest of the poem' [68, pp. 121–2]. This would *seem* to be unduly harsh on Pope.

It does however preoccupy itself with the *relative* values of sound and sense in specific contexts, and it does underline the fact that the critic is faced with a constantly fluctuating situation. One in which even, for example, 'the subjects on which it is possible to compose poems cannot be rigidly divided into those whose inevitable medium is high vowels and those whose inevitable medium is low' [422, p. 91]. The critic must apparently be a very supple empiricist in this field where impact is constantly redefined by use. So supple that he might find acceptable the impressionism of Masson's statement that '. . . in a suitable poetic passage, *night* and *Nacht* could illustrate a leap or the arch of the sky, while *nuit* cannot be used to illustrate anything so spacious'! [441, p. 13.] In any case it is evident that a variety of methods is necessary to cope with such an unstable subject. The alternative is the kind of exhaustive approach which Guiraud and Monique Parent have applied with such good effect to the study of poets like Valéry and Jammes [v. 270 and 517] and which, because sound is related to so many other things, allows us to perceive a poetic dimension which Spire, Grammont and Morier do not really communicate.

At this stage perhaps it would be wise to sound a cautionary note from a great twentieth-century critic: 'The relations of sound-effects to the rest of the happenings in the poem are too subtle and too mingled for any analysis to have much cogency. It is sad to have to discourage so harmless a pastime, but the facts are so'. [579 p. 136.] Such a statement should certainly curb our ambition (as that of Delbouille quoted above [p. 14] should limit any obsession with sounds). Should we therefore abandon any interest in what we have recognized to be an essential part of the poem? Should we not rather suppose that, in the forty years since Richards wrote those lines, progress has been made towards more precise methods of studying the interaction of sound and sense in a poem? The examples I have cited in this chapter so far would tend to support this. So too would the tremendous growth of linguistics over the same period—and this relates not merely to what has been achieved but also to what will be achieved in the future [389, p. 52]. Progress will indeed be very great if linguistics can manage, for example, to devote more attention to problems of meaning as well as to accepting that phenomena like rhyme, onomatopoeia and metre may be linguistically pertinent. These latter elements are constantly on the threshold of meaning where the poem is concerned.

The pages which follow will show something of what has been realized.

It was noticed at a very early stage by the Russian and Prague School formalists that rhythmical patterns need not be considered in isolation, that they had very real syntactical and therefore ultimately semantic significance. For O. Brik there were syntactic structures which were inseparably bound up with the rhythm [v. 196 and 86, p. 143]. Guiraud suggests that metrical patterns are indeed empty spaces to be filled in. The structure of the alexandrine is such that it excludes long words and certain types of rhythm (feet of two, three or four syllables). Rhythm continually restricts the way poetic language may be handled [270, pp. 24 ff.]. Taken to its extreme, this penetrating idea explains the workings of stereotyped verse, like many of Hugo's *Odes et Ballades*. These are often seen to be flat and uninteresting not only because they are full of over-familiar verbal formulae, but also because the formulae, like the rest of the language, fit too neatly without enriching tension into the metre of the poem. The example of Hugo's early verse shows too that such an approach is not without value for the history of literature. Hugo's formulae fit pat because his poetry is at the time imitative. Stereotypes have also helped Josephine Miles to show that the different sentence structures on the basis of which poetry can be periodized carry with them characteristic vocabulary and sound patterns which recur too [463]. Where an oral tradition of poetry is involved, these prefabricated sound-syntax-sense structures are even more evident: The singer/poet has a second language 'parallel to his spoken one but significantly different from it in that it has the added dimension of metre. Metre in this other language is almost an aspect of grammar: phrases do not "make sense" unless they have a certain rhythmical pattern. The basic element of this language is therefore not the word but the phrasal pattern of a grammatical and metrical value, a grammetrical unit.' [383, p. 170.] This would seem to apply in fact to many other forms or moments of poetry. It is indeed very close to Wexler's statement that in the French Classical alexandrine (not exactly folk art) 'all metrical units are ideally to be defined in terms both of numerical and syntactical components'. Hence the term 'grammetrics' which he proposes to define as the practice of analysing metre and grammar simultaneously [751]. Wexler shows how 'dislocations of grammetrical boundaries . . . may *as a group* be associated with changes of subject-matter generally, that is with *cues* in the widest sense'. These short falls and overruns have an even wider significance: not only do the former point, for example, to scene end cues, they are also a means of pointing to punch lines; overruns on the other hand are often related to enumerations. Such a phenomenon is peculiar to one moment in poetic time (there are even differences between Corneille and Racine): Cohen shows that the clash between metre and syntax increases from a mere 11 per cent in seventeenth-century French verse to 52 per cent in Mallarmé [141, p. 62].

The dislocations Wexler refers to will therefore have a different significance at other periods of literary history: in nineteenth-century French poetry they will serve rather more conventionally to highlight key words or ideas:

L'eau verte pénétra ma coque de sapin
Et des taches de vins bleus et des vomissures
Me lava, dispersant gouvernail et grappin.
[Rimbaud: *Bateau ivre.* My italics.]

In English verse, where line endings are less systematically marked by rhyme, this device, like that described by Wexler, will be less apparent. The fruitful tensions between ordinary speech rhythms and those of the poem as well as the rhythm/syntax deviations at any specific point in the poem will therefore produce varying semantic effects according to the language involved. In all cases, however, it is clear that they help in a variety of ways to clarify and define the meaning. They have, as Stein suggests, metaphorical value [666; v. 124]. They enable us for example to follow more closely the development of a character like Othello, as we compare 'the measured and orderly cadences of his speech of defence to the Senate and the broken, unbalanced rhythms of the speeches during the undermining assaults from Iago'. This results from and points to 'not only the destruction of his peace of mind but also the temporary disorganization of his noblest faculties' [543, p. 6]. Rhythms become part of a process from which the words cannot be divorced: '. . . the rhythm which we admire, which we seem to detect actually *in* the sounds and which we seem to respond to, is something which we only *ascribe* to them and is, actually, a rhythm of the mental activity through which we apprehend not only the sound of the words but their sense and feeling' [579, p. 229]. If Richards is here perhaps over-emphasizing the subjective nature of our experience, the semantic nature of that experience is very perceptively underlined.

It is evident that we should expect similar rhythms to vary in effect and significance from one poem or period to another. The platitudinous value of many of Hugo's early *Odes*, to which I have already referred, does not imply that, when Hugo later uses the same alternation of alexandrine and octosyllabic, similar failures are to be expected: the greatness (and the originality) of a poem like *A Villequier* speaks for itself:

Je dis que le tombeau qui sur les morts se ferme
Ouvre le firmament;
Et que ce qu'ici-bas nous prenons pour le terme
Est le commencement;
. . . .
Je ne résiste plus à tout ce qui m'arrive
Par votre volonté.
L'âme de deuils en deuils, l'homme de rive en rive,
Roule à l'éternité.

Stanzas like this make skilful use of the shorter lines to stress important aspects of the poem's argument. Subtlety of impact is assured by the fact that stanzas with lines of regular length alternate with those having lines of irregular length.

Rhythms are therefore associated with meaning. And yet this association is itself ambiguous and diverse, for ambiguity may well exist within the individual work, the rhythm pointing in different directions according to context, or may even, as Stein's article on Donne has shown us, hover uncertainly to stress the basic ambiguity of the words: 'metrical ambiguity [may be] a functional part of larger ambiguity'. Not all critics agree with this: Seymour Chatman claims that 'ambiguity lies in a poem's diction and imagery, not in its meter'. '. . . Stresses occur in characteristic patterns and signal meanings, they cannot be switched around . . . nor are they affected by the lexical character of words . . . meter cannot be a figure of speech . . . meter is artistically arranged stress intonation pattern, just as poetic diction is artistically chosen vocabulary . . . ambiguity cannot be vocally sustained.' [666, p. 442; v. 124.] And yet the fact that Donne's verse (like Shakespeare's or Mallarmé's) is packed with lines in which one cannot determine where the emphasis *must* lie would tend to refute these statements. 'To analyse the metre of a poem is not so much to scan it as to show with what other poems its less significant (linguistically speaking) formal elements associate it.' [310, p. 125.] Such paralleling might well take place within the poem—and would underline metrical ambiguities which might be present.

Again, variations from one language to another must be mentioned. In his study of French symbolist verse, Morier [485, vol. I, p. 48] suggests a distinction between rhythm and metre: the latter is apparently descriptive and 'narrative' and corresponds to the use of equal-syllable lines. Rhythm, on the other hand is expressive and explosive and relates to the use of unequal-syllable lines. Thus we can see the contrast between Racine's *Phèdre*:

> On ne voit point deux fois le rivage des morts,
> Seigneur. Puisque Thésée a vu les sombres bords,
> En vain vous espérez qu'un dieu vous le renvoie;
> Et l'avare Achéron ne lâche point sa proie.
> Que dis-je? Il n'est point mort, puisqu'il respire en vous.
> Toujours devant mes yeux je crois voir mon époux.

and Claudel's *Sainte Thérèse*:

> Dieu qui pour illuminer l'argile et la rendre capable du paradis et de l'enfer
> Y a joint, hors du temps et du lieu par elle-même, mais dans un rapport substantiel avec notre chair,
> Cette âme connaissante en nous qui fait le corps, ainsi qu'un appareil de désir
> Continuellement occupé à respirer pour ne pas mourir,
> Permit, à cause du péché antique dans l'Eden, que ce feu inextinguible
> Restât, pendant que nous rongeons la vieille pomme, lui-même sans aucun aliment accessible.

In a literature where metre is based primarily on syllable counts, such a distinction is no doubt more acceptable than it would be for English or German verse. At the same time comparison of Verlaine's 'Dans l'interminable/Ennui de la plaine' (five syllable lines, and descriptive) and Rimbaud's 'O saisons, ô châteaux' (which has a six syllable line and is 'explosive') shows the situation to be rather more complex. The old ambiguity remains, even if nomenclature has changed somewhat.

And this is a good thing, for, as we shall see repeatedly, ambiguity is by no means a negative factor in literary communication.

Phonemic patterns may similarly be looked at in their relationship to meaning. In this respect the function of rhyme is especially significant. Critics have become increasingly aware of this, thanks to the progress in analytical method since the beginning of the century. At that time, the typical study would be like that of Fromm on the style and structure of the *Trophées* [226]. The relative quantities of rich and poor rhymes would be studied; combinations of sounds would be listed, and their relative percentages calculated, rhyme-strengthening elements (enjambement, sound context of rhyming words and the latter's grammatical forms) tabulated [v. too 160, pp. 237 ff.]. Such description without reference to function is largely a waste of a critic's time. The repetition of terminal sounds must be studied rather as echoes which establish 'a unity of meaning over and above any apparent confusion' [141, p. 78; v. 334, p. 233.] When Mallarmé, at the beginning of *Toast funèbre*, writes:

> O, de notre bonheur toi le fatal emblème
>
> Salut de la démence et libation blême . . .

even the separation of the first line from that which follows it cannot mask the link between rhyming words (the gap makes it perhaps even more striking)—grammatical and semantic differences become secondary and the unity of the poem, which links the example of Gautier and the idea of death, is already beginning to be established. Instead of being unrelated items, the two words become very necessary elements in a particular structure. J. G. Cahen explains the general principles involved further: 'Phonetically *guerre* reminds one less of *combat* which evokes a related idea, than of *naguère* which evokes a completely different idea. This fact will perhaps be helpful in understanding how a poet can move on from the repetition of the same word to the repetition of the same idea (or an associated one), from the *echo of sounds* to the *echo of ideas*.' [109, p. 184.] The example I drew from Mallarmé shows that the process can ultimately be simultaneous.

Thus rhyme especially (but all sound patterning participates in this) can help the words of poetry to point in several directions: *teaching* evokes not only the semantic field to which it belongs (tutor, chalk, blackboard etc.) but also any word which echoes it, whether the parallel be grammatical (walking), merely phonetic (thing), or both (bleaching) [v. 703, p. 63]. In all this rhyme clearly affects both the grammar and the vocabulary of the poem [123, p. 136]. The reader of poetry is constantly beset by the clash between the meanings or the grammatical functions of words which rhyme together [v. 763] e. e. cummings shows just how far this can be taken:

> of all the blessings which to man
> kind progress doth impart
> one stands supreme i mean the an
> imal without a heart . . .
> [*Complete Poems II*, 1968, p. 544.]

Rather more subtly, the contrasting rhymes in Verlaine's *Colloque sentimental* point to contrasting emotions in the two protagonists:

> Ton cœur bat-il toujours à mon seul nom?

is opposed by the rhyming word 'non'. The extreme of:

> Ah! les beaux jours de bonheur indicible
> Où nous joignions nos bouches!

is deflated by the sceptical 'c'est possible'. The last conversational stanza reads:

> Qu'il était bleu le ciel, et *grand l'espoir*!
> —L'espoir a fui, vaincu, *vers le ciel noir*.
> [My italics.]

We should do well, therefore, when analysing rhymes, to ask, as Wimsatt does, from what semantic sphere rhyme words are selected: whether for example they belong to one or to several linguistic categories (parts of speech, different cases, or groups of objects . . .) [763]. The relative importance of rhyme words must also be examined: 'one can distinguish the degree to which rhyme is implicated in the total context of the poem, how far rhyme words seem mere fillers, or, at the opposite extreme, whether we could conjecture the meaning of a poem or stanza only from its rhyme words' [744, p. 161]—as in Baudelaire's *Vie antérieure* for example:

> J'ai longtemps habité sous de *vastes portiques*
> Que les soleils marins teignaient de *mille feux*
> Et que leurs grands piliers, *droits et majestueux*
> Rendaient pareils, le soir, aux *grottes basaltiques*. etc.
>
> [My italics.]

With the remaining rhyme words (*cieux*, *mystique*, *musique*, *yeux*, *calmes splendeurs*, *odeurs*, *palmes*, *approfondir*, *languir*) the poem's central mysticism, and its symbolic content become apparent. Moreover, the development of the poem is outlined by its rhymes: the shift from purely static, descriptive nouns and adjectives to the verbs which make up the last two rhymes, points, with the meaning of the words, to a slight impression of disquiet as the poem comes to a close.

The shift from nouns to verbs plays a similar rôle here to that played by changes in rhyme pattern in other contexts. One thinks of the sense of resolution, of a problem simplified and explained, which comes in many sonnets (or often at the end of a scene in the plays), when Shakespeare replaces crossed rhyme by a rhyming couplet [79, pp. 130 ff.].

What we have seen so far points to the value of the ideas of parallelism and contrast in the study of the relationships between sound and meaning. The individual poem is I think best approached from this point of view. Indeed it is interesting that wider, linguistic definitions speak of the poem as a code; it is made up of syntagmata of which the paradigms point to phonetically and semantically related words [403, p. 27], an extension of Cahen's point given above (pp. 21–2). All is based on the idea of equivalence and recurrence. The pattern thus established leads to the foregrounding of semantic similarities. The structure of the poem becomes meaningful, meaningfulness being not so much a matter of the 'importance' of the ideas expressed as of the richness of the interrelationships set up. And this, of course, includes sound: 'equivalence in sound, projected into the sequence as its constitutive principle, inevitably involves semantic equivalence, and on any linguistic level any constituent of such sequence prompts one of the two correlative experiences Hopkins neatly defines as "comparison for likeness' sake" and "comparison for unlikeness' sake"' [335, p. 368].

In this two-way traffic between sound and meaning, sound must always be significant. But whether we are always able to analyse this significance in any detail is another matter. When Verlaine writes:

L'ombre des arbres . . .

we appreciate that *br* sounds, together with the supporting vowel shift from [õ] to [a], more intimately interrelate the words than if he had used a more *specific* word for tree. But I doubt whether the precise impact could be accounted for. Moreover, the function of the word or words in other contexts plays an important part: 'The more the meaning of a word is known the more thought process associations will tend to stifle those associations related to the form of the word.' [163, p. 434.] The question of degree here, inevitably, is left vague.

Only the more objectively describable phenomena are therefore within our reach. But the results here can be highly significant. One thinks of Stephen Booth's analysis of 'To be or not to be . . .' with its pointed exploitation of the 'simultaneous likeness and difference in the sounds of words' [80, pp. 164 ff.]. Equally significant is Masson's study of the opening lines of *Paradise Lost*. In these, Masson discerns sound patterns to connect the ideas of the Fall and its 'instruments', the Fall and Redemption, man's original disobedience and its results [440, pp. 56 ff.]. J. J. Lynch goes beyond this and suggests that the characteristic sounds of a poem may be concentrated in the word or words ('summative' words) which are thematically central. In an analysis of Keats's *On first looking into Chapman's Homer*, the effects of 'orchestration' are examined: metrical and syntactical stress giving relative value to phonemes, repeated patterns (varying in importance according to the degree of separation) and the local or general significance of sound patterns are all used as a basis for establishing the poem's dominant consonants and values. This in turn points to the very great tonal stress on the word *silent*, the first word of the poem's last line. Sound points to this word around which the theme of the poem revolves. The word *cor* sums up the basic sound pattern of the first part of Vigny's poem of that name. For similar reasons *dances* and *daffodils* would seem to be significant words in Wordsworth's *Daffodils* [418.] They point to the dominant sound structure of the poem. Dell Hymes has extended this search for summative words to some twenty sonnets, and his findings help to place those of Lynch in proper perspective. For, indeed, if summative words are of extreme interest, they are not necessarily a permanent feature of all poetry (the highly diversified use of language in poetry must never be overlooked): 6/20 sonnets have summative words, 5/20 have key words (i.e. where the tonal emphasis is great but not overbearing), 7/20 offer an approximately summative effect, whilst in five cases out of twenty no clear results could be obtained.

Hymes suggests that a particular sound pattern becomes less significant with longer poems, and that this kind of analysis excludes the essential poetic devices of sound contrast and the effects achieved by sustained rather than culminating sound [329.] The idea and the methods of investigation involved are nevertheless important ones. They suggest methods of approach additional to those of Grammont (who notes that the sound patterns of a Racine character vary radically according to whether she is expressing emotions or ideas) and those of Guiraud, who has attempted to compare key and theme words in Valéry in their relation to consonantal groups [270, pp. 143 ff.].

These are some of the ways, then, in which sound contributes to the overall sense of poetry. It would be an exaggeration to say that it creates new contexts through which the words themselves are made new [210, p. 118]. But they are renewed in a real sense, inasmuch as in poetry, and therefore with the help of sound, they participate much more closely in what Susanne Langer calls the 'morphology of feeling' [v. 162, p. 17]. Sound offers a very complex process of imitation. Spitzer's analysis of Malherbe's 'rose elle a vécu ce que vivent les roses' sees in the repetitions a sense of inexorability and the suggestion of moral qualities. The stoic restraint alluded to here is also closely related to the short line, and through the combination of these effects we see that 'Poetry thus evokes the rhythm of purely abstract thought.' [650, pp. 212–18.] A markedly contrasting example is Valéry's line:

L'insecte net gratte la sécheresse.

This is not a simple onomatopoeia of torrid dryness:* sound cannot directly describe a tactile impression. We are rather faced here with an obsessive repetition of sense: l'in*sec*te . . . *sécheresse* and the further associations of *gratte* and *net*. The dry heat thus conjured up is then enormously intensified by the recurrent sound patterns: *sec*, *net*, *sécheresse*; in addition all vowels here may be considered to be short, consonants are closely associated: c,t,g,r. The combined impact of sound and meaning is also intense because of the unusual collocation of words involved (*net* with *insecte*, *sécheresse* with *gratte*) which makes sound and sense appear to have been brought together for some specific purpose [v. 441, p. 153 and 531, pp. 32 ff.]. In any case the line of poetry here *enacts* its meaning in a very telling way.

The language of poetry thus becomes a kind of reality in its

* Note: the idea of onomatopoeia tends to obscure the study of sounds in literature rather than to illuminate it.

own right: 'sound painting is in fact merely one expression of man's effort to annul the indirect nature of language . . .'; it expresses 'a thirst for tangible reality' [102, p. 113]. Or again 'It is language's duty not only to communicate poetic value which cannot exist without it, but also to place this value on a specifically concrete level.' [346, vol. I, p. 222.] It is in this sense that we might accept Spire's statement that sounds in poetry may have 'the physical form of their meaning' [645, p. 304], although Spire himself was less precise in his explanation. But it is now considered preferable that wider blocks of expression than individual words be considered, as in Masson's study of free phonetic patterns in Wilfred Owen [442]. This shows the extent to which signifier and signified, which never truly coincide in everyday speech, tend to become one and the same thing in poetry. And this is one of the reasons why the criterion of realism is totally inapplicable to poetry [543, p. 6]. Sound and sense combine to create a second sense. To take a somewhat flippant example (but one which shows that we are still dealing with poetic devices and not poetic qualities) Barnacle Bill only exists, is only 'justified', because he is 'from over the hill' (a rather unusual qualification for a sailor). His *verbal* reality is thus demonstrated. The contradictory nature of this demonstration is ignored in favour of rhyme and parallel rhythm.

One major problem remains and this relates to sounds in prose. Before I consider it, however, I wish to mention the way sound in poetry (especially that of less 'rational' words or effects) may be analysed not by the methodical critic who relates his statements as far as possible to objective phenomena, but by the gifted one whose sensitivity is matched by a penetrating ability to express himself. Leavis would be an obvious example of this if my study at this point were more wide-ranging. Nadal's book on Verlaine [498] is however an even more pointed example here, and is well worth detailed commentary.

Nadal distinguishes between two basic sound effects: symphony and melody. In the former (and Nadal refers to *Les Fleurs du*

Mal as a good example) 'all the harmonic values of language were brought into play. Words brought sense and sound to an extreme pitch in sumptuous combinations in which the reciting voice of the poet seemed to be at the service of some mysterious cult . . . Linked to the voice and by that token to the richness and mobility of thought, words were grouped together with their complex depths of sound; they became the tangible parallel, the analogue in sensorial terms of the world of the mind.' [498, p. 124.]

For example:

> Les soirs illuminés par l'ardeur du charbon,
> Et les soirs au balcon, voilés de vapeurs roses,
> Que ton sein m'était doux! que ton cœur m'était bon!
> Nous avons dit souvent d'impérissables choses
> Les soirs illuminés par l'ardeur du charbon.
>
> [*Le Balcon.*]

Verlaine attempts similar effects in the early *Poèmes saturniens.* But in some poems, different techniques are at play: *Crépuscule du soir mystique*, for example:

> Le Souvenir avec le Crépuscule
> Rougeoie et tremble à l'ardent horizon
> De l'Espérance en flamme qui recule
> Et s'agrandit ainsi qu'une cloison
> Mystérieuse où mainte floraison
> —Dahlia, lys, tulipe et renoncule—
> S'élance autour d'un treillis, et circule
> Parmi la maladive exhalaison
> De parfums lourds et chauds, dont le poison
> —Dahlia, lys, tulipe et renoncule—
> Noyant mes sens, mon âme et ma raison,
> Mêle, dans une immense pâmoison,
> Le Souvenir avec le Crépuscule.

'In place of a poem of descriptive cut, in place of caesurae which determine the meaning of words, instead of rhymes which give a body of sound to our response, in place of the hard outlines of a miserly beat with its strong and weak stresses, Verlaine brings in monumental orchestration where no break is felt. The line of thought is dispensed with . . . The same sounds as they recur . . . give symphonic balance to a poem where logical support is hard to find . . . This leitmotiv guarantees that signals of sound are recognized [even] when the variations in imagery and sound bear it off to regions too distant from the initial figurative pattern. . . . Objects themselves . . . are set out according to the sound value that language bestows upon them.' [498, pp. 126–7.] With the last ariette of the *Romances sans paroles*, however, a more radical change takes place:

L'ombre des arbres dans la rivière embrumée
Meurt comme de la fumée,
Tandis qu'en l'air, parmi les ramures réelles,
Se plaignent les tourterelles.

Combien, ô voyageur, ce paysage blême
Te mira blême toi-même,
Et que tristes pleuraient dans les hautes feuillées
Tes espérances noyées!

Incantation and harmony give way to melody: 'a modulatory art'; language becomes 'an organ of the voice and no longer an instrument of thought'. It is now 'whispered'. Rhyme is 'curbed', and is perceived more 'secretively throughout the whole body of the line', for 'the rhythmic outline is no longer controlled by the external law of a fixed form but rather by the shifting pace of word forms. . . . Assonance adds further to its presence and its impact inside the line; rhyme there is punctuated and delicately shaded by all the effects which syllable combinations can produce.' [498, pp. 132–4.] The metrical figuration of the *Fêtes galantes* and *La Bonne Chanson* is also worthy of note, especially its fluidity. This is achieved by the 'hesitation of the caesura between third and fourth, fourth and fifth, eighth and ninth feet caused by the most subtle use of the unelided mute *e*':

Les hauts talons luttaient avec les longues jupes,
En sorte que, selon le terrain et le vent,

Parfois luisaient des bas de jambes, trop souvent
Interceptés!—et nous aimions ce jeu de dupes.
[*Les Ingénus.*]

This contrasts markedly with Racine's permanent stress of the sixth foot, Chénier's ternary rhythms or Hugo's sense-controlled dislocation of rhythm [498, pp. 138–44].

Nadal, as can be seen, is not afraid of using impressionistic language (although he refers to very precise evidence). If this is normally dangerous and can lead to the kind of gush journalists often pass off as criticism, Nadal's ability to explain effects, which more systematic methods could perhaps not analyse, is apparent. The effects, and even the devices of poetry are not always scientifically demonstrable. Impressionism is evidently justified at times, and Nadal's is far from an isolated example. One thinks of Masson's statement about the role of sound patterns in Wilfred Owen's horrific war poetry (which could apply to many other poets: the Baudelaire of *L'Irrémédiable*, the Shakespeare of Sonnet 129, or the Rimbaud of *Bateau ivre*): '. . . these internal alliterative/assonant patterns with their kinesthetic and musical shapefulness, function (like the verbal mythopoeia) as a compensation, a counter-affirmation. As craftsmanship, they compensate for Owen's discordant half rhymes. . . . As creative art they oppose the dissolving chaos of war; for they support the heroic affirmation in his poetry and probably helped (through their ordered satisfaction) to defend the poet himself against the disintegrating forces without. They form as it were a litany or charm against panic emptiness.' [442, pp. 368–9.]

The study of the *impact* of sound is complex, as we can see. Objective techniques are useful in describing it and must be used whenever possible. But the experience of literature is a subjective one, and objective techniques are always dependent on the sensibility of the individual critic.

Nearly all the points I have raised so far are concerned with verse. This is to be expected for one more naturally associates sound effects with poetry. Their presence in prose should however not be neglected, as any reader of Flaubert or Jane Austen or Sir Thomas Browne will know. At the same time, it is clear that such phenomena may well produce quite different effects, or implications in prose. As Jean Cohen has shown in great detail, poetry is in many ways anti-prose [141 passim], and in prose devices which cut across the primary aim of communicating abstractable meaning may well be condemned. Thus Wimsatt points out that rhyming echoes like 'a baptism of optimism' or 'practically exclusively' are to be rejected because words here are not parallel. On the other hand such a statement as: 'we are swallowed up irreparably, irrevocably, irrecoverably, irremediably' is acceptable because 'behind each of these parallel sounds' implicit parallel meanings there is a parallel meaning'. We have thus a sense of the sounds' 'concordance with the structure of meaning' [765, p. 373]. Alliteration, which may be widespread in a prose work, is thus conditioned in a way which would not apply to verse, for, as Wimsatt shows elsewhere, counterlogical procedures such as repetitions of sounds or homophones are accepted in verse but not in prose. In poetry they imply and even impose similarity of sense. This clearly applies to such effects as metre [767, p. 13], but not to rhythm. Flaubert resolutely 'persecuted' all forms of repetition, except of course the characteristic ternary rhythms of *Madame Bovary* and the insistently 'lame' period endings which typify *L'Education sentimentale*, and which help, in the case of the former, to underline the heroine's stereotyped lyricism, and, in the case of the latter, to parallel the dead-ends to which all Frédéric Moreau's actions lead. Here the device is in no rigid sense logical, although it does not undermine the specifically rational value of words as assonance and metre would tend to do. As Philip Rahv points out: 'Poetry concentrates on the immediate affective associations of the word' whereas narrative or logical thought goes first to 'the object or entity symbolized by the word in order to draw its associations from that. . . .' The emotional associations in the novel are attached not to its words but to the mock reality which they bring into being [555, p. 294]. This is useful but it should be noted that in the case of Flaubert or Proust this mock reality may be literary: the movements of the characters' mind may well be 'expressed' by the balance of the sentences.

As far as more precise sound qualities are concerned, the use in Dickens or Balzac of evocative proper names requires yet further qualification of Rahv's assertion. We should also take into account the thesis put forward by Jean Ricardou in his *Pour une théorie du nouveau roman* that the productive ability is very much responsible for the final form a piece of writing takes. Links of a phonetic or orthographic nature may well play a substantial part in the way a text develops. But it is still correct that the sound of prose plays a noticeably less important part in its overall effect, as is inevitable in a medium where notions of realism (i.e. reference to non-verbal external reality) play an important part. One would suppose that the sound element of many novels (e.g. those of Dreiser) could be ignored altogether.

Terms of sound may be applied with justification to phenomena which are not related to sound effects: the rhythm of plot for example: the acceleration and deceleration of action, the alternation of action and description all produce a rhythmical effect. It has even been suggested that where narrative is concerned (and this includes the theatre), totally different and yet parallel phenomena may be at play to produce the aesthetically essential effect of unification: '. . . the effects I have described in *Hamlet* are of the same general kind as the non-significant coherences made by rhythm, rhyme, alliteration and others of the standard devices of prosody. For example, the physics of the relationship among Hamlet, Laertes, Fortinbras and Pyrrhus, the four avenging sons in *Hamlet*' may be compared to 'the relationship among *cat*, *rat*, *bat* and *chat*. The theme of suicide, for all its inconstancy . . . is a constant and unifying factor . . .'. [80, p. 172.]

A statement of such perceptive originality drives home the fact that prose and narrative require particular methods of analysis and that sounds must also command a different approach. Those methods involved in very broadly based studies will be best examined when I come to talk about the role of statistics and the computer in textual criticism. Less mechanised methods are not however unimportant [v. 250].

Jean Mourot, for example, in his *Le Génie d'un style; Chateaubriand: rythme et sonorité dans 'Les Mémoires d'Outre-tombe'* sets out to 'examine rhythm and sound patterns in the *Mémoires d'Outre-tombe* with a view to establishing what is typical of their author and personal to him'. He establishes relationships between intense sound patterns and the themes of exile and vast spaces and shows that the grouping of certain sounds, which have no specific meaning in themselves if they only occur once, crops up each time that an important and vital point in the *Mémoires* is reached [488, p. 365; v. 538, p. 311]. This, it must be stressed, is parallel to the idea of the summative word in poetry, but is not identical to it. The radical difference is of course that in Chateaubriand not only are the groupings recurrent, they also relate not to words but to ideas. Sound, here, is rather an evaluation of meaning than a direct component of it. Chateaubriand adopts a particular voice to express important aspects of his experience.

Other stylistic values of sound may be seen in Ian Watt's study, *The Comic Syntax of 'Tristram Shandy'*, in which we learn that Sterne creates a particular comic effect in the first paragraph by opposing the equilibrium of Augustan prose, with its 'balanced pattern of consonantal stops', and the colloquial looseness of disjointed and freely associated ideas [728, p. 321]. This is in some ways similar to that disintegration of the Ciceronian period which Croll describes in his study of *The Baroque Style in Prose* [pp. 344–5]. The impact here is however far from comic, for in Montaigne or Sir Thomas Browne such rhythms, linking as they do with a floating absence of syntactical connections, offer a new apprehension and expression of thought. Indeed with their lack of formalized structures, they reproduce much more closely thought processes in which the object of discussion is not deliberately reconstructed but rather named and then considered from many different, not precisely related points of view.

Spitzer's well-known study of Diderot's style is another useful example of the way prose rhythms may be interpreted. Initially he links rhythmic patterns, the self-accentuating rhythm in Diderot's writings, to the eighteenth-century doctrine of mobility. The author's stylistic (and nervous!) system is thus linked to the spirit of the new age. Spitzer goes further, however, for he relates the whole phenomenon to an 'urge for self-potentiation' in the characters which leads to a kind of 'mental stuttering' which is undoubtedly sexual, at least in part. Moreover, such a manifestation cannot be explained exclusively on an artistic level. Biographical data must be taken into account [657, pp. 135–91]. Thus the critic fits stylistic features into a framework where cultural, artistic and biographical elements are shown to play a determinant role.

All this is reasonably clear-cut and would seem to offer useful suggestions about the way we might approach the rhythms of prose. And yet it would be quite wrong to suggest that poetry and prose are in any way as compartmentalized as theoreticians would have us believe. Any art is full of half-way houses, and we should not confuse tendencies with the more abstract definition of genres. In reading Joyce or Céline or Virginia Woolf we should be prepared to recognize poetic devices and analyse them as such whilst yet seeing the work to which they belong as fitting, by action or reaction, into a tradition of narrative. The prose poem offers even more exquisite difficulties, for it may well 'disappoint' the narrative effect which the disposition of words on the page has led us to expect. This is indeed perhaps part of its function.

The solution to such problems is again empirical: to relate phenomena of sound and rhythm to the wider significance of the individual text. This is Lawler's approach in his analysis of Rimbaud's prose poem *Génie*. The rhetorical pattern which he sees to be the basic convention of the poem develops, in the first and second paragraphs, through a series of references to present, future and eternity. The support for these is a rhythmical progression and ultimately a series of exclamations [382, p. 77]. This is a much more valuable statement than any abstract suggestion concerning the nature of sound patterns in poetic prose.

This chapter is incomplete in two ways: on the one hand the points raised could have been expanded and exemplified in much greater detail; on the other hand it is inconceivable that a great deal of critical comment can be achieved merely by looking at sounds. The later chapters of this study must complete the picture. Sound is part of grammar, meaning, construction and the rest. Conversely, these areas should lead us to consider the relevance to them of sound effects.

This chapter will however contribute to making such an interchange possible. Already we have seen that methods of describing sound exist; that it is possible to examine the ways in which sound participates in the creation of literary meaning and impact; and finally that the careful study of sound in no way excludes the personality of the individual critic. These are facts on which the following chapters will build.

CHAPTER TWO

GRAMMAR

Sound, I suggested, is the most elementary part of a text. After that comes the grammar: the framework of linguistic conventions which expression has to take into account, the different functional types of word and phrase which a text may be made up of, and their varied combinations.

It is fair to ask to what extent grammatical analysis can be critically useful, and to look at some of the findings such analysis has produced. In addition it must be stressed that, like any other tool, grammar is not an end in itself for the critic. It is merely an element which should be considered (and which is often neglected) in the hope that it might supply information about the way a text produces its effects (but with the realization that it will not always do so). A further stimulus to this approach lies in the fact that, as time passes, grammar is becoming more and more adept at looking at and describing passages which are long enough for the critic to take them seriously [v. 216, p. 5].

Grammatical analysis is at all events another useful corrective to the kind of impressionism too many critics indulge in. It ties one down to the facts of a text and counteracts that 'tendency to read meanings into poems at random, regardless of linguistic limits' which I. A. Richards complains about [578, p. 335]. Statements about a text must be made on the basis of evidence, and if one is anxious to establish the presence or absence of a particular bias in a poem 'the best if not the only sorts of evidence are fundamentally linguistic—have to do with relations of words and phrases to one another' [578, p. 330].

Thus even unpretentious grammatical facts (like those in the appendices of the two volume Hatier edition of selections from Hugo (1950)) may not be without value to the critic who can see their significance, or who can relate stylistic effects to them. The critic must be grateful too when the language of a complex and dense writer like Mallarmé is systematically analysed for him, as in Scherer's *L'Expression littéraire dans l'oeuvre de Mallarmé* (1947). In this, Mallarmé's peculiar grammar, with its English and Latin influences and the special features of his syntax, is set out in a workmanlike way as raw material for the critic. Similar value can be attached to M. E. I. Robertson's grammatical breakdown of imagery in Hugo [597, pp. 77 ff.], which points to the varying importance of substantival epithet, present and perfect participle and prepositive or appositive expressions.

It will already be apparent that, in the main, grammar will be of more immediate importance to the critic when he is looking at a poem than when he is analysing a novel. It can be accepted as a fact that precise reference to language is the *instinctive* reaction of the poetry critic, whereas such considerations are in no sense so obtrusive in criticism of the novel. When the grammar of the novel is considered, the findings may be important but they will not normally reveal that language has been put to any strain or that grammatical categories have to be reassessed. Discussion of the novel will often concern itself with the 'moral' problems raised by the behaviour of the characters and the way the substance of the novel relates to the outside world.

It would be ridiculous however to go to the other extreme and pretend that in prose, stylistic considerations are not important. The present chapter and the next one should demonstrate that this is not so. One might reflect on Cressot's statement that '[a writer's] creations, borrowings and syntactical innovations always arise in answer to a need; by getting to know these needs the grammarian penetrates the most intimate and personal aspects of a writer and a period' [155, p. vii]. Lubbock's apparently exclusive concentration on action, episode and character in his *Craft of Fiction* would seem therefore to be misguided. I believe Sherrington and Cortland to be mistaken for similar reasons in their studies of Flaubert's *Education sentimentale* [635 and 151]. Another critic, Kibédi Varga, attempts to define baroque style without making any reference to syntax! [351]. It would seem essential therefore to underline the fact that 'the difference between the writer and the ordinary scriptor is that for the former writing is not a means of expression . . . but rather the very domain of his thought . . . The writer is one who can think only in the silent, secret world of writing.' [240, p. 246.] The kind of criticism which could be taken as a model might well be that of Nabokov, who in his study of Gogol is constantly aware that his subject's medium is language, and that, as we shall see further on, even characters may be seen as the product of syntactical devices [v. 497].

And yet the situation is far from clear, especially for the professional critic, who will be, of necessity, an amateur grammarian. He may well tend to take grammatical terms over-literally, to see grammatical value in purely morphological phenomena [v. 234, p. 65], whereas terms like noun, adjective, personal pronoun may have both a much wider and a more ambivalent value [ibid. p. 68]. He may tend to confuse the terminology of classical languages like Greek and Latin with the approach needed to describe the grammatical elements in a modern Western European (or American) text. This is perhaps why Cressot's study of Huysmans is somewhat stereotyped and uninspiring: the degree of conformity which Cressot explores relates to classical grammar and not to notions which might more precisely describe the linguistic content of nineteenth-century French literature, with its new approach to word order, sentence structure and even tense and noun usage.

Grammatical analysis often entails underlining elements which, because of their apparent unusualness or the fact that they occur with unaccustomed frequency, show the text examined either to be unique or to belong to a distinctive group. But I personally do not believe that it is always important for the critic to establish whether these features are *really* deviant or not. This is basically a linguistic problem. The critic is concerned rather with tracking down and describing striking (i.e. characteristic) elements, and whether he uses the term *deviation* (as Jean Cohen does) or *strangeness* (like Gérard Genette) is largely immaterial. Linguistics and criticism handle the idea of the norm differently: for the linguist, individual examples are primarily a means of proposing a more refined definition of the norm—for the critic, who depends to a greater extent on his own sensitivity, the text exists largely in its own right; the need for comparison is much less imperative. It is the fact of distinctiveness which is important and the value of that for the description of the text studied.

Once this has been established, it is worth noting that, as Leech points out [391, p. 140], literature (especially since Romanticism and the growth of experimentation) is distinguished by the high number of its deviant features. Some of them will inevitably be grammatical, and to study them is clearly to examine an important aspect of literature. The poet may well be creating patterns of grammatical distinctiveness. The way he handles and modifies the norms he has created will be a significant aspect of the language and structure of the poem, of his works as a whole or even of the period to which he belongs.

This need not of course mean that the degree of poeticalness in a passage is directly proportional to the weirdness of its grammar (this would seem to be the central mistake of Jean Cohen's study): such a view forgets the importance of any kind of grammatical patterning, which includes the above average repetition of 'normal' grammatical forms, a kind of divergence in itself. It does imply however that the description of grammar in poetry will produce useful results. In the case of 'difficult' poetry, in which the 'meaning' of words is hard to grasp, the essential medium of the verse may often be defined by grammatical description, for here the reader's experience has much more to do with the way language is handled than with the communication of ideas as such.

Prose works may be tackled in this way too. In all cases, the need for such analysis depends on the elements present in the work studied (and not on some aprioristic decision that poetry needs grammatical analysis and prose something else). Thus Cressot studies what he calls the aesthetics of improper linguistic forms in Huysmans [155, part II]. There are many other prose writers, from Petronius to Salinger, who invite similar treatment.

Such an approach is often a useful springboard for other studies. The way grammar is affected in the poem indicates the way the poem's meaning is handled and defined. A poem studied as modified grammar reveals inevitable and inseparable changes in vocabulary types and in syntax. We shall see below in greater detail how word groups or meaning groups become part of the syntax. We might note here that ideas which recur in similar grammatical categories become interrelated. McIntosh [425] thus describes how Hopkins's creation of *inscape* is closely linked to the dropping of modal adverbs and the insistent recurrence of verb + adjective + noun. In another sphere, and sticking to accepted grammatical categories, Zumthor offers useful information on Hugo's evocation of the Middle Ages by pointing out that, in *Eviradnus*, 'the majority of typical words and nearly every single decorative word are nouns and verbs', with adjectives playing a very minor role in each category. In this way, Hugo builds up a world of substances, functions and actions rather than one of qualities, 'a world whose basic values may be easily quantified' [784, p. xxvi].

The variety of possible results from such analyses is considerable. In the rest of this chapter I intend to offer samples of the information which we may glean from the study of the grammatical elements (categories and syntax) in a text and their critical significance, always remembering that the omission of this kind of element may be as significant as its striking inclusion.

'Vous avez mis le pied gauche sur la rainure de cuivre, et de votre épaule droite vous essayez en vain de pousser un peu plus le panneau coulissant.' In this first sentence of Butor's novel, *La Modification*, our surprise, the feeling that information is being given to us from a most unusual angle (unusual for a novel, of course, not for a lawyer examining a witness), is almost exclusively caused by the unconventional use of the second person plural (not quite exclusively, for we are also puzzled by the description, until we realize that it refers to a man pushing his way into a railway compartment). In contrast to first person narratives with their implied subjectivity and bias, and third person narratives with their omniscience and objectivity, Butor's use of 'vous' creates at one and the same time a feeling of distance, or distancing, *and* subjectivity. It is legitimate to consider that a man might here be addressing himself (the author would otherwise not have taken it for granted that a railway compartment was being described); at the same time however we are presented with an *object* for description: significantly, 'vous' is used and not the 'tu' which one would expect from a man talking to himself—also the obsessive preoccupation with minute detail in which the central character is set or of which he is a key spectator strengthens this impression. The initial choice of personal pronoun (which also replaces the more expected proper name) thus creates a radically new dimension in the novel. It is one, too, of great complexity, for the *vous* might also be the reader: he feels himself more directly addressed, involved in the substance of the novel than if either of the usual pronouns had been used.

This is an extreme example of how significant the use of personal pronouns can be. It is not, however, a unique example of the way an author can play off the impact of one alternative against another. Genette has pointed to the way Proust gave up the 'over centralized third person form of [his earlier novel] *Jean Santeuil*, in favour of the ambiguous decentralized first person of *A la Recherche du Temps perdu*, the first person of a Narrator who is definitely neither the author nor anyone else . . .' [238, vol. II, pp. 13–14]. Genette's speculation is no doubt supported by the fact that the Narrator in *A la Recherche* has the same first name as his creator. It would however seem fair to suggest that if, as is quite legitimate, we ignore the earlier novel and thrust aside biographical considerations, the first person in Proust fulfils a similar function to that of *Adolphe* or even

David Copperfield: subjectivity and partiality. The dominant pronoun underlines a point of view much more than it pinpoints a person.

In other works the effect may be different. In an unpublished thesis [138] David Clow has analysed the unstable function of personal pronouns in Lautréamont. Here, the narrator sometimes coincides with the protagonist (Stanza V in Blanchot's edition) [71], in other stanzas he is distinguished from him and then identified with him (e.g. Stanza III). In some stanzas *je* = Maldoror, whereas in others it relates to Ducasse, the author of the *Chants*. And very often the precise attribution of the pronouns cannot be established! Again this is a peculiarly literary situation (with perhaps in addition a paranoiac tinge): our response is being constantly shifted and distorted, pointed outward to some object offered for examination, which, it may be implied, is ultimately interchangeable. The third person singular here suggests a depersonalization of experience.

The example given is once again extreme but it links up very closely with what Barthes sees as a basic function of the third person narrative: the third person is always given in some degree as a negation of personality [41, p. 56]. Standing outside us, offered as an *object* for our examination and speculation, it will tend to invite direct identification with the writer or indeed with ourselves to a much lesser degree. Being placed outside us and being undistinguished grammatically (and therefore semantically) from other characters in the novel, the third person directs our attention more radically, as Barthes also points out (p. 55), towards human relationships. This is an existential experience.

Different genres and different linguistic and social conventions will inevitably invite consideration. Francis Berry [68, pp. 36 ff.] offers a contrast with our preceding paragraphs through his study of *thou* and *you* in Shakespeare's sonnets. He points out that there are twice as many *thou* sonnets as there are *you* sonnets. The former may be associated with a Petrarchan, immature style, the latter relate to a colloquial, Donne-like style. *Thou* points to a distancing effect and to a feeling of subservience. And this makes for greater impact when, exceptionally, an addressee like the fair youth is called *you* instead of the more expected *thou*. It signals the exceptional, direct approach. Used in rather different ratios, *thou* and *you* create different effects in the Dark Lady sequence, for here the former has a value of condescension. Berry's argument is at various points confused, and my account of it here is an attempt at clarification. The kind of contrast involved is however of obvious critical value. It is indeed one which McIntosh has taken considerably further in a study of *As You Like It* [424]. Here, the personal pronouns help to bring out the relationship between Celia and Rosalind. The former's regular form of address is seen to be *thou*, for she is 'impulsive and outgoing'. Rosalind, on the other hand, tends to use the more formal, protocol-observing *you*. There are some disturbing contradictions or at least contrasts here with Francis Berry's study —but these may well be resolved by reference to a poetic tradition which requires *thou* as a standard form of address, parallel to a colloquial tradition which in the theatre points to *thou* as a familiar form of address. In any case (and this suggested interpretation is far from adequate) the switch to the alternative form of address points to a change in situation or attitude. Celia using *you* is shown to be annoyed or 'full of petulant impatience'. Rosalind when she suddenly adopts *thou* reveals 'a lapse in her customary reserve'. The characters thus express deviations from their normal behaviour whenever a disturbance of some sort (the arrival of Orlando for example) occurs.

McIntosh tabulates all these deviations in detail, but some problems remain unsolved. For example, he does not refer to context in sufficient detail. He tends also to base his premises on the first scene of the play, which would seem to be much too restricted, for reversals, the 'abnormal' switching of personal pronouns, appear thereafter to be as frequent as normal usage. Neither does he invoke the (in this context) illuminating background of contemporary usage. For the impact of personal pronouns to be fully analysed, reference must obviously be made to this, and to their function in different genres and at different periods: the *vous* in *La Modification* would be much less strange in a poem; *thou* in a twentieth-century poem (by Walter de la Mare for example) contrasts violently in impact with that of a sixteenth-century poem; *tu* in French Classical drama indicates a sudden burst of emotion on the part of one or more of the protagonists, as in Phèdre's switch to *tu* when towards the end of Act II, sc. V, she is trying to seduce Hippolyte. Other languages more ready with this form of address (Spanish might be a case in point) could not perhaps achieve the same degree of impact by this means.

Such flexibility, or even instability, can be taken yet further. Even within one genre, different authors may handle the same pronoun with widely varying effect: 'Between the third person in Balzac and the third person in Flaubert there is a whole world of difference (that of the 1848 revolution); in the former we witness a spectacle harsh in its narrative thread but coherent and dependable; in it, order triumphs; with Flaubert we have an art form which in order to break free from its guilty conscience weighs down the convention or wildly attempts to destroy it.' [41, pp. 57–8.]

Personal pronouns rarely function in literature as they do in real life. The relationships between narrator, subject and reader/hearer are much more complex and variable. They may be deliberately established by the author's choice of pronoun and genre (or vice versa). Hypothetical experiences are angled in different ways. In old English, we are informed, the use of the first person singular is a mere genre device, something expected in elegies or riddles. It in no way relates to personal attachment [660, pp. 447 ff.]. Consider too the values of the first person in an epistolary novel (where different subjective points of view may be exchanged).

In poetry, *I* or *you* will therefore not necessarily point to a specific *I* (to be identified with the writer) or a particular *you* (to be confused with the reader). Susanne Langer states that 'in reflecting on lyric expression in the light of other literary work we shall find . . . that neither the person speaking nor the person spoken to is an actual human being, the writer or the reader; the rhetorical form is a means of creating an impersonal subjectivity which is the peculiar experiential illusion of a genre that creates no characters and no public events' [378, p. 260]. A centring or an expansion of experience are more pertinent notions here. Similarly the *I* of the novelist may relate to the notion of events witnessed, whereas the third person points to an actor, a participator. This is clearly not always the case, but we can give serious consideration to the suggestion that the third person singular is the basic convention of the novel [41, pp. 52–4] and that it points to notions of order or ordering, material dominated by the author, an illusion of reality, whereas the first person singular presents a situation which falls short of this or goes beyond it: the world then appears to be full of unknown factors (*Adolphe* or *David Copperfield*), is the over-systematic product of one individual brain (*L'Etranger* or *Les Mémoires d'Outre-tombe*) or makes no claim to reality at all (*Gulliver's Travels*). Thus in Margaret Drabble's novel *The Waterfall* the narrator's vain attempt to grasp the shifting uncertainties of her experience is brilliantly shown in the way she talks of herself at times from the more tendentious viewpoint of the first person and at others through the third person, which under normal circumstances would appear to be more 'dependable' and 'true' but which, when it is patently a character talking about herself, creates an extra area of distortion and tension. Flaubert of course achieves all these effects through third person narrative! And the convention is largely undermined in the twentieth century. But the general tendency would seem to be correctly defined, and there is no doubt that Flaubert himself, in the first sentence of *Madame Bovary* ('Nous étions à l'étude . . .'), seems indeed to be exploiting it by approaching the reader from an unexpected angle.

The use of pronouns is clearly an area which can be explored profitably. The need to be aware of genre and period conventions is very great. But perhaps the best approach is to realize that pronouns in literature have a special value which will tend not to be their everyday value. This can be examined empirically in individual texts, and will often give significant results [v. 100B].

Any study of the function of verbs in a particular passage or a poem will tend to take two aspects into account: their varying dynamism and descriptive qualities on the one hand and the way in which, in different genres, they handle the idea of tense which is inseparable from them. I intend to concentrate on the second aspect here, for it strikes me as being much less obvious or straightforward. It might be noted too that as soon as one turns one's attention away from the tense aspect of verbs, the category becomes much less easy to define. Dynamic, 'verbal' effects ('a sharp rap', 'footsteps') have perhaps even more impact, are perhaps even more 'verbal' because the verb is missed out. Verbs vary considerably in their dynamic potential: *flow*, *shatter*, *think*, and *eat* are hugely different. To describe them all as verbs is a useful way of distinguishing them from adjectives or nouns. But this distinction does not always mean very much to the critic (unless, say, the preponderance of verbs in a text is rather startling)—to group them semantically with words from other grammatical categories would seem to be much more rewarding. If grammatical analysis of verbs is going to have much sense critically, *tense* must be considered to be central. The first aspect fits more satisfactorily into the problems to be dealt with in the chapters on meaning and style and the computer.

As with personal pronouns, it must be emphasized that everyday and literary usage are in many respects radically different. In the first, tense is a sign of time relationship, the link in time between speaker and subject spoken about. In literature, it is much safer to assume that tense does not necessarily equal time but that conventional genre usage is an important determining factor. Thus it will be remembered that utopian novels (which we should expect to reflect life as it will be in the future) tend to express themselves through the medium of the preterite. As Weinrich points out in his book *Tempus* and in a lecture on tense and time delivered in 1968 in the University of Leeds (from which the main substance of this section is taken [v. 735B]), the preterite is as much as anything else a *sign* for narration. With the third person pronoun it therefore makes up a very explicit combination. We are immediately aware that we are being presented with a story, with a sequence of events rather than a lyric state.

The French narrative preterite, in this scheme, brings in ideas of remoteness: it suggests that the things, events and people described are there for us to examine, and are not a stimulus for our immediate action or reaction. As Barthes suggests, its role is to link up reality with one particular point, to 'cut away the mingled and superimposed moments of experience, and to extract from them a pure verbal act relieved of the existential roots of experience and set to link up logically with other actions, other processes, to create a general movement of events: its aim is to maintain a hierarchy in the domain of facts. The preterite form integrates itself implicitly into a chain of cause and effect . . .' [41, pp. 46–7]. The preterite, according to Barthes, would therefore (unlike his own style) tend to cut out any idea of the incomprehensible side of life. This can be demonstrated negatively by pointing to the way Camus, in *L'Etranger*, creates a deliberately meaningless succession of events merely by using the *passé composé*: the reader is affected by the fact that this tense is normally used in the disjointed discourse of everyday life, which relates to events which have just taken place, as they take place, as well as by the fact that he *expects* the preterite. Joyce Cary, too, in *A Fearful Joy* creates effects of unlogical sequence by setting the whole of his novel in the present tense. This is in one sense the equivalent of Camus's *passé composé*, for of course the contrast of preterite and colloquial perfect which Camus exploits is not possible in English. An English translation of *L'Etranger* might ideally be in the present. Once again expression would centre on what Barthes calls the density (rather than the significance) of life [41, p. 50]. Barthes is not completely right however: the use of the preterite cannot be said to exclude the absurd. The novels of Robbe-Grillet are enough to demonstrate that. It is rather a question of degree and style. The preterite is an almost exclusively literary tense in French. To use it is to imply some degree of organization, of abstraction from the incoherence of everyday life, or the description of some other kind of incoherence, verbal for example or pathological, or both combined.

Tense and genre should not therefore be separated in criticism. In this respect two typical classes of speech situation may be indicated: the narrative, which we have just looked at, and the discursive, relating more specifically to poetry. The tenses of discursive style relate to notions of response and action. If it is simplistic to say that the present tense is the tense of poetry, it would be correct to suggest that the present tense surprises us as little in poetry as the preterite does in the novel. Whilst the novel is likely to be preoccupied with a sequence of situations and states, poetry is inclined to show those which, in spite of their fluctuating complexity, are essentially stable. The alternative to the present in poetry is therefore not the preterite but the imperfect, which would not in this case be subservient to the preterite as it is in prose. The immediacy of the present, and its value for poetry, is brought out too by the fact that it is the common language for summaries, stage directions and scenarios.

These then are the norms which the poet, or the novelist, exploits or contradicts to obtain his effects. Susanne Langer has pointed to the way tenses are mixed in such heterogeneous forms as ballads or narrative verse [378, pp. 266 ff.]. Her very detailed analysis is especially interesting for its examination of tense shifts in *The Ancient Mariner*. At the end of the poem, the switch to the present is an indication of homecoming: the crisis is over:

> The Pilot and the Pilot's boy,
> I heard them coming fast:
> Dear Lord in Heaven! it was a joy
> The dead men could not blast.
>
> I saw a third—I heard his voice:
> It *is* the Hermit good!
> He singeth loud his godly hymns
> That he makes in the wood.

He'll shrieve my soul, he'll wash away
The Albatross's blood.
[My italics.]

Tense mixing can achieve a wide variety of effects. It can for example underline a sense of insecurity, as in some of Shakespeare's *thou* sonnets which, as Francis Berry points out, often move uneasily between imperfect, pluperfect and future. This is especially the case in those sonnets where the youth is not directly addressed but referred to as *he*. Pronominal complexity and the tensions of age and youth lead to a constant shifting of the time angle. In the *lust* sonnet, on the other hand (no. 129), a 'before and after' situation is sustained in part by a very powerful verbal switch from present to past:

Th' expence of Spirit in a waste of shame
Is lust in action, and till action, lust
Is perjured, murdrous, blouddy, full of blame,
Savage, extreame, rude, cruell, not to trust,
Injoyd no sooner but despised straight,
Past reason hunted, but no sooner had
Past reason hated as a swallowed bait,
On purpose layd to make the taker mad . . .

The perfect participles are too obsessively numerous after line 4 for them not to be a significant part of the sonnet's style.

In *Macbeth*, particular *moods* of the verb are contrasted: future indicative and the subjunctive point to the repeated conflict of future certainties and possibilities: 'If t'were done when tis done . . .' This of course develops with the play: tension between present and future now underlines the loss of certainty and its replacement by much less tangible hope [v. 68, pp. 48 ff.].

All this could well be shown without reference to grammar. At times indeed direct, non-grammatical analysis would be much less cumbersome. Reference to the linguistic devices involved does however have the value of showing how our experience of the play or sonnet is built up in verbal terms. Time, as Poulet has so admirably demonstrated, is an important dimension in literature.

To look at the way tense and mood are handled is a useful objective way of pinning down the temporal patterns of a particular work. It is a means of gathering preliminary or supporting information which must then be interpreted. Thus in Baudelaire's *Invitation au Voyage* there is a shift from dream evocation ('Songe à la douceur . . .') through possibility ('Déco*reraient* notre chambre . . .') to direct imperative ('*Vois* sur ces canaux/Dormir ces vaisseaux/Dont l'humeur *est* vagabonde . . .' [my italics]). The imperatives of the first and the last stanzas are very different semantically too: they underline the psychological development of the poem in which tense change plays an essential part.

The study of tense usage need not be restricted to individual authors or works. It can be a useful means of describing the mentality of a particular period. Tense simplicity in the seventeenth and eighteenth centuries has been noted by both Sayce and Berry [621, pp. 104 ff. and 68, pp. 119 ff.]. The frequent use of the universal present, the fact that the preterite is preferred to the imperfect and that verbal constructions in general are kept simple would seem to point to an age not much given to high flown imaginative speculation or an interest in the exceptional. Hence the marked contrast between pre-Cartesian Europe, the Europe of Romanticism and the period (1650–1750) which separates them.

It is also useful to examine the degree to which the verb (whether we emphasize its tense aspect or its dynamic quality) is a central element in style. This we shall see when we look at syntactical problems and when we come to the problems of computerized analysis. The aim, whatever aspect we are looking at, should be as always to establish significance. Potential verbal patterns are of little use. When Gaylord Jones writes '. . . formally, the sonnet [Shakespeare 30] appears to be composed of two symmetrically composed conditional sentences with the last protasis following the apodosis' he is right to add 'semantically, of course, the sonnet makes no sense when divided thus' [343, p. 1034]. Such an approach illustrates the dangers of looking for grammar as an end in itself. Categories and function should be defined in relation to the substance of a text and not by reference to an empty shell.

We have already seen (in chapter one) that grammatical analysis is a useful basis for grouping and analysing key or rhyme words. It enables us to establish links between groups of words, or to strengthen already existing patterns. The writer's world becomes, in that case, one where verbal, nominal or adjectival impact predominates, and grammatical grouping might thus be seen to have some sort of metaphorical value: it points to value and meaning which the individual word could not possess.

This is additional, but similar, to the implications behind the tense usage I have just examined—it links up, for example, with the fact that the use of the preterite in French may be considered to have metaphorical value: in the nineteenth-century novel, it implies that the world is to be described within an artistic convention and that the metaphysics of this world will remain within certain bounds.

But this is not the only way grammar and metaphor may be related. If one aim of textual criticism is to examine essential functions of style, then it is useful to look at the way grammar functions in metaphor: the varying procedures and impacts which arise when different grammatical elements stand at the core of an image. Such studies, which demonstrate the aesthetic dimension of grammar, must be associated primarily with the name of Christine Brooke-Rose who in her *Grammar of Metaphor* uses grammatical analysis to describe the structure of different kinds of metaphor. She is not of course alone in this particular field: Monique Parent's study of imagery in Barrès's *Colline inspirée* [518] splits up images according to whether they are based on a substantive, a verb or an adjective. Meuraud's study of plant imagery in Eluard's poetry [459] devotes space to the grammatical structures of imagery: verbs, adjectives, singulars, plurals etc., as the focal point of the image. Other protagonists are not hard to find [39 for example], but *The Grammar of Metaphor* still constitutes perhaps the most useful basis for the study of individual authors, and most of my examples in the coming pages are taken from it.

Brooke-Rose mentions the different accredited ways of classifying images: by species or genres; animate or inanimate; by domain of thought; by dominant trait. All these are purely semantic and contrast with the author's own linguistic approach, for if some of the categories she uses are not explicitly linguistic, the phenomena they refer to are. For example Brooke-Rose gives the name of simple replacement to the process whereby 'the proper term is replaced altogether by the metaphor, without being mentioned at all' [90, p. 24]: 'Loving Shepherd of thy sheep' for example, or 'the pit that doth await us all' or 'my mantle and my strength'. In modern poetry, especially where it is used in conjunction with less apparently figurative words, simple replacement has come to play an important part. One thinks for example of Mallarmé's sonnet 'Le vierge le vivace et le bel aujourd'hui' which is a sustained example of simple replacement: the terms of the first line and expressions like 'un cygne d'autrefois', 'le transparent glacier des vols qui n'ont pas pui' are at no point explained, although they do not represent stock metaphorical terms. Here is one of the basic elements in 'obscure' modern poetry since the middle of the nineteenth century, the sense of mystery which grows from words used literally and yet which *seem* to refer metaphorically to other things, to imply a great deal more than their literal meaning (a process often called the objective correlative):

> The river's tent is broken: the last fingers of leaf
> Clutch and sink into the wet bank. The wind
> Crosses the brown land unheard. The nymphs are departed.
> Sweet Thames, run softly till I end my song . . .
>
> [*Waste Land* III, ll. 1–4.]

—yet the meaning behind them is never elucidated by the poet (*and I think critics are wrong to try and elucidate it, for there is really no second meaning—only a vast pregnancy of the words themselves*). This is grammatically explainable. It can be related to the way the definite article appears to point to something precise and to be expected (although at the same time we are surprised by the unexpected, mysterious facts the article ushers in). Other grammatical elements (possessive adjectives, demonstratives) may also be associated with simple replacement, but none is so striking as the definite article. As another critic, G. R. Hamilton suggests in a penetrating and detailed study of this phenomenon, *The Tell Tale Article*: 'The poet's use of the definite article often suggests that he has become absorbed and isolated in his own vision', and yet at the same time 'paradoxically, the poet, when most solitary [because of his use of esoteric allusions], seems to take us closest into his confidence'. The definite article transmits a sense of uniqueness which again evokes the mysterious potency of the thing alluded to [p. 14]. This non-cataphoric (i.e. ultimately non-demonstrative) value of the article is clearly a value which helps us to characterize poetry in its difference from prose [v. 284, p. 59].

Christine Brooke-Rose's second category relates to the use of pointing formulae, often based on *this*, *thus*, *so*, *such*:

> A woman drew her long black hair out tight
> And fiddled whisper music on those strings.
> [*Waste Land* V, ll. 377–8.]

—but which may grow out of parallel constructions:

> Then all the woes and wrecks which I survive

where literal and metaphorical elements are placed side by side, and thus by implication closely related.

To be is also a regular grammatical basis for metaphor, as is *to make*: 'He is a very devil'; 'Je suis le ténébreux, le veuf, l'inconsolé'; 'Mon âme est un trois-mâts . . .';

> For love, all love of other sights controls,
> And makes one little roome an everywhere.

In the 'genitive link' Brooke-Rose sees 'the most complex form of all for the noun metaphor is linked sometimes to its proper term and sometimes to a third term which gives the provenance of the metaphoric term: B *is part of*, or *derives from*, or *belongs to*, or *is attributed to* or *is found in* C, from which relationship we can guess A, the proper term'; cf: 'That life, a very rebel to my will.' This is complex because 'the same grammatical links *of*, *in*, *with*, *from*, *out of* . . . are used to express many different relationships, even the identity of two linked terms: e.g. in the *fire* of love, love is the fire . . .' [p. 25].

The Grammar of Metaphor is highly detailed—my account of it can only be partial and sketchy. The author rightly puts most emphasis on the noun, for 'whereas the noun is a complex of attributes [some of which can therefore be abstracted for metaphorical purposes] an action or attribute [verb or adjective] cannot be decomposed. Its full meaning depends on the noun with which it is used and it can only be decomposed into the species of itself according to the adjective with which it is used.' [p. 209.] She nevertheless devotes great space to the behaviour of metaphors centred on grammatical categories other than the noun. Many aspects of dynamic or static metaphorical expression are thus explored—and this without at any time grammatical description appearing to be an end in itself. Christine Brooke-Rose is never afraid, as we have seen, of linking up grammatically disparate categories in defining metaphorical types. Similarly she is prepared to admit that variations of one type may come from paralleling procedures which dispense altogether with significant grammatical terms. She does not therefore exclude an alliance with semantic methods of analysis.

On the other hand her approach *is* one which sets out to establish extra-textual categories. Its lists of examples and variations may at times appear a little dreary. Wider contexts are of necessity excluded, and if the liking of different poets for different types of imagery is also studied, the deeper thematic motives (see my chapter on construction) are not really considered. If the book is therefore essential reading for those interested in close textual criticism, it is because, like so many of the methods examined so far, it provides a tool which the student may make use of *if the text so requires it*. It does not point to essential literary phenomena which must crop up in any text. Most seriously, perhaps, in spite of the fact that meaning is in no way excluded, Christine Brooke-Rose is not centrally preoccupied with it. Thus, although there are too many examples for the reader ever to have the impression that metaphor might be reduced to a series of empty patterns, the quotations are too short for the author to be able systematically to couple her analysis with those aspects of imagery (and poetry at large) which, since the early 1930s and Empson, we have come to consider as central: degrees of clarity and ambiguity, the clash between the implications of clarity and the obscurity of the idea. The whole question in fact of the *impact* and quality of metaphor. Hamilton's study of the definite article shows however that such undertakings are possible. Perhaps what is really needed is some combination of Christine Brooke-Rose's approach and the long-established categories listed above [v. too 81B, 303A, 393B].

The impact of individual grammatical categories is only one aspect of the problems I am dealing with here. Their various combinations are also important, whether one means by that the varying 'dosages' involved or the ordering of categories. Both these phenomena are of course known as syntax. For linguisticians like Chomsky [v. 131], syntax is the central element in grammar. Whether this holds good for grammar-based criticism may well be another matter, of course—the fact that syntactical analysis may ignore meaning altogether and deal in empty formulae should make one a little suspicious. Neglect of syntax is on the other hand difficult to justify and is becoming more so as concordances are more widely used. Indeed it has been suggested that in Empson's revolutionary studies of ambiguity in poetry [202 and 203] 'the omission of syntax is perhaps the only serious defect' [620, p. 126]. Up to sentence level, syntactical possibilities must very seriously restrict and determine a writer's mode of thinking and expression. Above that level, restriction may be much less noticeable but it still exists. A writer like Winifred Nowottny for example does therefore seem to be forgetting the importance of syntactical formulae associated with many types of writing and ideas when she claims that 'above the level of the sentence the structure of the language itself does not constrain a speaker's choice of the best way to arrange his discourse' [504, p. 73 see

179B]. We have already seen that tense usage, personal pronoun implications or the exploitation of sound in poetry all constitute real pressures on a writer working in a particular genre. It will I think become apparent that period and genre style are syntactically 'codified' not only for individual sentences but also for the *succession* of sentences which make up the writer's discourse. My chapter on computers should add further evidence of this.

The impact of a sentence or a group of sentences must relate to the ratios of grammatical elements found in them. Action or description, abstract event or concrete tangible scenes, physical or mental movement or immobility—these things might depend say on whether a noun/adjective combination dominates or a verb/adverb one. Compare the first stanza of the following poem with the second:

Tiny beside the enormous bole of the beech
Your back to the pre-war photographer, your head
Flopped back like a child's, you stare vaguely
Up into the universe of the summer leaves
Rehearsing a series of similar appearances
In doorways mines ruins avenues, confirming
That the Corinthian Order of the Lateran
Is gigantic, and Banteai Serai a toy.

The beech crashed that winter, but it's not only
That monument that you outlive, for yours is the face
That launched the ships and could not be got out of the mind.
Yours the eternal body in the doorway;
You are the temple goddess that settled dimensions,
The continuity girl of at least a hundred
Generations of architects.

[Lionel Brett, *To Give Scale*, London Magazine,
October/November 1971, p. 56.]

A whole question of weight is involved too. It has been pointed out that a 'nominal sentence is likely to be longer than its verbal counterpart.' In nominalization there are likely to be fewer clauses per sentence and the number of distinct sentence patterns will decrease.' [745, p. 216.] The statistical side of this problem will be left to a later chapter. But even with statistics it would still seem that this is a little explored area of style: 'the peculiar suitability of one rather than another grammatical pattern to a particular situation is less commonly considered' and, a point which is relevant to my remarks in the preceding paragraph, 'the subtle interaction of grammar and lexis has as yet received little attention' [427, p. 95]. The same could indeed be said of grammatical categories, for even the groups of opposing categories which I have just given are not always accepted. Konrad in her *Etude sur la métaphore* [p. 69] brings together verb and adjective as functions of another totality, the noun. The similarity between noun and adjective is considered to be much less important. In my chapter on computers, it will be seen that verb/adjective ratios are thought by another scholar to be the most important! Such apparent contradictions do not necessarily imply confusion. They merely point to the limiting relevance of grammatical categories taken at face value or individually. The study of differing combinations or opposing groups might merely allow one to pinpoint the impact of differing syntactical sets. For the purposes of criticism, grammatical categories never oppose each other radically or permanently. At most one can suggest that the same combinations can create widely differing effects (cf. *a sudden blow*! and *a sweet smile*!), whereas differing categories are much less likely to produce similar results.

It should perhaps be realized too that, as in so many other areas, grammatical analysis needs to draw on wider sources of information. The language involved, the stage of its development and the kind of social and aesthetic conventions controlling it must be taken into account, as Vinay and Darbelnet have shown in their *Stylistique comparée du français et de l'anglais.* Josephine Miles is, one feels, being a little crude in her methods when she points to the fact that the typical combination in Dryden of one adjective to two nouns and one verb is the same as that found in Vergil, Horace and Ovid [463, p. 185]. In two languages as radically different as Latin and English such facts cannot be very conclusive whatever the importance of Classical literature at the time when Dryden was writing.

Two examples will however point to the value of this kind of analysis once perspective is right. M. K. Halliday [281 esp. pp. 61 ff.] takes descriptions of rooms and furniture in John Braine, Dylan Thomas and Angus Wilson and shows that the varying effects they create can be expressed in terms of grammatical combinations as well as by reference to lexical sets, collocation and cohesion. The second example comes from a reading of Pushkin's *The Captain's Daughter*. In spite of a highly adventurous story, and in spite of the fact that the work dates from the Romantic period, the style is curiously flat. Such restraint, which is of considerable thematic significance, can be described grammatically—adjectives are very rare, nouns and verbs take the main emphasis. Movement and fact are thus given most importance. Deeper exploration of impression, emotion or character is excluded. We are reminded of Voltaire's style which, with its emphasis on auxiliary verbs, underlines the importance in the author's thinking of motivation and relationships between events [v. 621, pp. 34–5]. Such styles thus stand in very marked contrast to that of French novelists like the Goncourt brothers, Zola or Flaubert who for various reasons were strongly attracted to description. Here sentence structure, as Ullmann has shown in his chapter on the Goncourts [704], leads to much more sparing use of finite verbs, which tend in any case to be in the imperfect; substantive/adjective combinations and verbal substantives become of central importance. In place of the terseness of Pushkin we have passages like the following (from Zola's *La Faute de l'abbé Mouret*):

La clairière était faite de grands rosiers étagés, montant avec une telle débauche de branches, un fouillis de lianes épineuses tels, que des nappes épaisses de feuillage s'accrochaient en l'air, restaient suspendues, tendaient d'un arbuste à l'autre les pans d'une tente volante. On ne voyait entre ces lambeaux découpés comme de la fine guipure, que des trous de jour imperceptibles, un crible d'azur laissant passer la lumière en une impalpable poussière de soleil. [Pléïade, vol. I, p. 1338.]

The subject-matter is of course vastly different too. But differing combinations of grammatical elements do not need to handle different material to produce contrasting effects. The above passage could be rewritten as a series of short sentences, or present participles could merely be replaced by finite verbs and conjunctions, and the impact would shift immediately from the creation of a lush, sensual atmosphere to much more factual description; relationships between things would give way to relationships between events.

Such rewriting is revealing for other reasons. It leads for example to syntactical reordering and brings out the fact that ratios of grammatical elements are not enough in themselves. Emphasis through positioning is also very important [v. 141, pp. 182 ff.]. Thus, in a study of Thomas Hardy's style [486], J. Farrington Morris does not merely examine ratios of nouns, verbs, tenses, and types of phrases and clauses; he also considers the frequency with which verbs directly follow their subject and the grammatical nature of what follows the verbs. Four positions for phrase and clause modification are thus established and tabulated. Mourot too [488] takes key sentence structures in Chateaubriand and examines the importance of such underlining devices as punctuation and word order.

The emphasis of this chapter is shifting clearly from 'dosage' to word order. Questions of 'dosage' should not of course disappear when word order is mentioned. Both are simultaneously present in the text, and any criticism which looks at the one whilst pretending the other does not exist is in danger of producing strange results.

It is in part because she steers a middle course between these two poles that the work of Josephine Miles on poetic syntax since the sixteenth century is so important and stimulating in spite of its defects. Her main thesis (set out concisely in a major article [463], or in considerably more detail but perhaps more rigidly in her earlier book [462]), is that any sentence structure will fall into three main groups: *phrasal* (with its predominance of adjectives, nouns, subordinate clauses and participles—very much like the

Zola passage just quoted), *clausal* (which is predominantly verbal, a series of actions—one thinks of Pope or Racine) and *balanced* (a mixture, as one might expect, of the two—Keats for example). Josephine Miles examines noun/verb/adjective relationships and syntactical structures for 1,000 lines each of a large number of representative poets (10 per era, 130 in all). Her conclusions are that the succession of styles in English poetry between 1500 and 1900 is as follows: clausal — clausal — balanced — clausal — clausal — balanced — phrasal — phrasal — balanced — clausal — clausal — balanced [463, p. 179]. Josephine Miles also expresses the fluctuations on a graph and this helps to cut out the excessively sharp transitions or the over-similarity between one period and another. She agrees that variations of style within one particular period exist and that there is greater fragmentation of styles at some periods than at others (1670–1700; 1770–1870), but she points out that in the past these features have been stressed to the neglect of her suggested categories. [463, p. 178.] Thus the history of post-Renaissance poetry in England would seem to be made up syntactically, stylistically, of an alternation, with various intermediary stages, between *clausal* poems, which are stanzaic, active, offering 'argument or narrative in clearly defined stages and formal external order', and *phrasal* ones which exhibit 'line by line progression and cumulative participial modification in description and invocation without stress on external rhyming or grouping. So the strongly stanzaic verse of the sixteenth century became moderated in the more skilful blank verse and couplets of its last generation.' [463, pp. 182–3.] Of course the effect of these modes of expression will vary from one period (or era) to another—changes in vocabulary and subject-matter ensure this. Indeed vocabulary is the last likely element to recur, whereas syntactic structure is the most likely. But an essential dimension of poetry in different periods can be compared, as Josephine Miles demonstrates when she sets Shakespeare and Wyatt side by side: the former achieves greater balance in his verse by using phrasal constructions and verbs where the latter uses clausal constructions and adjectives [pp. 13–14]. The author also points out that many poets

(Donne, Dryden, Thomson, Keats, Eliot) tend to keep to one sentence structure. This may well be due to the strong conditioning factors present in language and literary convention at any one time and which only 'allow' the writer to modify the standard mode within certain limits.

All these findings and the methods behind them are fascinating. They have the great advantage of being applicable to relatively small pieces of verse as a normal part of close critical work. Indeed, the method involved is even more effective if one shifts slightly from the attempt to make sweeping statements about literary history to the task of describing one poet in relation to his named contemporaries or to poets from another period. There is no doubt that other literatures would greatly benefit from similar studies. But some points in the approach would have to be improved: the way Josephine Miles breaks up the four centuries she studies is to say the least worrying. For example Donne and Shakespeare are both classified in the 1570–1600 group, which would seem rather early especially for Donne; Wordsworth and Blake are both made to belong to the 1770–1800 period, which neglects the fifty years the former still had to live; Poe (who died in 1849) is classified in the 1840–70 period; whilst Chaucer, who presumably had to be brought in somehow, belongs to the period 1500–40! One result is that people like Shakespeare and Milton appear to be anomalous.

I wonder whether Josephine Miles's conclusions would not have been more impressive still had she studied prose works rather than works of poetry where genre, metre and notions of suitable vocabulary (and therefore perhaps even preference for one grammatical category over another) tend to distort the 'natural' propensities of the language. Had she, whilst retaining verse, eliminated narrative verse, her results might again have been more dependable.

The other problem is a semantic one: Josephine Miles tends to see each grammatical category as being semantically stable. The difference between transitive and intransitive verbs, verbal and static nouns, flat and dynamic adjectives, the value (verbal or otherwise) of prepositions or adverbs—all these variations, and others, are ignored. And yet they make for a radical difference between the following two extracts (which are *grammatically* similar):

For Godsake hold your tongue, and let me love,
  Or chide my palsie, or my gout,
My five gray hairs, or ruin'd fortune flout,
  With wealth your state, your minde with Arts improve,
    Take you a course, get you a place,
    Observe his honour, or his grace,
Or the Kings reall, or his stamped face
  Contemplate, what you will, approve,
  So you will let me love.

[Donne: *The Canonization.*]

The woods decay, the woods decay and fall,
The vapours weep their burthen to the ground,
Man comes and tills the field and lies beneath,
And after many a summer dies the swan.
Me only cruel immortality
Consumes: I wither slowly in thine arms,
Here at the quiet limit of the world,
A white-hair'd shadow roaming like a dream
The ever silent spaces of the East,
Far-folded mists, and gleaming halls of morn.

[Tennyson: *Tithonus.*]

More positively however, Josephine Miles, by highlighting the constants in a genre and their variations, offers further information for those who are anxious, not perhaps to produce the ultimate definition of poetry (that would seem impossible), but to show what its basic characteristics may be. The texts she quotes seem to establish that poetry may be defined by the way certain types of subject and vocabulary necessarily link up to a phrasal or a clausal 'mode'. This could of course signify that poetry can only be defined for a particular period, and that wider definitions are a waste of time. Syntactic analyses of Pope or Wordsworth would clearly produce a wildly varying set of norms. And yet there does seem to be a general overall norm: for the four centuries involved, the fact that clausal and balanced modes far outweigh phrasal ones points perhaps to something fundamental about the structure of poetic language in English. Unless of course changes in periodization, which I personally feel to be necessary, produce a different sequence of norms (and therefore perhaps a different overall norm!). Faced with such bewildering alternatives, it is useful to remember that fact is always flexible in criticism. I am not sure that a clear-cut answer, even if it were possible, would be more useful than the realization that such questions exist and must be taken into account.

The value of sentence structure analysis (or at least the stimulus it gives to the way we look at a text) should now be clear. If we look at syntax as sequence (rather than as a variety of combinations of different grammatical categories) other possibilities appear. These will now relate to pattern and motif. The technically minded (those who are perhaps more interested in linguistics than in criticism) might here be tempted to bandy terms like syntagmata and paradigms, but there is little need for this. It is enough to suggest that (as with sound motifs) the syntactical elements of different parts of a poem may echo each other (or set up contrasts) and thus point to parallels or contrasts in meaning. Or they point to meaning *tout court*—meaning for the poem as distinct from the meaning the same expression would have if detached from its poetic context. The statement 'he sees the dog', followed by 'he hits a cat' offers parallels of a semantic nature. But if these two sentences are followed, in a poem especially, by 'I buy this box', syntactical similarities (the sequence: personal pronoun, verb in the present, noun direct object) will suggest that the statements are not unrelated in spite of very real dissimilarities of meaning and syntactical differences. In a varied form these very simple examples illustrate a common phenomenon in a huge number of poems, whether they are narrative or lyrical. The stanzas of Hardy's poem *In Tenebris* begin respectively with 'Wintertime nighs', 'Flower-petals flee', 'Birds faint in dread', 'Leaves freeze to dun', 'Tempests may scath', 'Black is night's cope'. The syntax of one and two is the same; three and four are similarly parallel. In addition the first four openings have many similarities: initial noun subjects with no article immediately followed by a verb in the present. The fifth begins in the same way as its predecessors. This underlines the fact that the poem is still moving in the same context. Only the last stanza begins in a totally different way, stressing perhaps its importance as a summing up. Other elements, vocabulary and rhythm especially, ensure a wider general unity. But it is significant that each stanza but one of the poem begins with signs which beyond the isolated meaning of words indicate that it is handling the same subject-matter as its predecessors [290, pp. 24–5]. And this of course is only the first point one can make. In the last three stanzas of the poem the repeated pattern 'But friends can not turn cold', 'But love can not make smart', 'But death will not appal' extend and deepen the poem's unity. 'Friends', 'love', 'death' on the one hand, 'not turn cold', 'not make smart' and 'not appal' on the other, because they are parallel because of syntax and other grammatical features, combine and contrast and progress in a way which would be impossible if these parallels did not exist. This kind of analysis helps to show that the text being looked at is poetry and not some other literary form. It would seem therefore to be a useful part of any close criticism of poetry. When in *Gerontion* T. S. Eliot writes 'An old man in a dry month' and then a little later 'An old man in a windy house' the syntax plays a crucial part in the echoing of what would otherwise be less tightly related expressions (for they could have been expressed by varying syntactic sequences). As in the other examples I have mentioned, it takes the words that crucial step further: its insistent similarity suggests to us that *we should not take the words literally.* Syntactic patterning is a frequent and effective basis for metaphor. The 'dry month' and the 'windy house' are (at least) an expression of the sterile, uncomfortable dead-end in which the old man finds himself. This is one of the essential functions of what Levin in his study on *Linguistic Structures in Poetry* calls coupling (i.e. the meaning/

grammar parallels I have just described). Jakobson's insistence that poetry concentrates on 'the tangibility of the language as such', which he also calls the 'set towards the message', clearly relates to this as well as to the sounds of verse. This is why he underlines the predominant importance in poetry of combination over selection [v. 335 esp. pp. 302 ff.].

Such descriptions become even more interesting, of course, when they are added to the more conventional moulds of rhyme, rhythm, alliteration and the like, and emphasis will vary according to the poem. But as I suggested in the last chapter, rhythm and grammar may be expressed in terms of each other: they certainly are in *In Tenebris* and *Gerontion.* Methods become useful when they intersect in this way, because within the poem, rhythm, rhyme and grammatical parallels interact at a practical level to create meaning which would otherwise be far more diffuse, far less pointed.

The central importance of grammar and perhaps especially syntax is worth stressing, however. Meaning depends much more on them than on other elements I have just mentioned. Grammatical complexity together with grammatical equivalence are perhaps just as important as the rather more famous notions of ambiguity and deviation which will come up later [60, p. 78].

The importance of syntax as a key to the way literary prose works may be even greater, if in a different way. Paralleling disappears (or diminishes radically) as does verbal ambiguity. This is quite logical, for the syntactical similarities which imply parallel meaning in apparently dissimilar statements suggest at the same time that words are being used ambiguously.

The syntactical analysis of prose will therefore bring out other things, and again this should result from the critic's practical needs rather than from any abstract or a prioristic wish to be original. He may, for example, be preoccupied with the stylistic implications of Montaigne's development from the short, rather impersonal *Essais* he wrote initially to the more expanded, wandering and at times very subjective productions like 'Des Coches', which he was writing some sixteen or seventeen years later. Syntax can be very useful indeed here as will be seen by referring to Croll's study already mentioned [158, pp. 341–61]. For it is clear that the shift from a balance of idea and statement to the process whereby an idea is approached from a succession of widely varying angles implies syntactic changes. Croll points [p. 346] to 'the varying length of the members within the period' leading to a real sense of asymmetry. This latter is also caused by 'conspicuous differences in form with or without differences in length'. The writer may 'begin a succession of members with different kinds of subject words'. There will be radical switches in point of view some of which will be marked by grammatical jumps, say from first to third person. The style will be jerky—conjunctions will be used 'without any plus force' [p. 348]—that is to say that the ideas are linked together loosely rather than related in logical extension or contrast. Thus the subordinate members of the sentence will tend to exist in 'greater independence and autonomy'. As a result of all this, one of the prime characteristics of Montaigne's later style (that it is an adequate vehicle of the author's attempt to paint a true portrait of himself) can be expressed grammatically—the shifting associations of the author's ideas are directly represented by the loosened syntactic structure just described. For other writers this will have other less subjective implications, although basic intellectual assumptions (i.e. how to go about expressing one's ideas) will remain the same.

Sometimes the results are not merely a confirmation or an explanation. They offer startling correction to subjective impressions. It might be thought for example that the contorted prose of a Mallarmé and the mysteries of surrealist writings (not very distant from each other in time) make use of the same grammatical distortions. Norman Paxton shows convincingly however that such devices as truncation, condensation and distortion of word order play an important part in Mallarmé's prose style [524]. The surrealists on the other hand tend to be impeccably 'grammatical'. Their sentence structures are often quite normal, or they may adopt the (again rather more unexceptional) technique of stringing together absolute or determinative clauses. They make great use of verbs in the present and may on occasion cut out link-words. So even when they do diverge from the norm, their tricks are quite different from Mallarmé's. The real roots of their esotericism lie elsewhere (especially in unusual word combinations) [36, pp. 238–9]. Obscurity itself may result from many factors: subject-matter, genre norms, the ordering of material and language. Syntactical analysis is one useful means of exploring them [v. too 141, pp. 182 ff.].

Some dangers should be avoided however. Poetry cannot be analysed grammatically if the terminology used is itself vague and loosely handled. Terms like *syntax* and *grammar* should be allowed to keep their usually accepted meaning, and should never be used impressionistically. An exemplary culprit here is Donald Davie who in his *Articulate energy* talks about syntax like music or mathematics or even about modern poets rejecting syntax completely [p. 67]! Rather than such confusing generalization, the isolated point is often much more satisfying. The breathless, scrambling drive of Shakespeare's sonnet 129 is in part due to systematic use of unfinished syntactic units [79, p. 151]; Villon's elliptical language can similarly be put down to incomplete sentences [220, pp. 78 ff.]. Such facts are a direct description of the texture of the poem.

The value of grammar and especially syntax for historical studies should be reasonably clear. It has been very well demonstrated by Stephen Ullmann (see especially his chapter on new patterns of sentence structure in the Goncourts [704]) or by Richard Sayce in his *Style in French Prose*. Grammatical information is illuminating in widely differing domains: Colin Clark's demonstration that in *Sir Gawain and the Green Knight* syntax is a method of characterization [135]—or the brilliant pages where Nabokov shows that 'the peripheral characters in Gogol's *Dead Souls* are engendered by the subordinate clauses of the novel's various metaphors, comparisons and lyrical outbursts. We are faced by the remarkable phenomenon of mere forms of speech giving rise to live creatures' [497, p. 78].

Nabokov's analysis remains firmly anchored in the way sentences behave. Syntax is taken literally. There is however a tendency in modern criticism to use the term metaphorically, which Barthes mentions [43, pp. 27–8] as does Todorov [686]. This tendency is, of course, neither as new nor as French (Barthes ascribes it to Greimas) as one might be led to think. Sayce a good ten years earlier gave a much more lucid and complete account of this idea: 'in a typical novel, the hero might be considered as the noun or the pronoun subject in the first or third person; the action or plot as the verb (active or passive); the external world and the other characters as the object or complement. The other characters in turn may be represented by relative pronouns and their doings by relative clauses. Descriptions of time and setting correspond to adverbial and adjectival clauses. Transitions are the equivalents of conjunctions, their omission produces the effect of asyndeton . . . Tense [and, one might add, mood] governs the whole work as well as a single sentence . . .' Thus one can follow 'the expansion of the linguistic patterns of the sentence into the structural patterns of the work' [620].

This is not of course pure speculative metaphor. It is firmly justified by the fact that grammatical categories are unnecessarily cramped if they are reduced to single words. Verbal, adjectival and nominal functions and the rest may well be expressed by much wider units. The realization that different aspects of the novel may have varying grammatical force is a very useful indication of the way its different tensions, its dynamism or stasis, are created.

The basic principle involved here is the diversity and freedom of grammatical categories and sentence structures which may break free from their normal framework and restrictions. It is perhaps an indication of the adaptability of grammatical analysis that syntax may be looked at from a completely different point of view: the attempt to express style in an author as the variation of basic sentence patterns. Sayce's sentence pattern diagrams [v. 621] are an early and successful suggestion of this. More recently, however, the emphasis has shifted to the value of transformational or generative grammars. The author's sentences may for example be rewritten in order to reduce them to their simplest syntactical forms: e.g. 'The man with the blue hat standing over there came to see me yesterday' becomes 'The man has a blue hat. He is standing over there. He came to see me yesterday.' The writer may then be seen basically as producing *transformations* of the resultant simple forms. These, it is said, allow the critic to supplement the parallel patterns I have already mentioned by revealing more permanent syntactic structures in a given writer.

Such principles have been well demonstrated practically by Ohmann [509]. One should, he suggests, think of transformations as 'manipulations . . . [of] fully formed sentences rather than as ways of getting to parts of fully formed sentences from incomplete abstract symbols . . .' [p. 429]. Complex sentences are a build-up of simple ones, style being very much concerned with alternatives. Ohmann shows the value of his approach by reducing part of a sentence from Faulkner's *The Bear* to its simplest grammatical form. The necessary transformations are then described. It is noted that they produce drastic changes in the style with little change in the meaning. Relative clauses, conjunctions, comparatives are the important elements which disappear. They are therefore shown to be central to the style of Faulkner's original sentence. To put it another way: Faulkner may be considered to be taking simple sentence forms and producing his sentence by making a characteristic choice of certain types of transformation. *These the critic has reversed* and in so doing highlighted. The conceptual orientation of Faulkner's expression is revealed. This is the way he organizes experience, and it can be expressed grammatically. Ohmann recognizes (in *Literature as Sentences*) that there are stylistic differences between alternatives, that different versions 'structure and screen the content differently'. He also points out that the sentence the author wrote acquires part of its unique character by resounding against unwritten alternatives (especially the sentence in its most basic form) [p. 233, v. too 281, p. 65]. The neatness of transformation as a tool is confirmed when Ohmann goes on to contrast Faulkner with Hemingway. The stylistic difference between the two authors is profound. With the latter, transformations are significantly straightforward—the simple sentence forms produced (mainly by eliminating indirect speech) do not differ greatly from the original. It is interesting that huge stylistic differences can be explained (a better word would be *described*) so simply. The simplicity and therefore the wide general usefulness of the method is impressive, although Ohmann does say that Henry James, for example, because of the high number of intercalated subsidiary clauses, phrases and interrupting qualifiers, could not be analysed in the same way as Faulkner, for the very large number of these 'embedded' elements outweighs, and may contain more information than, the main sentence. The interrelated elements, once in their simplest form, are therefore written in a different order to maintain the emphasis of the original [v. too 123B]. Sentences pointing to simultaneous parallel preoccupations are thus established, and this is a rather more complicated procedure. But the complications are not enormous and one might suppose that the authors concerned (James, Proust and some baroque authors mentioned above) are in no sense as numerous as those to whom the simpler procedures may be applied.

Styles thus depend in part on the kind of transformational operations (addition, deletion, reordering and combination) on which they are built. [509, p. 437.] If a critic restricts himself to syntax, he will inevitably leave out important elements, a risk in any grammatical approach: image, sound, articulation of ideas above sentence level, type of vocabulary, tone, the varying semantic values of the same syntactical pattern [v. 64]. All this Ohmann accepts [v. 511, pp. 406 ff.], but it would be rash to follow Riffaterre or Hobsbaum in their rejection of grammar because it is thus revealed to be a limited and fragmentary approach [v. 584; 590, pp. 474–5; 309, pp. 188–207]. We might rather see Riffaterre's attitude as no more than a timely warning which should qualify the value and success of Josephine Miles's or Ohmann's work. He does not hide the fact that transformational analysis, like grammatical analysis in general, may be a highly versatile method in whatever language one is working, and whether one is preoccupied with literary history, the development of an author's style, or the style of an individual work.

Ohmann suggests that transformations are not only a means of describing the author's technique, but that 'since critical understanding follows and builds on understanding of sentences, [they] should eventually be a reliable assistant in the effort of seeing just how a given literary work sifts through a reader's mind, what cognitive and emotional processes it sets in motion, what organization of experience it encourages' [510, p. 238]. Yet again, it would seem clear, from what we have already seen, that most grammatical methods of analysis could be described in a similar way.

Describing the grammar of a text is often a straightforward affair. If it is sufficiently detailed, it offers solid objective facts about style, especially when one is dealing with an esoteric piece of writing. Grammatical analysis is very versatile: prose as well as verse may profitably be studied from that angle as may period styles (provided, of course, that criteria peculiar to each of these are borne in mind). It would be foolish to separate grammar from other aspects of a work, but it is clear that the analysis of sentence structure and the functions of different parts of speech can produce results which make the major areas examined in the coming chapters noticeably more significant.

CHAPTER THREE

MEANING I: WORDS

Neither sounds nor grammatical elements can have any real critical interest in themselves. We need to look at them because they act as a support to meaning—their importance varies from one text to another. In connected language, they are of course inseparable from words. But the essential part of any message must be in the words themselves and the relations between them. This would seem pretty obvious, if the contortions of some critics did not at times lead one to think otherwise!

This chapter and the next will look at ways in which meaning in a literary work may be approached. *Meaning I* is concerned with what may be achieved by looking at the vocabulary of a text, words that is, in some degree of isolation. *Meaning II* will look at the ways in which wider questions of meaning are relevant to criticism.

As may be expected, some critics have pointed to the defects of a lexical approach: Milic, asserting that style is the appreciation of quantifiable and mainly subconscious phenomena, rejects the author's choice of vocabulary (along with rhetorical devices, imagery, metrics and prose rhythms . . .) because it is conscious and context-bound [472, p. 83]. In a totally different approach, Susanne Langer suggests that literature is made up of events, 'virtual' events, and that these are what we should be looking at, not words [378, pp. 208 ff.]. Many other critics tend purely and simply to ignore vocabulary. And yet the impact of style is achieved by words, as are virtual events.

The vocabulary of literature would seem to be worth even more attention than it has so far received. It certainly allows one to see a work in greater depth and complexity than grammatical categories could generally do. Words are much more complex than the grammatical categories to which they belong—it is useful to examine an author's vocabulary to find out whether it is abstract, concrete, flattering or pejorative, lyrical or flat etc. [v. 437, pp. 114 ff.]. Barbier [39, p. 422] has pointed to the frequently philosophical value of Péguy's adjectives. Vendryes, in *Le Langage* written fifty years ago, suggested that words might be set up in a kind of hierarchy according to their poetic value, going from the proper noun which calls up a place or a person to the morpheme (which for him was not a word) with its rudimentary value as a grammatical tool [v. 645, p. 292]. This goes well beyond the descriptive powers of grammar. In fact we might even follow Bally and suggest that as a word increases in expressive impact, its purely grammatical significance decreases [37, p. 75].

The crude semantic categories I have just mentioned point to another aspect of words which must be borne in mind: the relation of words to the things or concepts they designate. This is a complex problem which I do not need to examine here in detail, for it has been done with complete clarity in Stephen Ullmann's *Semantics* [703, pp. 56 ff.]. The basic point which we must retain here is that the word and the thing it designates are in no way equivalent. Words are symbols, not replacements. Words are at one and the same time more general (in comparison with the precise physical nature of the object, or the complexity of the concept evoked) and more particular (for they imply in varying degrees an attitude, an emotional charge). They may indicate a multiplicity of different things, whilst a multiplicity of words may point to the same thing.

These facts should be in our minds whenever we consider the ways in which meaning is communicated in literature. When individual words are examined, the fact that they are so free-floating and potentially vague might lead us to wonder whether words may be looked at individually, in isolation at all. English linguistic philosophers, urged on by Wittgenstein, have suggested that a word changes its meaning each time it changes context. Reluctance to take this into consideration has led to strange results: Lawler seems to consider some aspects of Rimbaud's vocabulary to be fixed and unchanging from one poem or period to another [382, pp. 87–94]. Within one author, a given term may vary widely in associative value [303, pp. 10–11]. Although clearly words have a core of meaning which they carry about with them ('chair', 'life', or 'happiness' cannot mean 'window', 'death' or 'misery'), the impact of context, especially literary context, must be very great. The heightened value of sound and grammar is but one indication of this.

It is useful therefore to look for a form of analysis which highlights the word as an independent item of meaning but which firmly maintains its links with all other words in the work, or works, studied.

This could be seen as one possible definition of a concordance, or an index. Modern concordances, or indexes, of which there is a vast quantity, are normally produced with the help of a computer. They present a variety of information. Good ones like those offered as a basis for the study of literary French and produced by the University of Besançon, situate each word in each of its different contexts (this is the basic meaning of the word concordance)—which is syntactically and thematically significant. They also offer an index of words classified grammatically, a list of dialectal and foreign words, an index of variants and an index of rhymes. They provide statistics too: an index of the 500 most common full words; a table grouping words of equal frequency, and one showing the frequency of words in alphabetical order [551] Seven volumes in this series have been published to date: *Les Fleurs du Mal*, *Le Cid*, *Phèdre*, *Polyeucte*, *Calligrammes*, *Andromaque*, *Cinna* [v. too 276, 321 and 493B].

It is perhaps most important of all to note that concordances are a tool and not an end in themselves. They may enable one to establish basic facts: the central themes in Valéry (order and disorder, being and non-being) are directly indicated according to Guiraud [270, pp. 112 ff.] by the two most frequently used words: *pur* and *ombre*. But words are often too unstable for their frequency to be significant without reference to anything else. Important findings can be made, especially if one considers the stages at which particular words come in the work, and their links with other apparently important words. Garnet Rees [562] does this and is able to point out that concordances of Apollinaire's *Calligrammes* (1918) and *Alcools* (1913) reveal the 'evolution of Apollinaire's poetical ambition and the change in his obsessions. For example the word *automne* and its derivatives appear 22 times in *Alcools* but only 3 times in *Calligrammes*, *avenir* 6 times in *Alcools* but 19 times in *Calligrammes*, [whilst] *amour* has almost the same number of mentions in both volumes, 51 in *Alcools*, 49 in *Calligrammes*.' These results are especially interesting because the dates would lead one to expect frequencies to be the other way round, given the normal process of human psychology! At other times concordances provide confirmatory evidence, but offer it in a new way. They show for example that idealism in Wordsworth is as much expressed by the rarity of 'realistic' vocabulary (*ugly* occurs once, *ugliness* never) as by the use of words like *beauty* which run to several columns [78, p. 56].

Here numerical comparisons or comparisons between subject-matter and vocabulary are clearly useful. Such wide-ranging surveys are possible only with a concordance, which would seem therefore to be an essential instrument for the study of style. And yet concordances are not enough to handle the wide variations in meaning which a word might offer according to its varying contexts. The information they give could be further refined by offering subgroups of the same word according to its different meanings [v. 78 p. 59]. One has to take the nevertheless very useful raw material offered by them and work on it, paying particular attention to context. Thus, in Baudelaire's *Fleurs du Mal*, the word *souvenir* recurs over twenty times. A study of its impact shows, however, that at times it expresses optimism, at others pessimism; that it may refer either to a precise event in the past or to a *state* of remembering; that it may be personified or impersonal, subject or object. The word thus becomes much more fragmented than mere frequency would have us believe.

The converse may also be true: a variety of words may be important because of the similarities which bring them together rather than because of their specific distinguishing features. Hugo's poem *Navarin* in *Les Orientales* mentions a vast number of different kinds of ships. The concordance which classified them separately would be as unhelpful here as the conventional standard edition note which tells you how many masts or banks of oars a particular ship may have. It is the evocative, exotic quality of these terms which is important, and therefore the critic must especially highlight the variations on a central topic which they set up.

Another aspect which needs caution is the fact that frequency is not an absolute clue to importance (see *Counting*)—the examples I shall take below from Empson's *Structure of Complex Words* show that words which crop up in the mouths of important characters at crucial points in the action may well be especially significant (and not necessarily the most frequent). The distinction should be made between these key or pregnant terms and the theme words which are important solely because of their unaccustomed frequency [v. 270, pp. 155 ff.]. Words may be common because they are essential elements of any discourse—they only become really important if they crop up with surprising frequency. Rarer words will be significant similarly if they occur more often than they might be expected to, if some sort of necessity has brought them into the work. Our criteria for appreciation will vary according to the word in question. Thus Guiraud suggests that in Valéry *fuir* which occurs 20 times is much more significant than *voir* (encountered 37 times). It is also legitimate to suppose that abnormally high frequency in a rare word is much more striking than in a common one.

There must be a real element of individual assessment even in this. If Empson's study (of 'honest' in *Othello*, 'fool' in *Lear* and 'dog' in *Timon of Athens* etc.) is initially based on the numerical importance of certain words, their key function is also evaluated. And this depends to a great extent not on the stable, recurrent aspect of these words but on the multiplicity and richness of their various associations (an aspect which, as we have seen, is not quantifiable). This does not mean that Empson subscribes to I. A. Richards' ideas on the emotional content of poetic language. Empson especially stresses the links between emotional and cognitive aspects of language (as well as ambiguity and connotations). Such an approach applies to a wide variety of poetry: for example it allows such a term as 'wit' in Pope's *Essay on Criticism* to be seen in much greater depth and with many variations in meaning. Meanings are indeed given which go beyond the experience of modern readers, for Empson's approach is in no sense based on purely subjective response: contemporary meanings are given considerable prominence. 'Honest' in *Othello* is situated 'in the middle of a rather complicated process of semantic change': 'at once hearty and individualist . . . common amongst raffish low people . . .'. The word is related to natural behaviour, generosity, trueness to friends. In Shakespeare, however, it never relates to 'simple hearty use between equals'. It is 'condescending when applied to Iago. Rather than being concerned with the idea of truth-telling, it may point to slight stupidity, and Iago thinks that this is the sense applied to him. It thus contributes greatly to the contexts of dramatic and class irony which inform the play' [203, pp. 218 ff.]. Empson similarly shows how 'fool', the varying values of 'foolish', the idea of 'making a fool of' and the interplay of these notions with that of madness combine to establish a master symbol in *Lear*. 'Dog' in *Timon* is on the other hand less central [pp. 177 ff.]. It 'does not . . . become a symbol that includes cynic and flatterer, flattery and affection so as to imply a view of [characters'] proper relations. It remains a bridge over which they exchange puzzles and the generalization of it amounts mainly to letting you feel the same kind of distaste for a variety of different people.' [p. 183.] This is too slender an account of what is a brilliant and at times a difficult study. Empson offers an outstanding example of what the examination of individual words can achieve in literary criticism. But his study does have some defects inherent in the isolation of words: the works are broken up into a series of examples—examples are given in an order dictated by semantic groupings rather than by the development of the work. In this it resembles less enterprising works like Barbier's study of Péguy's style and vocabulary [39].

Empson does not however neglect the importance of *word combinations*—seeing key words as likely to bring in with them a limited number of other terms. Words may thus be considered to be part of what Guiraud calls stylistic fields—if Baudelaire uses the term 'gouffre', for example, it will tend almost exclusively to be qualified by such words as 'noir', 'ténébreux' or 'glacé' and to be associated with such words as 'horreur', 'nausée', 'vertige'. Words may be grouped according to their synonyms too: the typically Baudelairian contrast of 'gouffre' and 'azur' leads to a highly developed language of anguish and euphoria, height and depth, damnation and redemption, in which the terms used point implicitly to other terms which parallel them or contrast them [274, pp. 20–1; v. too 282, p. 219].

The advantage of looking especially at combinations of words from the point of view of their meaning is that an excessively grammatical approach is avoided [216, p. 5]. The true basis for literary study (*groupings* of meaning) is thus established.

And yet we should beware of taking this as too neat a solution. As Ullmann points out [703, p. 249], words in one language do not necessarily cover the whole of a particular semantic area evenly or even completely. Colours are a good example of this, as we can see from the constant struggle of clothes designers to describe their products adequately. The rarity or otherwise of interrelated words (to mention but one aspect) will produce widely varying degrees of impact.

In addition, the examples quoted from Guiraud show that word combinations may not be particularly striking—we rather expect the associations of 'gouffre' to be what they turn out to be in Baudelaire—pretty similar to what they are in Victor Hugo . . .

We should therefore constantly set this kind of critical material against our experience of language in general and literature in particular—the facts may not be particularly useful unless they point to the development of certain literary clichés in a given period.

I find that the stylistic field approach is very useful when (with the help of a concordance or otherwise) it notes the fact that two or more unrelated words recur with unexpected frequency, and encourages one to try to see the links between them: 'souvenir' and 'parfum' in *Les Fleurs du Mal* for example. The stabilising effect of putting words into a semantic group (the semantic group created by the context that is, and not by Roget's *Thesaurus*) is here at its most effective—perfume is set by Baudelaire in a temporal dimension—it is an agent of memory—and may not be seen as a purely sensual experience (see *La Chevelure*); memory conversely may on occasion show itself to be associated with a specific type of sense experience. In this way, the wider context of the individual word is seen as determining its precise literary significance. The characteristic vocabulary of the text or texts can be made to show the most significant aspects of the work.

Grouping (or listing) is all important. Even modest and to us slightly out-of-date approaches may be of great use—like those studies of Hugo's metaphors undertaken by Huguet at the beginning of the century [324 and 325]. Here images are grouped under such general headings as dawn, fire and lightning, water, ice and snow in the latter, and, in the former, men, animals, deformities, the sea, buildings. This enables one to see where the emphasis in Hugo's terminology lies in relation to the major areas of experience. Zumthor offers a useful and more up-to-date example when he points to the links in St. John Perse between the word sets 'aube' (with its connotations 'orient' and 'exil'), 'aubain' (connotation: 'exil') and 'aubaine' (connotations: 'don', 'grâce', 'création', 'fraîcheur') [785, p. 33].

Such examples are numerous, and it would be tedious to list more than a representative selection. One which is especially worthy of note, and which is close to Empson's work examined above, is Ehrmann's study of Corneille's *Cinna* [195]. This is a political play about the search for power, favour, revenge and forgiveness. One of its basic motifs is seen to be embodied in a series of turns of phrase expressing notions of purchase, sale, exchange and the like. In the plot, acquisition is set against taking—the ideas of prizes and rewards are given prominence, as are the notions of taking and giving.

Quite wide contexts can be characterized in this way. Once again the value of concordances becomes clear, for a concordance makes it possible to look at even wider areas, a man's complete works for example, and search for similar constants in theme and vocabulary (providing of course that such elements as chronology are borne in mind). A lexical breakdown of Jane Austen's novels would allow one to determine whether the vocabulary of manners which David Lodge points to in *Mansfield Park* [411, pp. 100 ff.] is a permanent feature (as one would suspect) or a phenomenon which distinguishes this novel from, say, *Pride and Prejudice* [v. too 514B]. The *varying* emphasis on the unreal in Huysmans might be similarly established [155, part II].

The idea of cohesion is central to such an approach. Certain stylistic conditions may however make the *lack* of cohesion, the fragmentation of language significant in more or less the same way. Many modern works according to Guetti [264] point to a breakdown in language, a demonstration, on the part of the author, that language is unable to come to grips with, or explain reality. The opening of *Moby Dick* (*Etymology*, *Extracts*) with its lists of words and their definitions, creates in the reader not a satisfaction that all is defined and explained but rather the need to go beyond words and seek elsewhere for what Ahab and Moby Dick are. Such a critical approach would seem to be especially useful for an understanding of modern fiction (I shall take it up in the next chapter) for it establishes a direct contrast to the methods by which more traditional authors attempted to define a particular character or event by using rigidly constant formulae to designate it. Homer's 'rosy-fingered dawn' is one example. Another is the way novelists like Dickens or Balzac use proper names as precise analyses of their owners: Crevel, Steerforth, Séchard, Murdstone etc. Here the world and the word fit flush. Cervantes uses proper names to similar but rather more subtle ends, as Spitzer has shown [651, pp. 28 and 41–85].

Ordinary nouns may have a comparable power to stimulate a fixed attitude towards a particular character. Mitterand has demonstrated this brilliantly in a study of the way Zola in *Thérèse Raquin* contrasts the words 'face' and 'visage' [477]. Starting with the kind of statistical evidence which could come from a concordance, but taking care to associate relative frequency to the different characters involved, he shows that the 'mobile', lively 'visage' is used especially to describe Thérèse, whilst the more fixed 'face' is used to describe Camille (her husband murdered by Laurent her lover) and characters linked to him. The associations (in adjectives or adjectival phrases for example) developed through these two words are moreover an opposition of life ('visage') and death ('face'). Mitterand tabulates this not only for faces described in general but for the different parts of the face: lips, mouth, hair etc. And this, by linking Thérèse and Laurent (who are described in a similar way), strengthens the opposition of the two groups of characters yet further: positive and negative characteristics are set against each other. Thus, suggests Mitterand, over and above the fact that Zola is using realist techniques, 'it would seem that he develops his portraits not on the basis of direct observation but of an established system of descriptive elements, which are *clues* pointing both to physical traits and associated psycho-sociological factors' [p. 27]. Such a cross-section makes it possible for an important aspect of Zola's novel to be very precisely described. It is significant too in that it shows to what extent the vocabulary of the work of art may be considered independently of its usual connotations: ' "face" and "visage" are broadly synonymous in everyday life, but this is no longer the case in *Thérèse Raquin*' [p. 23].

This kind of approach would certainly be worth applying to any works which stress the logical relationship between the tangible external world and psychological or moral states. Dickens, Balzac, Tolstoy and George Eliot (and indeed most novelists of the nineteenth-century tradition) are authors who spring to mind. Outside such a tradition, vocabulary 'codes' are still conceivable wherever systematically contrasted groups of characters, emotions or tensions are to be found (although other contrasting techniques are possible, as Empson shows).

A less original tack is to consider vocabulary in the light of its provenance. Its impact examined thus relates to the outside world and not to any strong semantic changes which an author may have imposed on vocabulary. This is useful because it indicates the types of experience and the kinds of association most emphasized in a given work. Scherer thus breaks up Mallarmé's vocabulary into common or even vulgar terms, archaisms and rare words. Huysmans's liking for rare words [155, p. 3] is also stressed by Cressot. However there is a real danger in these studies for such facts are merely noted, their thematic implications (see my chapter on construction below) are hardly gone into. The grouping is an *a priori* one, not imposed by the work. Spitzer on the other hand, talking about Rabelais's liking for invented words, links this with some justification to the unreal world which Rabelais creates at one level [652, pp. 14–18]. Words here are at least set in a human context.

The bias towards the outside world inherent in work by scholars like Cressot and Scherer would seem to indicate that they are most useful not ultimately as a basis for the precise understanding of individual works but rather as background information and as a pointer to traditions in literary history. The human context referred to is a wide one. The vocabulary of a given work may thus relate to the way the world was looked at at a given moment in history. In a sense it must: if Dámaso Alonso [10, p. 194] suggests that personal and 'group' reactions in a particular period are irretrievably intermingled, 'traditional' features which link one author to another must have some significance. Josephine Miles sees vocabulary as being a feature which with grammar and sound is worth looking at in this light [462, p. v]. She underlines a 'relational pattern of clausal sentence with stanzaic sound and conceptual vocabulary' and a 'cumulative pattern of phrasal sentence with internal and onomatopoeic sound and with sublime vocabulary' [463, p. 184]. This establishes a cyclic idea of literary history: vocabulary tends to recur from one period to another. Recurrent terms often crop up at the same time as recurrent sentence forms (but not always): 'the early Tudor vocabulary of concept in words like "mind", "thought", "word", "thing", "time" and "world" recurred strongly again in the clausal poetry of the nineteenth century'. In England, sensory and observational vocabulary seems to have cropped up in the last generation of each century [463, p. 183].

It is also possible to set the authors in a particular period and to explain them by reference to contemporary tendencies. Barnwell's perceptive study of a passage from *La Princesse de Clèves* points implicitly to a vocabulary of moral attitudes in society at large as well as in Mme de la Fayette [40, pp. 166 ff.]. R.-L. Wagner shows that Baudelaire's use and semantic reshaping of the word 'mystique' can be more closely defined by examining the word's shift from a religious to a poetic value (partly under the influence of 'magique') during the Romantic period, as examples in Hugo or Sainte-Beuve show [722]. Guiraud uses similar clues when he attempts to decode Villon's *Ballades* and *Testament* by reference to contemporary slang [269; 275]. Matoré shows how colours and the vocabulary of light in Camus and Gracq fit into and are in turn explained by the tendencies of a particular moment in time [444]. On a much broader scale, we have the example of Matoré's study of the vocabulary of literary prose in the 1830s and 40s, with special reference to Gautier [446]. Matoré looks at the influence of the new living habits of the period and points to that exerted by such widely varying areas as politics, fashion, the arts, exoticism, foreign languages, slang, middle-class language and working-class expression. In Gautier these borrowings were the result of the desire to particularize his descriptions and to point to strong contrasts. Matoré suggests that Gautier's novel *Mlle de Maupin* is packed with artificially oriental vocabulary more for the fun of it than anything else. The main search was for impact at any price. The priorities of a new style and the way that need satisfied itself are thus defined in detail. But the study is not completely satisfying for me, mainly because Gautier and his time are not approached in depth. Terms are collected rather than examined in context and related to theme (see *Construction*). They are not supported by any sort of concordance-type evidence and, being thus out of context on two counts, they tend to be held at the level of impressionism. They help us rather to assess a period than an individual [v. too 4B]. Cahen's study of Racine's vocabulary [pp. 251 ff.], which is more tightly organized, tends nevertheless to suffer from the same defects: external criteria are the dominant basis for classification. What is offered is basically a very useful extension of Brunot's massive *Histoire de la Langue Française.* It is interesting to compare Cahen's study with that of Aron examining Racine's *Phèdre*, Pradon's *Phèdre et Hippolyte* and Thomas Corneille's *Ariane* [v. 110B and 702]. He points to the fact that Racine's play, although the shortest, uses about 20 per cent more words than the other two and about twice as many proper names and that 79 words of the sample examined (20 concrete and 12 belonging to the language of violence) are peculiar to Racine. This clearly established one real basis for the distinctiveness of Racine's play within the vocabulary tradition of his times.

The true meaning (or meanings) of a text begins with the words which it is made up of. Even when we look at them independently of such basic elements as syntax, they may well provide a tangible indication of a text's main preoccupations. We can group them according to their recurrent areas of meaning; we can look at their literal or evocative, original or stereotyped values; we can examine their degrees of abstraction or concreteness; we can classify them historically or according to the level of style and registers [v. 4B] to which they belong.

The main point is perhaps that words should indeed be grouped and not looked at in the isolation of individual sentences. It is clear too that if you classify words in a literary text according to a check list of pre-established norms, the result will be primarily linguistic. The text itself must dictate the categories, and for this, as elsewhere, the perceptiveness of the individual critic is of central importance.

It must also be realized that words represent, individually or even in groups, a very restricted area of meaning and that to complete the picture it is essential to look at the wider contexts dealt with in the coming pages.

CHAPTER FOUR

MEANING II

In this chapter, I shall be examining how meaning is most frequently communicated in a novel or a poem. In the chapter on style, I shall consider *devices* writers use to express themselves. This division is very artificial, as are all the divisions in this book: like them, it should be seen as a 'heading' to be taken into account when looking at a particular work. I shall however try to keep clear of the danger Messing points to in his review of *Style in Language* (edited by Sebeok and considered to be a major contribution to the subject). He suggests a little unfairly that this book is 'largely a waste of time and money' especially because it mistakenly separates style and meaning [v. 457, p. 257]. I have rather chosen to look at literary meaning from two different angles: semantics and style.

In both cases, the great need is to consider meaning only with tangible literary examples in mind. Largely under the influence of Saussurian linguistics, too many critics (notably the French and survivors of the Prague school) were for a long time over-preoccupied with elaborating abstract theories and patterns. This is no doubt a temptation when one is confronted with a foreign literature, but to let patterns oust meaning is perhaps as dangerous as to overemphasize (like Sartre) the message-bearing quality of words [615, pp. 63–4]. However it is much less arduous than to try to describe the meaning a work really communicates to a reader. I shall return to this when we come to the chapter on construction. The main point here is that, as we shall see, literature is not *exclusively* verbal in impact; it cannot be scientifically categorized and catalogued: 'How can you catalogue what is not said but merely suggested?' [512, p. 69.] As American linguisticians subsequently realized, all subject-matter must be taken into account if one is to understand what a text is about in the normal sense of the term. Poetry is included in this too, for the nature and source of poetic impact may also be non-linguistic, wider than language [v. 60].

This raises great difficulties, but it is less ludicrous than some theoreticians would have us believe: '... as no science can go beyond mathematics, no criticism can go beyond its linguistics. And the kind of linguistics needed by recent criticism for the solution of its pressing problems of metrics and stylistics, in fact, for all problems of the linguistic surface of letters, is not semantics ... but down-to-the-surface linguistics, microlinguistics not metalinguistics' [755, p. 415]. Linguistics' traditional fear of dabbling in meaning is well illustrated here. It is a little like trying to talk about a meal without mentioning its taste. But whilst it is easier to list ingredients than to describe the effect of their combination, we have already seen that the same grammatical pattern or identical sounds do not guarantee similarity of meaning.

Saying what a work means is the most difficult aspect of criticism. Jakobson underlines this: 'We stand before [*sic*] a nearly unexplained question of [the?] interrelation between message and context' [399, p. 159]. So, more idiomatically, does Dámaso Alonso: 'If the signifier [i.e. for our purposes language] is a tangible substance which can be pointed to and listed, the "signified", what language is talking about, is merely our own intuition of the poem ... the signified is not analysable, it cannot be seized upon; it is ineffable' [10, p. 196]. Thus, in a sense, it is not surprising that the most blurred and question-begging section of *Essays on the Language of Literature* [128] is that devoted to literary form and meaning. This is a field in which critics like Barthes, J.-P. Richard, Poulet, Genette, in spite of the fact that many of them are over-preoccupied with theory, come off well, for they have been concerned with the precise, but wide-ranging semantic impact of different words without restricting themselves to the individual sentence (which is all many linguistic critics dare to tackle) or other purely linguistic elements. They are not shy of seeing human communication as something unscientific and tackling that 'very important emotive and primitive content of literary experience' which Ransom has pointed to [558, p. 202]. And this can be seen to include 'the aesthetic effects towards which literature is aiming' [737, p. 417].

This vast, vague problem, relating rather to languages (i.e. all sorts of means of communication) than to one individual language [v. 176, pp. 25–6], is concerned moreover with a shifting, impermanent situation. Historical semantics points to this in the social group. But it is also part of each reader's experience, as my quotation from Dámaso Alonso would seem to imply and as Empson's description of subsequent or different readings of Pope's *Essay on Criticism* suggests: 'In the first the words are merely English and not governed by any sense of what the style wants—you are feeling your way about to see what the point of it all is, and many of the effects won't come. In the second the author (I think) has to seem prominent as poking his meaning at you, and you feel that various words have Moods in them. But no doubt there can be a third in which the style to which you have become accustomed is viewed as a sort of dialect with its own rules and structure of meanings and the author partly fades out.' [203, p. 98.]

It might be concluded that the only possible approach (nightmarish thought it may seem) is an exhaustive appreciation of all aspects of a work's meaning. This kind of thing has of course been attempted, but I am not at all sure that this is the right solution. The welter of information is crushing and de-humanizing and the relative importance of this information is insufficiently worked out; such methods can in any case be applied only to very short texts (if the writer and his reader are to stay sane). They are a useful indication, on the other hand, of the advantage of accepting the way a work expresses itself, of describing what is there and not jumping to conclusions about what should be there.

Let me begin with a non-verbal approach: the meaning of a work of art is everything it contains or implies. Meaning is produced by the total context to which a statement belongs and which it evokes. If the work must *always* be the starting-point and supply the fundamental evidence for anything we wish to say about it, we must also be prepared to go outside the work in order to clarify the associations which it sets up.

As a result we may well have to link a work with the literary tradition to which it belongs. Josephine Miles shows to what extent poetry from a given period tends to share common features. Even more orthodox approaches to literary history show that plays written in late Elizabethan England or those produced in mid-seventeeth-century France will have many elements in common. Some works are really comprehensible only in relation to a tradition—many early *Odes* by Hugo for example and the late Classical tradition of which they are such a notable pastiche, with all the verbal and rhetorical clichés they exploit. This is a crude example but it serves to point to the fact that *no* work exists in isolation: 'In any poet, and this is very clear during the Renascence, direct reactions to the stimuli of life are so closely bound up with those communicated by cultural tradition that any clear-cut distinction between the two is impossible.' [10, p. 194.] Many formal devices so clearly bear this out that critics have suggested that any analysis of these must be comparative [v. 310]. It is certainly clear that the idea of genres is neither dead nor useless, a fact which is especially true if the idea of genres is expanded to include typology, common practice, stereotypes and clichés—for the work's dependence on complex traditional elements can be more precisely described, and seen to be a specific element in the work [v. 380B]. Elements like Maud Bodkin's archetypal patterns (to be examined in the chapter on construction) are also of great value here, as are studies like Hildick's *Thirteen Types of Narrative* and Wayne C. Booth's *The Rhetoric of Fiction.*

All this should in no sense be seen as a plea for describing literary works purely in terms of the genre to which they belong. It is rather that *the individual work makes use of traditions of expression.* To describe this use is to describe one aspect of the work's uniqueness.

Barthes's theory that the work of art is not a product but a sign, 'the sign of something "beyond" the work' [v. 637, pp. 9–10], is only partly true, I think: traditions *in the widest sense* must condition the way an artist expresses himself. Indeed Barthes [41 and 45] describes tendencies (we have seen the example of tense in the novel) which point as much to the community or tradition to which an artist belongs as to his independence. Julia Kristeva too shows the extent to which the novel when it emerges in the fifteenth century is a modification of already existing forms [366, p. 443]. That there is a certain danger in forgetting the idea of tradition can be seen in, say, Todorov's description of the function of letters in *Les Liaisons dangereuses* which is in no sense as exclusive to that novel as the Bulgarian critic would have us believe.

The problem is perhaps made more acute (and at the same time more clear-cut) by the fact that modern literature (i.e. since the early nineteenth century) has witnessed an enormous multiplication of traditions and tendencies. This does not, however, mean that the individual work is thus susceptible to a more exclusively specific description. It is rather that, as Barthes puts it, 'these "bits" of literature take on meaning only if one can relate them to something much wider'. And this is a complex undertaking for '. . . it is possible that the historical significance of modern literature will become apparent only when it is possible to group together, for example, surrealism, Sartre, Brecht, "abstract" literature and even structuralism as so many variations on a single idea' [48, p. 261]. Hence the tendency in modern criticism to reject genres and literary history! [v. Barthes himself in 41, p. 122.] But this is a rather sterile baby-and-bathwater approach. It leads at times to complicated restatements of the obvious. Genres and traditions can live with (and be refined by) new ideas of the way texts may be grouped. The specific qualities of an individual sonnet or a five act classical tragedy can best be worked out if we know what may normally be expected of these forms.

Two rather more old-fashioned approaches can help here. The first is Thibaudet's use of comparison. 'When I am not comparing I am not making a critical judgment' [70, p. 337]. Clearly to compare and contrast one text with other similar texts is to define its specific as well as its general qualities. Leavis's brilliant comparison of the barge scene in both *Anthony and Cleopatra* and Dryden's *All for Love* [385] is ample indication of the value of such a technique. Spitzer's method is broader in scope for he sees the experience of reading not as the rather oblique awareness of and reference to anything outside the individual work (as is the case with critics like Poulet or Richard) but as a constant to-and-fro movement from text to externals.

This suggests notions of tradition which go beyond literary form and into society itself. Hill [308, p. 390] says that 'meaning in literature is things as a culture sees and values them'. He is talking mainly about poetry, but this is even truer of a novel, which can only be criticized properly if one is prepared to discuss such things as ethics, manners and motives (comprehensible only if they can be linked with and compared to similar elements in the outside world). We have already seen that individual words can often be classified socially, depending on whether they are slang, crude, familiar, academic or literary [v. 445]. Any critic who does not consider these aspects is not doing his job [309]. Sartre asserts that 'a work of art is both the product of an individual mind and a social fact' [617, p. 33]. It would therefore be wrong for a student of Renaissance literature, say, to ignore the facts of social psychology that Henri Weber supplies [731, p. 160] when he states that 'for the seventeenth century after 1660 truth is basically psychological, whereas for the sixteenth century it consists in being faithful to the constantly shifting appearance of the world'. Such information is an anchor which firmly links works to the period which produced them: they are all the more real for that.

There are other advantages too: in a famous article [357, p. 12] L. C. Knights took another critic, Morgann, to task for talking about the *wholeness* of Shakespeare's characters by asserting that '... instead of realizing that this quality sprang from Shakespeare's use of words ... Morgann referred to the characters' "independence" of the work in which they appeared ...'

Knights would seem to be going too far [v. 505B, p. 111]. Characters *do* belong to the outside world (otherwise we should not be able to understand them): 'they resonate with suggestions and images which cannot be contained' [191B, p. 99]. And yet, they are not as independent as Morgann would suggest (Shakespeare does not tell us enough about them which is not exclusively relevant to the play). A play like Tom Stoppard's *Rosenkranz and Guildernstern are Dead* does have to supply extra information in order to come off as a fascinating 'back-stage' extension of *Hamlet*. Serge Doubrovsky would seem to strike the happy medium in all this: 'Writing . . . is not cutting oneself off from the world in order to shut oneself up in language: it is rather an attempt to shut the world up in language . . .', to express the world in words [176, p. 100]. Both the distortions and the similarities must therefore concern us.

This sounds reasonably straightforward. We must of course beware of one great temptation: *bringing in information which the work does not call for*, which is imposed by the critic from the outside. Books like Raymond Williams's *Culture and Society*, M. Bradbury's more recent *Social Context of Modern English Literature* and J. Raban's *The Society of the Poem* merely show that literature, being the product of a society, must relate to things which are present elsewhere in that society. The products of even recent societies sometimes need background elucidation. The fact that so many of Trollope's novels take place in and around parsonages reflects the social reality of a period when, much more than today, the important events of a community were centred on such buildings. The substance of literature is not pure invention. It is only by bearing this in mind that close textual criticism can make sense. A thorough background knowledge is at times considered necessary: 'How is a critic to grasp his Kafka, Proust, Mann and Joyce unless he is learned in history and language and well read in anthropology, sociology, philosophy and psychology?' [558, p. 190]. This varies from one period to another, for, as Ransom goes on to say, 'James and even Dostoievsky are simple by comparison . . .' But the difference relates to the abstruseness of the facts involved, not to whether they are there or not.*

We still need to be able to appreciate James's references to sources of wealth, or to know why he so seldom mentions servants (key elements in his characters' lives yet so much taken for granted)—we must also be aware of the important tensions coming from the abolition of serfdom which Dostoievsky refers to (without going into details) in several of his novels. Critics have been so mesmerized by the notion of the independence of the work of art that they have been ashamed to mention such indispensable facts. Valéry is (even with reference to poetry) making much too extreme a statement when he says that 'the only reality in art is art itself' [707, vol. I, p. 613], and Urban is correct to insist that 'art is not important nonsense'. Poetry contains real propositions, and questions of truth and falsity must come into it [705, pp. 470 ff.]. Dubois's assertion that poetry is completely non-referential and that when it refers to anything outside itself it ceases to be poetry is a useless statement as far as practical criticism (i.e. real words in a real text) is concerned.

Truthfulness is perhaps a different matter. Mukařovský feels that truthfulness is useful only in determining 'the extent to which the work has documentary value' but it would perhaps be more correct to say that, as with literary form, the reader's response to the subject-matter of the novel is conditioned by the knowledge which he may already have of that subject-matter [492]. We are presented with something which is at one and the same time familiar and unexpected. This is I think a valid way of interpreting and extending Graham Hough's statement that 'literature is meaningful fiction, an imaginary presentation that has nevertheless some meaningful relation with the real world' [318, p. 44]. In *La Curée*, Zola's portrayal of high life and double dealing in

* Note: I must stress one point here—whether one is familiar with the specialized subjects mentioned or not all the authors mentioned are still comprehensible to a very large extent. It is as unhealthy to give the impression that a work of the past is inaccessible without the help of vast erudition as to suggest that it can exist in a vacuum.

Second Empire France may well not be permanently accurate as fact, but it *is* an accurate expression of an *attitude* towards the activities of a particular class at a specific moment in history.

In a sense literature always *copies* the outside world, for language must always be referential. The idea that 'art imitates nature', although an acceptable statement, is however a highly flexible one, as Harvey has shown [294, pp. 11 ff.], for the ideas of imitation and nature are both open to wide interpretation. They certainly do not imply that we can only understand details with which we are *specifically* familiar—otherwise Rabelais's phantasy world of giants and magic voyages, like Swift's, would be gibberish for most people, as would the writings of Tolkien or Mervyn Peake. This is not the case simply because their descriptions offer an extension of what we already know. We also accept them because they are logical and coherent within the framework of the book.

The right approach, I think, is to develop this idea of extension and underline the important and obvious fact that art entails a profound modification of recognizable reality. Rousset makes a useful correction to Valéry's statement given above when he claims that '. . . art has recourse to reality only to abolish it and put another reality in its place' [604, p. 111]. But with his talk of abolition, he is still going too far, for the original raw material is always visible, even where modern literature is concerned. Picon is nearer to the mark, although his terms are excessive: 'The work, in modern art, is not an expression but a creation: it shows what has not been seen before, it forms rather than reflects' [530, vol. 2, p. 289]. And again Paul Bourget: 'A novel is not a representation of life but an account of life' [quoted in 682, p. 24]. 'Form', 'account'—these are ideas which will concern me greatly for the rest of this book (as they have done so far) for they show that any work is *at one and the same time* independent and derivative. It is therefore essential for the critic to describe the facts retailed in a work and to look in detail at the way in which they are presented. The transformation may be very great: Proust has been able to claim that Balzac's *Comédie Humaine*, despite its huge welter of information, is much more concerned with a striking effect than with the portrait of an age [547, pp. 241 ff.]. Balzac in other circumstances even goes so far as to demolish what is possible in everyday life: when in *Une Fille d'Eve* or *La Cousine Bette* or at the beginning of *Illusions perdues*, he halts the action and for many pages takes us back in time, he is in fact stopping time—the characters will still be as he left them when his flashback is over. Such a technique may well be 'realist' (cause and effect are looked at closely, nothing is left vague) but it can scarcely be called reality.

Looking at the problem from a different angle, we can point to the fact that the narrator in a novel by, for example, Fielding or Thackeray or Stendhal does not represent the novelist himself. It is rather a put-up job: the artist takes on a personality to fit the circumstances. He gives the work a *point of view* which may be all-knowing, ironic, partly in the dark or even from a multitude of angles: compare Balzac, Henry James, Flaubert, Dostoievsky (especially in *Karamazov*) and Virginia Woolf (*Mrs. Dalloway* for example). *Each kind of approach implies not what the author is but rather what reality is like.* The same things happen in poetry in an even more extreme way. Although S. Langer exaggerates differences between poetry and prose, a quotation I have already given is worth repeating: 'neither the person speaking nor the person spoken to is an actual human being, the writer or the reader; the rhetorical form is a means of creating an impersonal subjectivity which is the peculiar [?] experiential illusion of a genre that creates no characters and no public events' [378, p. 260; v. 141, p. 162].

Impact is radically affected too by *choice* of detail. Despite what critics like Lubbock might say (about Balzac [415, p. 221]), no writer, not even Robbe-Grillet, can describe everything. He may even choose to hide important facts like Camus, who in *La Peste* does not tell his readers until the end that his narrator and one of the central characters are one and the same person. He may not attempt to elucidate his character's confusion, as in Flaubert's

Education sentimentale. This contributes to the work's point of view which I have just mentioned. The writer's presentation is inevitably biased and partial (in both senses of the word). So many things are *ex*cluded that those actually described must be very different in impact from those in everyday life (where this essential notion of deliberate choice cannot operate, although even in everyday life our perception is selective). This is perhaps the fundamental difference between art and life. Choice implies exclusion and therefore strong emphasis. When a Racine character, in the very first line of a play says 'Oui, seigneur . . .' he is answering words and confirming statements which *do not exist*. The pressure is exclusively in the confirmatory nature of his statement. Our whole experience of reality is changed as a result of choice: 'Whatever is described . . . tends to be more actual than actuality and whatever is not described—even though implicitly there . . . is much *less* actual than actuality' [57, p. 348]. Not just 'actual' but also 'meaningful'. If a writer chooses to mention the presence of a table in a room or the fact that a character smiles or that the weather was fine, we may take it that these details are significant. Not in any dramatic way perhaps, but people in books do not smile for nothing (or if they do, it is because the writer has chosen the empty smile to signify an empty head)—and the table or the mention of the weather may well be elements chosen to signify that the world in which the action is taking place is a real, tangible one where such things fit naturally. We do not take them for granted therefore in the way we accept their real life equivalents. They are part of those descriptive elements which, like colours or precise references to time, enable us to make a general statement about the work in which they occur, and thus point to its significance [v. 58, pp. 39–53]. They express broadly the kind of reality which the work is related to (but they do it in a way and with a suggestiveness which are foreign to reality itself). Nothing in a work of literature is literal. When a nineteenth-century novelist (Tolstoy, Henry James, George Eliot, Balzac) goes to great pains to describe a character's physical appearance, this is admittedly a straightforward way of familiarizing us with him; but it also implies the notion that reality is best interpreted by careful attention to physical details (an idea which eighteenth- or twentieth-century novelists, and poets of most periods, would not necessarily accept). It even implies that it can be interpreted at all—a fact which is not universally accepted today.

It is clear that such aspects do not exist in isolation. Indeed a great deal of their ultimate significance depends on the different elements of which the work is made up: for example, it is the *combination* of a swan, Andromache and the disappearance of the Paris of the 1840s which makes the true basis of Baudelaire's poem, *Le Cygne*. The impact of the poem depends on the fact that such disparate ingredients echo each other.

This brings us to a central aspect of literary meaning which the preceding pages constantly hint at: association, one thing linking up with another, or being shown to be similar to another.

Association of course is prevalent at the levels of sound and grammar, as we saw in earlier chapters: links of sound or syntax point to links in meaning. But literature is associative or evocative in many other ways too. Indeed one notion of any particular style is to suggest that it results from choices being made with an eye to what has already been said and what will be said later [438, p. 1288]. The term often used to describe this is *connotation*, and this is acceptable provided it is not restricted to purely verbal phenomena, for literature plays on all the associations and cross-references which our experience (verbal and non-verbal) sets up within us. Of these at a given time, there is a fund common to all people, so much so that Martinet [438, p. 1292] suggests that 'culture is not in denotations, the precise things words and (to my mind) events in literature point to, but in connotations' [v. too 45 and 258].

The idea that meaning is really what is left in and not what is left out [v. 504, p. 152] is another way of saying this. The work ends up as a semantic field of great complexity, creating *inside and outside* links which are much more numerous and varied than the rather elementary examples which I mentioned in *Meaning I*, for the links are as I have suggested between events, ideas, characters and facts as well as between sounds, words or phrases. This is one result (to take a simple example) of the lack of punctuation which modern poets (Mallarmé or e. e. cummings and many others) indulge in: it allows sounds, words or phrases to be more easily linked with others and in so doing makes even the broader events or facts or attitudes which the poem is dealing with more potentially interrelated. The different 'contexts' to which any element in a poem may belong are thus multiplied because each individuals one is not over-defined. The associative impact of context, in this way, supplements the strong associative value which a few words or events have [v. 243, p. 141]. It may be difficult to know where to stop with this kind of approach, or rather only a misguided notion that criticism is primarily a scientific undertaking would imply that there is any real need to stop at one particular point—the individual critic's notion of what is significant should be the basic guide. The first stanza of Baudelaire's *Voyage* sets up an infinity of reverberations:

Pour l'enfant amoureux de cartes et d'estampes
L'univers est égal à son vaste appétit.
Ah! que le monde est grand à la clarté des lampes!
Aux yeux du souvenir que le monde est petit!

Our precise personal experience of expectation and disappointment, of future and past is here linked literally and symbolically with the fascination maps and prints may or *may not* have for us, in a combination which we see in various degrees as something subjective and objective. The following first stanza from a poem by Donne is similarly complex:

Tis the yeares midnight, and it is the dayes,
Lucies, who scarce seaven houres herself unmaskes,
  The Sunne is spent, and now his flasks
  Send forth light squibs, no constant rayes;
    The worlds whole sap is sunke:
The generall balme th'hydroptique earth hath drunk,
Whither, as to the beds-feet, life is shrunke,

Dead and enterr'd; yet all these seeme to laugh,
Compar'd with mee, who am their Epitaph.
[*A Nocturnall upon St. Lucies Day*.]

The complex and precise associations of light and darkness, sickness and death and even (for the modern reader) Guy Fawkes's night all interplay within the poem and link it simultaneously with the outside world, and the ever varied state of our individual sensibilities.

Connotations should be looked at closely for another important reason: if it functions by pointing to a network of associations, the impact of these links will depend on *the extent to which they are expected*. All events, characters, grammatical features etc., occur more naturally in some contexts than in others. The combination which Baudelaire sets up in *Le Cygne* is a good example of unusual *collocation*, and of course the elements involved produce a totally different impact when they are taken separately, for we are made to move backwards and forwards in time and civilization: Baudelaire thinks too of an exiled negress at the end of the poem (which in addition is dedicated to Victor Hugo, yet another exile . . .).

This process should be looked at from a wide variety of angles and related to literary traditions as well as to the natural relation of words in a sentence, whether this be grammatical (one expects a definite article to be closely related to a noun) or more specifically semantic (blue is a colour one expects to see linked with the sky rather than with an apple). At all times consciously or unconsciously the artist is either satisfying our expectation or surprising it.

This brings us back once again to the question of deviation with reference to non-verbal elements. It would be surprising if deviation (that most typically literary device) were purely verbal, for this would imply quite erroneously that style was a purely verbal element and not related to the organization (structure, sequence, combination) of material which is such an important part of all novels and most poems. Style, i.e. the meaning of a work, is a total effect [v. 273, pp. 78–9]. Indeed it has been suggested that before one can talk about stylistic effects one has to move away from purely linguistic features [345, p. 379]. The kind of impact the writer creates may depend as much on a manipulation of traditions as on an exploitation of language.

The reading of a novel by Robbe-Grillet, or Joyce or even one like Conrad's *Outcast of the Islands* must be conditioned by what we expect a novel to be, by our experience of the genre (that is to say our notion of what the novel tradition is). Our prejudices define the impact of the work. John Fowles, in *The French Lieutenant's Woman*, achieves a peculiar effect by pastiching the Victorian novel (suspense-laden chapter endings made even more so by characteristic flash-backs in the following chapter) and by offering alternative endings within a particular tradition. It is thus a comment on (rather than an implicit acceptance of) that tradition, and it questions our tendency to see the novel as a piece of real life: alternatives exist in real life only as possibilities and not as equally realized *events*. All this is interspersed on the one hand with precise (and not allusive) sociological comment and on the other with references to *later* literary and even philosophical tradition, with Robbe-Grillet, Proust and Sartre mentioned by name. The full impact too of a novel like Salinger's *Catcher in the Rye* can be appreciated only if the reader is aware of the assault on our pre-existing idea of the first person novel which Salinger launches in the very first sentence:

> If you really want to hear about it, the first thing you'll probably want to know is where I was born, and what my lousy childhood was like, and how my parents were occupied and all before they had me and all that David Copperfield kind of crap, but I don't feel like going into it.

As with *Le Cygne*, incongruous combinations of elements give these works a special flavour (in both cases traditions are cut across in a most original way). Philip Rahv states that 'in prose the relation between the word or sign and its referent is more firmly fixed and necessarily conventionalized than in poetry where this relation is continually maneuvered so as to exploit the discord no less than the concord of sign and referent' [555, p. 293]. This is quite acceptable so long as one sticks to verbal considerations, but as soon as subject-matter is looked at, the novel may well be doing with it what the poem does with words—are not Fowles and Salinger 'exploiting the discord no less than the concord of sign and referent'?

So the meaning of a work will almost certainly involve departure from a norm. It may relate to the social attitudes current at any particular time—Defoe's *Journal of the Plague Year*, for example. Or it may be a more personal phenomenon: it is difficult to read *Salammbô* without remembering that Flaubert's preceding and following novels deal not with 300 B.C. Carthage but with the France of the 1840s. Or of course it may be traditional, as we have seen.

The process of reading is therefore one in which the conventions set up by the author (through genre or the elements encountered in the work so far) are constantly scanned in order to work out our response to individual elements [v. 69]. The refrain offers us an example of the way a writer may deliberately impose this on us: as we read a poem like Baudelaire's *Invitation au Voyage*, new information is constantly communicated. Our attitude shifts at the same time: we move from the lover's dream of the journey to a description of the room he and his mistress might live in and then to the actual sight of ships and a sunset. But we are made constantly to consider these developments in the light of the refrain:

> Là, tout n'est qu'ordre et beauté,
> Luxe, calme et volupté.

Here is a constant value insisted upon at each stage of the poem —another example of meaningful tension created between an established convention (or reflex in the reader) and its changing context. Similar effects of contrast with the norm are produced by the introduction of a character into a social group to which he does not really belong: Marlow into the corrupt world of *Heart of Darkness*, Lucien de Rubempré into the unscrupulous society of Parisian journalism in *Illusions perdues*.

In the light of all this, it is difficult for the critic to be as squeamish about the idea of deviation as some linguisticians are. The fact is rather that everything may be looked at in terms of it. Stankiewicz may well claim that 'poetic language need not violate any rules of language and still remain what it is, that is a highly patterned and organized mode of verbal expression' [659B, p. 70]. The only mistake here would seem to lie in separating language from the rest. It may well be that even in poetry 'normal' language may be used—it must however be used to create constant patterns of expectancy—more complex than in real life—and in such circumstances the use of language itself ceases to be 'normal'. A reading of some of Rimbaud's prose poems, *Après le Déluge* for example, from *Illuminations*, would demonstrate the truth of this. In addition to strange verbal collocations, details, pieces of information which do not seem to belong together are linked in a way which is only an extreme extension of, say, the use of the unexpected in the novel: the failure of Isabel Archer's marriage in *The Portrait of a Lady* or the comic encounters in surprising circumstances of homosexual lovers in Proust.

This notion is very important for the understanding of the way a work of art affects us. It can also be used as a means of getting to the individuality of any particular writer, when it occurs in a startling way. Spitzer uses the notion of an author's aberrant expressions, his obsessive turns of phrase to point to Charles-Louis Philippe's reliance on pseudo-objective motivation, or (through his delight in making up new words) Rabelais's preoccupation with a world of irreality [652, pp. 10 ff.]. Here again, consciously or unconsciously, the writer, in order to draw attention to his modes of thought, must, as Doležel points out (his remarks relate to language but are much more widely applicable), 'destroy or at least shift the conventional relationships between sign and referent . . . means and rules become significant because they are used in an unusual creative manner' [171, p. 98].

The implications behind this manipulation of instilled reflexes are very great indeed—the particular way an individual writer exploits such reflexes points to a reshaping of one's notion of experience. I have suggested that the abnormal insistence in novelists like the Balzac of *Eugénie Grandet* or *Illusions perdues* on facts, externals, material things and their dynamic nature implies that values, action, character and the like, the meaning of the world in fact depend especially on the visual, the tangible, the countable. In another context, the modern poet's use of unconventional external detail ('the objective correlative') to put over the states of mind or ideal states suggests *now* that the visible world has symbolical value—it no longer explains actions and attitudes (as in Balzac)—it *is* them. Our way of looking physically at things is thus meaningfully distorted in two ways—a glance at the French new novel would show that there are others, with other implications: precise description of the outside world instils a sense of meaninglessness! Elements which normally merge into our blurred everyday perception of life are pushed into the foreground and change their significance in the process. Again, if we think of the way that grammatical patterns or a particular part of speech may be 'foregrounded' [391, p. 144], linguistic and non-linguistic processes in literature are not dissimilar.

The needs and criteria of linguistics and those of literature are however clearly different. Not only is deviation a *norm* in literature, but collocation and connotation, which abstract linguistics may prefer to separate, are to a large extent merged and their value diversified, for they relate to phenomena which go wider than language: Balzac's significant world of tangible facts distorts our normal experience of the world but it echoes similar elements (actions, attitudes etc.) in other passages or even works by the same author. Within *La Comédie Humaine*, therefore, we come to *expect* such distortion . . . In the circumstances, connotation and collocation may not always seem to be particularly useful terms.

Much of what I have said so far would suggest that at one

level form and content are separable and that many of the mechanisms in literature are derived from that fact. Is it not obvious, however, that once this has been established, once a work's debt to various conventions, traditions and external sources of information has been worked out, by far the most important critical work remains to be done? The deviations I have been discussing point to the fact that what matters ultimately is the difference between the individual work and the conventions from which it stems. Sonnets by Mallarmé and Ronsard are startlingly different, as are novels by Thackeray and Henry James, although the form may be said in all cases to be 'conventional'. Close scrutiny of any work makes the distinction between form and content very difficult to pinpoint. The fact that some works (novels more than poems, Pope more than Mallarmé) are more referential than others must be important—but the specific value of what is said in these is still unique. The same event described in two different ways will produce an effect as widely varying as different events described in the same way. Raymond Queneau has shown this in his *Exercices de style* [v. too 367 and 704, p. 9]. This is true of the novel in spite of Valéry's confession that '[he] finds it almost impossible to read a novel without feeling as soon as [his] active attention becomes involved, that alternative and equally acceptable sentences are taking the place of those on the printed page, without this having any particular effect on the novel's impact' [707, v. I, p. 1468]. Valéry is excessively preoccupied with language—in the novel patterns of behaviour are all-important and they are non-linguistic. Even Jane Austen's irony is only partially dependent on the words she uses. Events may be significant not because of a particular vocabulary but merely because they come in a certain order: David Copperfield's second marriage, to Agnes, is all the more stable and mature because of the nature of his first marriage to his 'child-wife' Dora, a fitting conclusion to a work which basically describes an experience of growing up. (The chapters on structure and sequence will explore these questions further.)

E. R. Wasserman, long before Barthes, stressed that 'the final goal of a critical reading is not to discover the universe in which the work functions, but the way in which it functions in that universe' [727, p. 7]. As Guiraud suggests, 'the work is not merely an experience, it is the peculiar form of that experience' [274, p. 14]. Hence the importance of criticism concerned with the *medium of expression* 'le signifiant' rather than with the raw materials to be expressed, 'le signifié' [v. 48, pp. 268–9; v. too *Meaning I*, pp. 77 ff.]. This is why I said earlier that over-erudite criticism is perhaps unhealthy: it exaggerates the external context to which a piece of writing belongs and does not allow us at least to try to see what permanent notions of humanity, humour or experience it might, and if it is worth reading, most certainly would communicate.

It is preferable to bear in mind I. A. Richards's insistence that the form of an utterance is inviolable [575 passim] and the notion that in the broadest sense, synonyms do not exist in literature [243, pp. 133 ff. and 42, p. 249]—and this of course relates to events as well as to words.

One's aim is therefore to describe the specific nature of the work, and that means the different ways in which various elements are handled [v. 196, p. 217]. These need precise and detailed description (whose principles I shall go into especially when I come to the chapters on structure and sequence). Otherwise one falls into the trap Sartre sets for himself (and springs) in *What is Literature* when his description of the social role of the artist up to the present day becomes so schematized that *it could not really be applied fairly and squarely to any individual work.* This is not acceptable in literary criticism except at the preliminary stage of the description of traditions and genres. Many critics have turned a work inside out and used it with others as a basis for literary history, or, as is the case nowadays with Jakobson or the *Tel Quel* group of critics, in an attempt to define 'literarity'. But if such definitions as have so far been rather murkily arrived at are turned upon the work itself, the result is yet again to reduce a specific work to its lowest common denominator, to a tradition, in fact.

One can thus appreciate the great value of the kind of approach adopted by Empson: 'Analyzing a double sestina of Sidney's, he remarks that the six end words, each of them repeated thirteen times in the poem, are "the bones of the situation" . . . these words "circumscribe [the characters'] world". What Empson implies is that the sestina *form* itself, instead of being a mechanical and difficult fixed form into which the poet fits his content . . . is actually the heart of the content, that the *form* is the attitude being expressed.' [328, p. 243.] Rigid forms have no rigid value—their meaning changes according to their content.

None of this is clear-cut. It would be impossible to produce a formula precisely applicable to every work. This is not merely because each one is unique in a special way, a unique combination of a variety of 'internal' and 'external' elements. It is also because, however clearly we may define these elements, we are dealing with a significant level of emotional content and impact. 'Apparently objective ideas, when they come into contact with real life, i.e. for example when they take on the concrete forms of literary expression, become filled with emotion.' [37, p. 18.] Even conceptual prose has a persuasive element in it [v. 309, p. 203]. As for poetry, it is 'the production by language constructs differing from normal speech [deviation again!] of adumbrations of a metaphysical world in which the laws of science, causality, practicality as we know and need them in our workaday world would seem no longer to obtain and in which we vaguely come to visualize other laws' [650, pp. 209–10]. Richards was therefore right to suggest [see *Meaning I*, p. 76] that poetry is a preponderantly emotional process. Indeed *any* meaning would seem to be strongly emotional when broken down into the component parts Richards establishes of sense, tone, feeling and intention. Ullmann has shown that meaning can be broken down further into such elements as the phonetic quality of the words and their contexts, slogans, emotive derivation (pejorative forms etc.), phonetic devices, imagery and syntax [703, p. 128]. And this is true of the communication of ideas too: 'In stylistics emotional and conceptual elements cannot be separated' [10, p. 194]. Again we are in an area which linguistics can point to, but it can scarcely undertake to analyse the *individual* cases which a literary critic will wish to tackle.

The fact is, as I have already shown [see above, pp. 95 ff.], that the decision to talk about something immediately invests that thing with meaning, significance. The thing is not what it was before anyone decided to pay any specific attention to it [v. 615, p. 72]. Speech is not things but the awareness men have of those things—this is an extension of the idea of connotation I mentioned above. Sartre even says that naming a thing invites people to act, or points to a need for change. Not all would agree of course. My insistence on the *uniqueness* of the work of art can for example be taken to the other (to my mind excessively purist) extreme of seeing art as a technique rather than a way of seeing or feeling. Yvor Winters is another important critic who shows himself to be indifferent to a work's emotional effect [v. 312, p. 64], but with him the interest is in its ethical significance, and this would seem to be inseparable from emotional effect.

As a working hypothesis, I. A. Richards's approach would seem to be more promising. He suggests that 'many, if not most, of the statements in poetry are there *as a means* to the manipulation and expression of feeling and attitudes, not as contributions to any body of doctrine of any type whatsoever' [579, p. 186]. Richards pushes this argument even further: 'There are types of poetry (Swinburne's *Before the Mirror* for example) where the argument, the interconnection of the thought has very little to do with the proper effect of the poem, where the thought may be incoherent and confused without harm, for the very simple reason that the poet is not using the argument as an argument and so the incoherence may be neglected. There are other types where the effect of the poem may turn on irrationality . . .' [579, p. 64]. But I should prefer to say that *if any poem is incoherent that incoherence will be part of the poem's character.* The critic cannot therefore neglect it. He must describe it. It is one of those aspects of the work which ensure its inevitably emotional impact [v. 615, p. 159]. If therefore Cuénot points to refrains in Verlaine as underlying the *idea* of the poem [160, pp. 242–3], this can only mean 'idea' in the sense of the general attitude which the work embodies, the kind of mood which Hugo explores in a poem like *Extase* (*Les Orientales*) or even Spenser in his *Prothalamion*, where slightly modified repetitions of the last two lines of each stanza shift the sequence of events towards what is better described as a constant situation, a state of mind, where ideas play a part which is far more complex than their conceptual value would seem to allow.

But of course we do not need to go so far: the events in Spenser's poem or events in a novel or a play are also like ideas in literature. What Richards and others have said above could quite easily be applied to them: the decision to talk about them, the fact that they too come in a particular sequence (which may be straightforward or justifiably 'confused' (as in *Ulysses*) and are represented through certain types of character—all this once again makes the content an inevitable communication of attitudes and therefore values. As Susanne Langer has pointed out [378, p. 223]: 'virtual events are qualitative in their very constitution'. This is another reason why critics of the novel are so wrong if they attempt to see works merely as factual documents, however 'unemotional' and factual the *raw materials* may be. The critic's job must be to describe the *function* of these elements, the relation between them and the attitudes they express. Which brings us back in a sense to the idea that the individual work of art may be considered to be unique. Whether we are dealing with prose (which may be as Greimas suggests 'the form of content') or poetry ('the form of expression in addition to that of content') [256, pp. 271–82], this uniqueness is maintained.

The word which I have perhaps repeated too much in the last few pages is *emotional*. My aim has been to point to the inevitable aura fact has once it becomes part of a wider fiction—it has not been to suggest that fact, concrete recognizable elements be in any way forgotten. Nor am I putting forward the kind of *poésie pure* abstraction which marred so much French criticism in the early part of the century [v. 361, pp. 39 ff.]. Ideas are not excluded as irrelevant to poetry—they merely have a different function from what might be expected from them in a textbook or a philosophical treatise. The fact that Victor Hugo's theories of a universe based on metempsychosis and a manichaeanism where good will eventually triumph over evil (see *Ce que dit la bouche d'ombre* in *Les Contemplations*) may be considered to be rather ludicrous does not for a moment invalidate them as a technical and metaphorical basis for great poetry which describes a world where all things have life and are set in patterns of basic dynamic opposition and change. It would be wrong to neglect the concrete elements from which the work's attitude is developed. Brian Lee has stressed the idea that poetry is a mixture of both description and emotion [389, p. 38]. We must avoid the kind of lyrical impressionism Anatole France indulged in or the excessive liking for metaphor and striking formulae amongst some modern French critics. Attitudes must be related to concrete facts. The interconnections between emotional and intellectual content must be analysed too, as Empson has insisted in the opening pages of *The Structure of Complex Words*, amongst other things to show how Richards's pseudo-statements actually work. It also helps to correct Nadal's reluctance (see my chapter on sounds) to consider the identifiable meaning which exists together with 'musicality' in a poet like Verlaine [498, pp. 127–134]—the emotional use of 'reference' and the 'referential' use of emotion which Umberto Eco talks about [193, p. 220].

Il pleure dans mon cœur
Comme il pleut sur la ville

is thus *at one and the same time* an echoing (referential) pattern of sound, and a statement which compares the idea of tears in the heart (emotion) to rain falling on the town.

It might be claimed that these unique combinations of sense which is also feeling and feeling which is also sense could be analysed objectively. Indeed, one can make a start by considering those elements implied in my chapter headings. But the idea that meaning in a literary work is completely stable must be limited in scope—it cannot take into account an element which varies constantly: the personality of the reader which changes not only from one individual to another but, if we are to believe Montaigne, from minute to minute *within* the individual. The work of art only reaches full realization when it comes into contact with this. *Part of the meaning of any work is the sensibility, culture, mood of the reader.* If these must be less important than the stable elements in the work, they must nevertheless be taken into account. Jakobson [335], suggests usefully that the unity of the work of art results from the way the reader puts together the elements provided by the work. Kenneth Burke has said something similar: for him the poem is a symbolic act leading to the re-enactment by the reader of the poet's original 'deed' [104, pp. 283–6]. Once again the personality of the reader is a key element. Two experiences of the same poem will not be radically different [194, p. 222] but they will have differences.

Criticism of a text must therefore be personal. *But it must be a personal response to the elements which are objectively there.* Perhaps Spitzer's idea that an element is there because he feels it [v. 656, vol. II, passim] is only really justified if you have as rich a critical mind as he. The intuition, Dámaso Alonso [10, p. 122] insists, is part of any stylistic analysis, is a means of giving more weight to one aspect of a text than to another. This is what I have been pointing to all along: the precise value of sound in relation to sense in a poem; the relative importance of tradition and original matter in a novel; vocabulary set against wider blocks of meaning—and so on. These factors must vary from one person to another. If this were not the case, literature would not offer the rich human experience it does [v. too 558, p. 192]. Once the concrete evidence for our attitudes has been worked out, it is as justifiable for there to be divergent views about a novel or a poem as it is for there to be real differences of opinion about the way real people behave or the quality of a real landscape. I happen to believe that the end of Solzhenitsyn's *First Circle* (political prisoners being loaded into a meat van) is a lapse into

E

anecdote unworthy of the rest of the novel—no one I have met agrees, but this makes me neither more nor less right than they. I am not talking about abstract criteria but about *my* specific reaction to a specific event, and in these circumstances absolute notions of right and wrong are impossible.

So many things point to the fact that the meaning of a work is unstable. It is impossible to tie a particular element down to one meaning. In addition to what we have already seen, the words may have more than one value, one scene may remind one of another, sounds (and therefore sense) may echo each other, grammatical patterns may be taken in several ways and so on [v. 703, pp. 154 ff.]. In theory one might even fear that the result might be chaos. But this in fact rarely happens, basically because of the interplay between semantic variables which relate to such naturally unstable things as attitudes, and semantic constants—basic notions of sentence structure or the function of the definite article for example—which are not very flexible. I have already mentioned the idea of *ambiguity*. It is necessary now to underline its central importance in literature—and therefore in criticism.

The idea which goes way beyond crude notions of punning has been current in English language criticism for the last forty years, and on the Continent perhaps for the last twenty. Its importance was demonstrated in a brilliant work entitled somewhat alarmingly *Seven Types of Ambiguity* by William Empson. I do not intend to analyse the book systematically, not so much because this has been competently done already (for example by Hough in his book on stylistics, or Hyman in *The Armed Vision*) but because I think the initial premise which Empson established is considerably more important than the categories he worked out—although the detail was needed at first to stress the general importance of ambiguity. Since 1930 when Empson's book first appeared it has been considered axiomatic that nothing happens in a poem, or indeed in any literary work, which is not multiple in implication, for the individual reader as well as from reader to reader. Empson was of course preoccupied with the *verbal* ambiguity inherent in words or phrases or encouraged by the syntax into which they had been placed: the way in which the poem exploits the notion that the meaning of a word is in fact the various contexts in which it may be found. He quotes for example the well-known lines from *The Rape of the Lock*:

> There thou, great Anna, whom three realms obey,
> Dost sometimes council take, and sometimes tea.

The comic effect is created by forcing the verb *take* to relate to high affairs and trivial, with of course the latter coming second for maximum effect. This, in spite of Philip Wheelwright's assertion to the contrary, shows that Empson was well aware that more than one meaning can exist simultaneously [v. 753, p. 252], an essential principle, it would seem, whether verbal or other ambiguity is being considered. Indeed it is almost inevitable psychologically—one value cannot be obliterated by another, and it would be a wrong critical decision to follow Empson in other parts of the *Seven Types* in suggesting that one is faced with some kind of an alternative.

Ambiguity depends too on uncertainties of words and syntax, like Mallarmé's:

> Toute l'âme résumée
> Quand lente nous l'expirons
> Dans plusieurs ronds de fumée
> Abolis en autres ronds
>
> Atteste quelque cigare
> Brûlant savamment . . .

where it is impossible to work out whether the subject is in the fifth line or the first line of the sonnet (with similar ambiguities about the object . . .)—the poem is enriched in this way because we do not know whether to take lines 2–4 literally or not. Something similar is happening in Hopkins's:

> dapple dawn-drawn falcon . . .

for we hesitate about relating 'dapple' to the dawn or to the bird: it thus covers both in varying degrees.

Eluard's:

> O tour de mon amour autour de mon amour
> Tous les murs filaient blanc autour de mon silence
> [*Giorgio de Chirico* in *Capitale de la Douleur*.]

uses exactly the same sounds in the first half of line one as in the second half—the sounds point therefore in the direction of two things at once—read out loud the two halves are interchangeable. This is a vastly extended application of the kind of technique Shakespeare was using in:

> Therefore I lie with her, and she with me
> [Sonnet 138.]

The examples are innumerable, they may well be much more complex, and all are carefully classified by Empson. Even when they are at the level of puns, they should be taken seriously for, as in Dylan Thomas, they may well be 'basic to the structure of the poems which "make simultaneous statements of antithetical themes or compress two stories into simultaneous motivation"' [v. 503B]. Hugo achieves similar effects in Ballades XI and XII of the *Odes et Ballades*:

> Daigne protéger notre chasse
> Châsse
> De monseigneur saint Godefroi,
> Roi!
>
> Si tu fais ce que je désire,
> Sire,
> Nous t'édifîrons un tombeau
> Beau; . . .
> [Ballade Onzième: *La Chasse du Burgrave*.]

Stephen Booth links words and wider meanings to point to

the way, in Shakespeare's 89th sonnet, the meaning of the verb *will* shifts and moves 'like pulsating alliteration, [and] evokes a sense of insecurity, flux, . . . motion' [79, pp. 90–1]. Parallelism and non-parallelism thus exist simultaneously as well as notions of readiness, future action and desire:

> Say that thou didst forsake me for some fault,
> And I will comment upon that offence:
> Speak of my lameness, and I straight will halt,
> Against thy reasons making no defence.
> Thou canst not, love, disgrace me half so ill,
> To set a form upon desired change,
> As I'll myself disgrace; knowing thy will,
> I will acquaintance strangle, and look strange;
> Be absent from thy walks; and in my tongue
> Thy sweet beloved name no more shall dwell,
> Lest I, too much profane, should do it wrong,
> And haply of our old acquaintance tell.
> For thee, against myself I'll vow debate,
> For I must ne'er love him whom thou dost hate.

The words at the same time keep their literal values. This is a neat example of the way ambiguity grows out of the everyday values language must have (for it is not an exclusively literary tool) and the specific ones superimposed upon it in a specific literary context [v. 46, pp. 262–3]. When we are dealing with literature, our idea of what meaning and language are about changes: 'The whole art of literature consists in turning language (which is a somewhat expeditious means of communicating knowledge and opinion) into a thing of uncertainty and questioning' [238, vol. I, p. 203]. Perhaps Genette here underestimates the ambiguities of everyday language (though the example of advertising shows that these are toyed with much more in English than in French), but the shift in emphasis is well brought out by what he says. Language, which functions through *denotation* in everyday speech, exploits at times its *connotations* in literature in a much more systematic way. Richards has shown the way Swinburne inverts the normal associations of time and grief, so exploiting the connotations of both:

> Before the beginning of the years
> There came to the making of man
> Time, with a gift of tears;
> Grief with a glass that ran.
>
> [579, pp. 195–6.]

The idea must be seen as having fundamental importance therefore. If no work can be reduced to one meaning it is better to say that a work is meaningful than to talk about its meaning [v. 331, p. 91]. The objective elements of the poem are varied in implication not only because of the reader's personality but also because of the shifting emphasis which may with perfect justification be placed on the implications of one single element. 'Night is falling', as Mukařovský has pointed out [493, p. 99], is double in meaning, but infinitely varying degrees of literal and metaphorical combination are possible, except, in literature, the downright exclusion of the one in favour of the other.

In poetry the same kind of potential exists in the devices used. As early as 1929 Slav philologists were talking about 'the diverse functions fulfilled by tropes and rhetorical figures' [v. 277, p. 61]. All critics would not of course attach such importance to ambiguity. Harold C. Martin [437, p. ix] talks about critics' excessive ingenuity in reconciling different elements 'as though obliquity and deviousness were the only *lingua franca* of the artist'. But again perhaps the difficulty concerns not so much the idea of ambiguity as a refusal or an inability to see that literal meanings remain at the same time as their ambiguous potential is realized. Two points should be made at this stage. The first, as Cohen has pointed out, is that the degree to which ambiguity is exploited will vary greatly from one period to another: especially since Romanticism, the extent to which the secondary, non-literal, meaning of a given statement is seen as being important has increased. The gap is clearly great between Boileau or Pope, in whom the literal meaning predominates, and Mallarmé or Dylan Thomas, where literal meaning is at best fragmentary and mysterious.

The second point is an extension of the first. It is that it would be a fundamental mistake to see all poetry as being divorced from logical processes or experience—or even logical argument, as many Shakespeare sonnets show. As Donald Davie has suggested, poetry may well 'describe' a logical process, but whether it does this to the extent that conceptualized vocabulary should be seen as having purely conceptual value is highly debatable. The very coherence which poetry establishes (through techniques looked at in earlier chapters) ensures that it means more than its literal value [162, pp. 52 ff.].

Marvell's plea *To His Coy Mistress*:

> Had we but world enough and time
> This coyness, lady, were no crime

rises well above the pure statement of haste. 'Time' and 'coyness' are associated by rhyme of thought with a powerful word: 'crime'—so strong that it might be seen to introduce a note of wit. In addition 'world' is, at this stage, of uncertain meaning. In a very complex way, therefore, the ideas of these two lines are stretched in various directions well beyond their literal value.

Some critics have fallen into the trap of seeing ambiguity as some sort of fault in the work [v. 434]. What must be realized is the extent to which a writer's search for coherence and the interrelationship of elements makes it necessary for statements and scenes, characters and actions to be double-edged. A particular scene can only be accurately defined if these interrelationships are established, as with the play on the word *will* in Shakespeare's sonnet quoted above. Ambiguity thus becomes a form of accuracy. The ambiguities do not scatter our attention: they point to the associations we must bear in mind if we are to understand what the passage studied really means. The writer in this way takes the prominently illogical nature of language (especially in poetry) and rather than making the best of a bad job, exploits it. Other kinds of accuracy are involved too. In Shakespeare's 94th sonnet 'the reader's essential experience of lines 1–8 is the experience of his own mind in flux' [79, p. 161]—in this way the shifting frames of reference of Shakespeare's works comes nearest to those of real life [79, pp. 171–2]:

> They that have power to hurt and will do none,
> That do not do the thing they most do show,
> Who, moving others, are themselves as stone,
> Unmoved, cold, and to temptation slow;
> They rightly do inherit heaven's graces,
> And husband nature's riches from expense;
> They are the lords and owners of their faces,
> Others but stewards of their excellence.

Language which aims to create this kind of effect could not be accurate if it were to remain logical in a conceptual way. The logic is that of the emotions explored—tensions are set up between an apparent effort towards logical statement and the disruption of this through emotion shown by obsessive repetition and 'overlapping' syntactic structures. Ambiguity is once again at work here —it does not create uncertainty in our minds, but rather points to added complexity in opposing forces.

As in so many areas where striking linguistic examples are needed for support, I have like quite a few of my predecessors fallen into the trap of talking almost exclusively about poetry. Let me redress the balance and insist that *the idea of ambiguity is essential to good prose criticism too.* It is behavioural as well as verbal. We know we can say that everything a work of prose offers is significant in the context of other elements in the work which at times may appear to be unrelated (see my chapter on construction). Prose is not a purely logical discourse, as we have clearly seen—there are too many attitudes involved. The outside world may be more important in a novel, but the novelist is constantly playing on the gap between reality and what lies behind it, or a situation and the interpretation which is being forced upon it. Julia Kristeva has suggested that duplicity in all senses is an essential part of the novel [366, p. 432]. Analysing Katherine Mansfield's *The Fly*, Bateson and Shahevitch point to the 'increasingly ambiguous implications of the boss's character'. Affable at first, he appears to be selfish, cruel and distressed before the story is complete [58, pp. 50–1]. Julien Sorel in *Le Rouge et le Noir* is permanently caught between the need to act hypocritically to further his own ends and the way his real personality keeps breaking through (e.g. his indignation at Valenod's exploitation of the poor or his impulse to kill Mme de Rênal)—and at times the reader's uncertainty as to how sincere he is adds a further dimension to the ambiguity. Dorothea in *Middlemarch* finds that her high ambitions are at war with the sterility of marriage to Casaubon. Mme Bovary at the Vaubyessard ball is blind to the decrepitude around her.

Here event does for the novel what language does for poetry. If the examples given have general value, the notion of ambiguity can be immensely widened by pointing to the fact that choice, the inclusion of a particular element in a literary work, implies its significance, as we have seen. This means that it must be taken on face value (i.e. by bearing in mind its links with the outside world) and at the same time evaluated in its links with the rest of the work: Julien Sorel's pity for the prisoners is one way of prefiguring his own fate. Mme Bovary's sordid little trips to Rouen parallel her dreams of an elegant life in Paris. The whole fabric of the work is thus implicitly drawn together; characters may be in opposition to others, but there will be points of similarity too, for the characters belong to the same world. The novelist takes the fact that the description of human behaviour can never be circumscribed and exploits it to describe (with an accuracy which cannot otherwise be achieved) the way differing elements cohere. Mme de Rênal may be as sweet and attractive as old Sorel is hard and grasping, but Stendhal implicitly shows them both to be adept at deceiving others [748]. Incidents in a novel (or a play) tend generally to have this kind of value. The pointlessness of the kind of criticism which 'tells the story' is clear.

Verbal ambiguity does occur in the novel. It does not normally work however in the same way as in poetry. In Sterne there is a constant tension for example between the idea of a novel as a story to be told and the work's tendency to discuss what writing a novel is all about. Flaubert persistently presents us with characters who fail verbally to describe the world and their experience of it —slogans, catch phrases, theories, manuals of painting or gardening are all of no help. The novels Guetti describes in *The Limits of Metaphor* deal with similar problems. Language here is ambiguous because it is at one and the same time the only possible medium for the telling of a story and the expression of its own shortcomings—the uncertainty as to what *real* events are is also acute. Language must be both taken literally and met with suspicion.

Much ambiguity in the novel is clearly related to irony (the gap between ideal notions of reality and direct experience)—examples from *Mme Bovary* or *Heart of Darkness* and the example of Dorothea mentioned above show that this may be verbal or related to a confrontation of events [v. 353; 630; 358; 341].

So Cleanth Brooks is perhaps being too restrictive when he points to the all-pervading nature of irony ('that recognition of incongruities') in poetry without mentioning its importance in the novel [96, p. 171]. One aspect of this kind of ambiguity is more present in poetry than elsewhere, however, and this is paradox [v. 96, pp. 1–16], born very often of a romantic preoccupation with newness and surprise to be extracted from familiar experience [v. 96, p. 4].

In a brilliant analysis, Cleanth Brooks sets out to explain the last lines of Keats's *Ode on a Grecian Urn*:

> 'Beauty is truth, truth beauty'—that is all
> Ye know on earth and all ye need to know.

He shows that the idea of the permanence of beauty is strikingly and logically put across by the paradoxes which run through the poem: the eternally motionless lovers, the forever still town, the cold pastoral [96, pp. 124–35]. Brooks's approach is useful because it encourages one to question statements and when they seem illogical, not to reject them as an aberration or to skip over them as incomprehensible but to see what deeper meaning they may offer for the works in which they are found. The examples from the Keats Ode show this, as does Brooks's study of the naked babe and cloak of manliness images in *Macbeth* [96, pp. 17–39].

Terms like ambiguity, paradox, irony (and many others) are, of course, pretty crude. A linguistician or a semantics expert could demolish them without too much difficulty. When we talk about the meaning of literature, however, we are dealing with problems much too complex for any scientific linguist to be able to tackle adequately. The terms critics use are not intended to be scientifically accurate [594, p. 115]; they are rather an indication of tendencies which we should keep our eyes open for and then, as in the examples above, describe precisely according to the context in which they are found.

The idea of ambiguity is not only useful in relation to these fundamental ideas. By underlining the way literature exploits the instability of language and the multiple meanings of events, it also enables us to see *imagery*, and especially *metaphor*, not as an isolated element but as something implicitly integrated into the basic meaning of any literary work. Metaphor is a form of ambiguity [v. 704, p. 15 and 504, pp. 140 ff.].

A metaphor can be seen as a direct statement which, because it is strange or merely because it is in a 'poetic' context, implies that a comparison is being made with something else, or that something else is being evoked. The statement cannot be accepted on face value:

> Je suis le Ténébreux,—le Veuf,—l'Inconsolé,
> Le Prince d'Aquitaine à la Tour abolie.
> Ma seule *Etoile* est morte,—et mon luth constellé
> Porte le *Soleil* noir de la *Mélancolie*.
>
> [Nerval: *El Desdichado*.]

Except for terms two and three in line one, none can be taken literally—this leads us to reject a purely literal, non-associative value for those in the first line. Concrete statements are thus seen to be pointing to and *tangibly* describing the sense of despair and desolation with which the poem begins.

I went into a major aspect of metaphor when I examined Christine Brooke-Rose's book in the chapter on grammar. The complex problems of semantic motivation involved in metaphor (and metonymy) have been dealt with thoroughly by Ullmann [703, passim]: the way metaphor exploits the ambiguous part of a statement and ignores the rest. Cohen too goes into great detail [141, esp. pp. 105 ff.]. They and others underline (at times unwittingly) the extent to which a purely linguistic description is inadequate: 'No linguistic warranty can be found for metaphor: instead the compensatory connexion is to be sought outside language in some kind of psychological, emotional or perceptual relation between the literal and figurative meanings of the item(s) concerned' [391, p. 154]. Once again we must go beyond words to things (or we must not be content to talk about words alone), either because there is a direct resemblance between two elements or objects to which words draw our attention or because two dissimilar things create an equal response in us—one supposes that this is involved in the French use of cabbage as a term of endearment. Richards [577, pp. 107 ff.] talks about a process of contiguous inflammation, the intertransference of properties from one thing or notion to another. We are faced therefore not with the much freer process of association which we looked at earlier but with a more systematic technique of identification of one element with another.

The participation of the reader may of course vary. Bachelard offers an extreme example of such participation [31, pp. 1–4] by cultivating an almost passive dream state which builds up and develops from the impact of individual images. For those of us whose sensibility is not so rich, descriptions based on more general principles are a better ground for criticism. Cohen, for example, points to the importance of 'irrelevance': the variable gap between the unacceptable literal meaning of a statement and the true significance which the reader must work out—as in the Nerval stanza quoted above. This gives individual metaphors part of their character: 'Le Prince d'Aquitaine à la tour abolie' is a strange and powerful expression of loneliness and isolation because

Nerval does not refer to an immediately recognizable person or a known place; the implication of the statement is thus not immediately established. Cohen uses this as a basis for suggesting that the more 'irrelevant' to each other the components of an image are, the more poetical the image is (this being one aspect of the notion of deviation by which, according to Cohen, all poetry is defined). This would seem to be untenable when a great poet can write like Pope, and yet Cohen's approach is useful for describing individual metaphors: it allows us to examine the extent of intellectual or emotional impact in them. Baudelaire's 'La nature est un temple' is not only more immediately perceptible emotionally (and therefore less powerful) than Nerval's metaphors, it is also more rational: trees (the 'vivants piliers' of the same line) may logically be seen as the pillars of this particular temple.

If we are careful not to isolate individual metaphors, the notion of logic is seen to be important in other respects: images may be strange, but they will in a particular poem (or novel) tend to be interrelated—they are logical therefore within the framework of the individual poem, as the stanza from Nerval helps to demonstrate. This is even true of the most outlandish metaphors of all, as Riffaterre has shown in his study of surrealist poetry [587].

Such modern articles show how useful it is to follow the long established practice of looking at the areas from which an author's or an individual poem's imagery are drawn: deciding whether they are animate, inanimate, concrete, abstract, visual, mental, related to one particular sense impression or a particular type of experience or activity etc., and whether both 'sides' of a simile or metaphor are drawn from similar areas of experience (see *Meaning I*, p. 79). Huguet's, Robertson's and Mabilleau's studies of Hugo's imagery [324; 325; 597; 419] like so many others are perhaps too much like catalogues for present-day critical minds, but they do have real value in helping to point to the coherence of an author's thinking, the semantic areas to which his associations tend to belong. But it is in Shakespeare criticism that this kind of classification shows its revolutionary possibilities. Caroline

Spurgeon's *Shakespeare's imagery and what it tells us* [v. also 328, pp. 161–96] and Clemen's study of the *Development of Shakespeare's Imagery* both point (perhaps a little unwittingly in the first case, for Caroline Spurgeon was to some extent interested in the real-life sources of Shakespeare's inspiration) to the logic behind the imagery, dominating images in individual plays and even obsessive images throughout the works [v. too 383B]. To describe such constant phenomena is to describe what a work *means*, as will be seen in the chapter on structure.

It is useful to search for the other ways in which imagery shows itself to be logical or illogical—the ways therefore in which it may seem to be disturbing. In the case of surrealist imagery I have just mentioned it has been pointed out that if the combinations of ideas involved ('la terre est bleue comme une orange' [Eluard, *l'Amour la poésie*] or 'Les archaïques carcasses de chevaux en forme de baignoire passent et s'estompent' [Char, *Le Climat de chasse ou l'accomplissement de la poésie*]) are highly deviant, or 'irrelevant', the grammatical context is very rarely disconcerting [36, pp. 238–9]. Cohen establishes that there are two basic types of metaphor: those which explain and those which have a more affective impact [141, pp. 127 ff.]. But is is clear from these examples that the character of each individual image will vary a great deal.

All this concerns the different connections and therefore tensions which are set up in the poem between literal and metaphorical or figurative meanings, and includes trying to square normal syntax and wild associations of ideas. For the rational or the metaphysical poet this may well involve an extension of literal statement into metaphor ('The blue of her eyes was cloudless') or it may be the other way round, as with romantic or symbolist poets—see the way Baudelaire or Rimbaud (in *Le Voyage* or *Bateau ivre*) take the idea of a sea journey as a symbol of life or experience and then develop all ideas in the poem literally from this.

My examples of what may be involved in metaphor show, I think, that as Leavis suggests '. . . we have to think of metaphor as something more immediate, complex and organic than neat illustrative correspondence' [385, p. 169]. Imagery is not mere illustration. It offers varied and complex forms of meaning. In Anglo-Saxon poetry for example, the gap between literal and figurative values even disappears altogether, there is no distinction between fact and figure, allegory and reality [v. 660].

Any attempt to 'translate' images into simpler meaning will be damaging therefore. In the following lines, some astrological knowledge is indeed useful but over and above this, there is the way one word (Goat) hinges the stanza *simultaneously* round its two *literal* values:

> You lovers, for whose sake, the lesser Sunne
> At this time to the Goat is runne
> To fetch new lust, and give it you,
> Enjoy your summer all . . .
> [Donne, *A Nocturnall upon St. Lucies Day*.]

The process involved is not the crude negative idea that imagery avoids the literal expression of things. It is much truer to say that *imagery creates new meanings*—the values set up in the examples quoted above cannot be found elsewhere because *the combinations of ideas involved are in the main unique*. Cecil Day Lewis claims that 'the image cannot . . . reproduce the soul of things: what it can do is persuade us, by the force of its own vitality, and our own answering sense of revelation . . . that there is beneath the appearance of things a life whose quality may not be apprehended in our everyday intercourse nor be gauged by the instruments of science' [407, p. 107]. Other general elements are involved too—the feeling that the image is a means (Wheelwright would see it as a tentative means [v. 753, pp. 257–8]) of putting over ideas, truths which more straightforward expression could not achieve. *Controllable*, *checkable* truth does not come into it. I would even suggest that it goes further than the exploration and reassessment of reality which C. Day Lewis talks of [407, pp. 58–9] in connection with the romantic image. Although clearly imagery must link with tensions in society at a particular time, and be especially adventurous or deviationist in a period of instability, the process involved is not one of stating the expected in an unusual way (a contradiction in terms in literature in any case) but rather of creating new areas of experience, associations *which did not exist before.* Surrealist examples given above are an extreme form of this, but even Marvell's linking of love and geometry is adequate illustration:

> As Lines so Loves *oblique* may well
> Themselves in every Angle greet:
> But ours so truly *Paralel*
> Though infinite can never meet
>
> [*The definition of love.*]

Another, associated with Eliot but widespread in modern poetry, is the use of the objective correlative, the description of externals which implicitly points to an inner state:

> Here is no water but only rock
> Rock and no water and the sandy road
> The road winding above the mountains
> Which are mountains of rock without water
> If there were water we should stop and drink
> Amongst the rock one cannot stop or think
> Sweat is dry and feet are in the sand
> If there were only water amongst the rock
> Dead mountain mouth of carious teeth that cannot spit
> Here one can neither stand nor lie nor sit
> There is not even silence in the mountains
> But dry sterile thunder without rain
> There is not even solitude in the mountains
> But red sullen faces sneer and snarl
> From doors of mudracked houses . . .
>
> [*The Waste Land*, ll. 331–45]

Except for one metaphor in line 339, the description is quite literal and yet the sense of desolation and torment takes us far beyond the facts of the scene described. Naming a thing, as we have already seen, implies that it should not be taken literally; it takes on metaphoric value and therefore changes its significance—here the change is so great that it creates a new conception of the thing implied. Similar examples (see Baudelaire's *Vie antérieure*, *Invitation au Voyage* or *Spleen II*) are very numerous.

At the beginning of this section, I mentioned the need to avoid isolating metaphor from other elements in the work of art. The example of the objective correlative points to the image's double role in a particularly relevant way inasmuch as it must retain its descriptive value in spite of its metaphorical impact. It is perhaps not enough to follow W. J. Harvey's injunction to 'preserve a firm sense of the relation of imagery to its total linguistic context and to realise that the concept of imagery contains a range of different forms, functions and content' [293, p. 223]. Once again the mistake lies in implying that linguistic and non-linguistic elements in a work are somehow separate. In a novel this creates all sorts of difficulties, for '. . . one of the functions of realistic art is to bring both *dramatis personae* in an essentially positivist and antimetaphysical world to a point where they are faced with metaphysical questions not in the abstract but as "proved on the pulses"' [254, p. 345]. This implies that action and events have a real metaphorical value; that, as is so explicitly the case in Balzac, objects which belong to the tangible, everyday world point to the characters who use, wear, inhabit them and to the criteria according to which the world is organized. They are much more significant than Barthes with his 'effect of reality' [44] would have us believe. In a novel like Conrad's *An Outcast of the Islands*, seascapes or the behaviour of flames or the sight of a man groping his way through the jungle, the systematically established close links between inner mood and external description, all referential rather than verbal, are similarly metaphorical. The mysterious shrouded figure looking out to sea at the beginning of John Fowles's *The French Lieutenant's Woman* cannot be taken literally (and because a real person is involved who will have other qualities, this can be no empty symbol).

Philip Rahv is right to suggest that symbol and image hunting is a bad aspect of much modern criticism of fiction [555, p. 280]. This is because the metaphorical dimension of prose, as we have seen, works in a totally different way. The critic of prose is therefore very often concerned with the wider significance events and descriptions may point to whilst they retain their literal value. This is metaphor still but it is largely non-linguistic and biased towards a form of the objective correlative. Excessive emphasis on the verbal associations poetry depends on so crucially (even the paralleling effect of rhythm is metaphorical) would be misplaced.

This does not, however, imply that more straightforward, obvious imagery does not exist (only the French New Novel seems deliberately to have excluded it). Indeed Stephen Ullmann [698, pp. vii–viii] suggests that images may at times formulate the main theme of a work (not the same thing as its main texture). 'Imagery may therefore take the critic by a short cut to the very core of the work, and the metaphors arising around these central themes may develop into major symbols.' Once again the listing of areas from which images are drawn is a useful procedure. Ullmann shows how Proust draws on medicine, science, art, animals and plants [698, pp. 128–9]. But it is also essential to notice that 'the contexts in which an author uses images are just as important as the sources from which he draws them . . . subjects in which we are intensely interested tend to become centres of both expansion and attraction: they will suggest analogies when we talk of other matters, but will also require the support of images from other spheres if we are to describe them precisely and effectively' [698, p. 195]. Images are a sign therefore that an important point is being made, that a significant event or element is being introduced. A recurrent image will suggest that a central aspect of the novel is being broached repeatedly. In Gide's *L'Immoraliste*, as Ullmann has pointed out, the image of the palimpsest, the conjunction of the superficial and the hidden, underlines a major recurrent preoccupation, as does the image embodied in the very title of *La Porte étroite*. In Dickens's *Our Mutual Friend*, a critic has suggested that the river constantly confronts us with ideas of death and rebirth, whilst dust mounds express the rotten foundations of riches and the power of the corrupt [491]. If this looks rather like what Philip Rahv was warning us against, Barbara Hardy's study of *Imagery in George Eliot's Last Novels* is much more satisfactory. The images (principally those of water, dark narrow spaces (including tombs and labyrinths) and mirrors) have a unifying function because they are taken from objects which have a natural presence in the novels. Characters' feelings that they have been trapped or the impression that their vision has been distorted, for example, are expressed by recurrent images and are a basis in both *Middlemarch* and *Daniel Deronda* for what Barbara Hardy calls 'a private ironical understanding between author and reader' [p. 6]. The significance of a variety of events is made clear to the reader by the recurrence of familiar imagery. Guetti offers an interesting variation on this: the characters of the works he studies are often seen to be trying to reduce their experience to a metaphor, the novels being in a sense a study of the extent to which the metaphor fits [264, pp. 148 ff.]. This leads to an ironical situation in which, for example, *Moby Dick* is defined as 'the denial of the possibility of metaphorical perception' [264, p. 112]. Guetti points at the same time to the need to square the use of metaphor in a novel with point of view: is the image a definition of experience offered 'objectively' by the work or is it imposed by a character and therefore primarily an indication of the latter's make-up? I have tried to show for example that in Flaubert imagery is always the representation of a character's view of the world and never an indication of the general or 'correct' meaning of experience [747].

Rightly or wrongly I have made no real effort so far to separate simile and metaphor, although what I have said has been mainly with the latter in mind. This is partly because we can often tackle both by referring to similar principles: values and sources of comparison for example. (The mechanisms of simile were looked at too when I mentioned Christine Brooke-Rose's book in the chapter on grammar [v. too 81B, 303A, 393B].) The association of ideas involved in simile is much more explicit, although the things associated (as we saw in the quotation from Eluard) may be startling. Concepts are brought together too in a more tentative way: it is *suggested* that they are similar, no more. The intellectual impact of the simile will therefore tend to be greater because the relationship established is toyed with instead of being perhaps thrown into violent affective identity. One can see this even by transposing 'la terre est bleue *comme* une orange' into 'la terre *est* une orange bleue'.

The transposition shows too that the mode of association of ideas involved changes from simile to metaphor. Moreover, when both terms are mentioned (and the objective correlative shows that with metaphor this is not always the case) the basic units of association in a simile may vary in position and emphasis much more. Eluard could have written 'la terre est comme une orange bleue'. Permutations of the metaphor on the other hand would not seem to be possible without a much more radical change in its effects (as Christine Brooke-Rose's book demonstrates). Winifred Nowottny says that the simile is a better mechanism for suggestion and that the means of comparison are more varied [v. 504, pp. 50 ff.].

This greater subtlety should not however be dissociated from the greater rational effect produced. It is significant that modern poetry makes great use of metaphor: the drop in the use of simile between Baudelaire and Mallarmé is quite radical, and even Hugo with his increasing taste for substantival combinations (of the 'pâtre-promontoire' type) shows a similar tendency. The relative use of simile or metaphor should therefore be seen as a convenient short cut to the *way* the experience described is being approached (over and above the different *types* of simile and metaphor involved). If Nerval had written 'je suis comme un veuf' instead of 'je suis . . . le Veuf' a much less 'unique' situation would have been described.

One further aspect to which I have alluded briefly here and there, but which (like simile) might well have merited a section of its own in this chapter is the problem and analysis of obscurity in poetry. For a variety of reasons I feel that, like so many other loose ends in this and other chapters, this may be best approached within the framework of the chapters on construction and sequence—especially as this book does not aim so much at abstract definitions as at practical critical method. What might be retained here is basically that 'difficult' poetry is not easy poetry mixed up. The last approach one should think of adopting is the prose transposition. Mallarmé criticism demonstrates that this is not as obvious as it might seem—Mme Noulet for example devotes vast energies and ingenuity to telling us what Mallarmé 'really' meant [431]. Any obscure poetry will tend to attract this line of approach, but what the poet said is on the page and what the poem means is what it says; our purpose should be to describe it, using the kinds of criteria mentioned so far in this book: types of vocabulary, the impact of individual words which are in a sense freed by ambiguous syntax, image constants and development, syntax, combinations of ideas and collocations as they manifest themselves in the course of the poem. Deviation is an idea which will inevitably play an important part here. The obscurity of an obscure poem is part of the experience of that poem—it must therefore be *described*, not eliminated or 'solved'. When Mallarmé writes:

A la nue accablante tu
Basse de basalte et de laves
A même les échos esclaves
Par une trompe sans vertu

Quel sépulcral naufrage (tu
Le sais écume mais y baves)
Suprême une entre les épaves
Abolit le mât dévêtu

Ou cela que furibond faute
De quelque perdition haute
Tout l'abîme vain éployé

Dans le si blanc cheveu qui traîne
Avarement aura noyé
Le flanc enfant d'une sirène.

the 'tu' at the end of line one may well be the perfect participle of 'taire' and may well qualify the shipwreck of line five and be a lead-in to the ideas of line four. But to reconstruct the syntax in this way is to neglect the very powerful position 'tu' occupies, one of extreme insistence and ominousness (because we do not know what it relates to), and one of bewildered ambiguity. In this it fits into the anticipatory phrases of lines two and three (which again do not seem to relate to anything) and the holding back of punch lines (shipwreck is not mentioned until line five) which characterizes not just the stanzas but the tercets as well (with a marked contrast between the climax of line eight and the anti-climax of line fourteen). Ominous uncertainty keynotes the poem. It is inseparable from the order and impact of the ideas. Crude rewriting destroys it.

The need to maintain this kind of approach in the novel (where obscurity is a rarer phenomenon) is equally great. Any attempt to work out what is so often being discussed just out of Frédéric Moreau's earshot in *l'Education sentimentale* or who really killed old Karamazov is misguided. The works, in their hugely different ways, put over an *experience* of uncertainty, mystery, confusion and underhand dealing. As I have already said, rather than deviation in language and concepts, it is now the way we expect people, or, especially in the twentieth century, the novel itself (the way it orders and explains its material) to behave which may result in obscurity. The way this kind of expectancy is 'dis-appointed' should be a suitable basis for tackling the work in question [v. 643B].

The basic approach to any work, whether it is straightforward or very obscure is: *when in doubt describe.* Esotericism being the extreme demonstration of the inseparability of form and content, such a formula cannot fail to produce results.* This furthermore will be most useful when the obscurity involved is of the modern, 'personal' kind, relating to private impressions and forms of

* Note: Clearly 'description' does *not* here mean telling the story. It means rather drawing attention to the basic means which are brought into play to put the story, attitudes or 'ideas' across.

expression and not to the codes of meaning of the kind found in say Maurice Scève or Guillaume de Lorris. Their obscurity is largely due to the passing of time—here a more literal meaning is involved and straight scholarship is essential, although once again the poem's final form is unique and should be described as such.

Conclusions in such a long chapter are best made as one goes along. This is what I have tried to do. And yet because the chapter is so long it would be useful briefly to underline some of the points which come out of it.

The most important point is that in the meaning of any particular work a massive diversity of factors is potentially involved. I have only been able to provide a sample. This will not offer much detailed explanation of the way factors will *combine* to give a work its meaning: each work will be different inevitably and must therefore be looked at on its own terms.

I have preferred to mention the basic semantic mechanisms which we may expect to encounter: meaning *is* context; it is an emotional as well as a factual thing; it depends on the relationship between the reader and what he is reading; meaning in literature exploits ambiguity as a positive asset (whether that ambiguity be verbal or situational); imagery is part of ambiguity as is esotericism, which is not so much a coded message as a different kind of message and it should be described as such.

All these factors can be illustrated further by reference to points in other chapters, including (and perhaps especially) the chapters to come. They too are broadly based and must therefore with meaning be central to this kind of study.

CHAPTER FIVE

STYLE

It would be difficult to imagine a book like this without a chapter on style, and yet, I am not sure that it is necessary here. To attempt a short but reasonably comprehensive survey of the different practical approaches to style is a frightening task, as any glance at bibliographies of the subject quickly shows [v. 295; 34; 298; 471]. The many thousands of entries given point to the wide and varied notions behind style analysis.

So many aspects of the subject are already covered by the other chapters which make up this book. It is a good start when looking at a literary text to see what can be gleaned from an examination of its sounds, grammar, lexis and semantic functions. All these overlap with each other, of course; they are fragmentary accounts of aspects of a whole which might be called style.

But this does not necessarily mean that stylistics and textual criticism are one and the same thing. The best general introduction to stylistics for the literary minded is undoubtedly the first chapter of Stephen Ullmann's *Style in the French Novel* which shows the extent to which different stylistic devices can be pointed to and named [v. too 274 and the introduction to 505]. This would perhaps seem to indicate, amongst other things, that orthodox modern stylistics tends to be a much more factual and formally precise discipline than all-out textual criticism. It is a much more objective affair. It is interested in very important mechanisms in literature, but it focuses rather on categories and classification than, say, on the reader's reaction. It always runs the risk, therefore, of separating different elements of a work from the wider notions of meaning which we looked at in the last chapter.

One reason for this (apart from the fact that it is always easier to describe objective features than to analyse one's response) may be that, as Guiraud points out [273, p. 94], 'stylistics is as yet aware neither of its aims, its tools, nor its methods'. That was in 1954—it would be a little harsh on Ullmann, Riffaterre, Ohmann and even on Guiraud himself to suggest that the situation has not changed at all since then. And yet the search for greater inclusiveness of stylistic analysis still has not covered the whole phenomenon by any means. It is doubtful whether even a comprehensive survey of the ingredients will provide an adequate description of the finished cake. What is left over is a huge area which the categorization of stylistic features cannot really help to define (and stylistics is, by definition, categorization).

The stylistician's approach offers two real dangers: on the one hand, as I have shown in earlier chapters, over-preoccupation with one particular feature may well minimize the significance of others which are equally important; on the other hand, any attempt to see a text as a mere collection of stylistic elements (even if all are analysed with equal emphasis) will tend to ignore the other ways whereby its meaning is produced.

One must especially avoid the biggest time-waster of all: the attempt to define style according to external criteria. Perhaps the most healthy approach is that of R.-L. Wagner when he admits himself 'incapable of giving a coherent definition to the word'. [723, p. 9.] Others, however, *have* attempted it, like Coleridge: 'Style is nothing else but the art of conveying the meaning appropriately and with perspicuity, whatever that meaning may be . . .' [141A, p. 320]. This is a description of style as effectiveness. I am not sure that the criteria of that effectiveness are easily established. Middleton Murry's definition is also inadequate: '"Style" is a quality of language which communicates precisely emotions or thoughts or systems of emotions or thoughts peculiar to the author.' [495, p. 65.] The only thing such statements can achieve is a general free-for-all.

This is not to suggest that intuitive criticism is a bad thing—as J. C. Ransom points out, it is wrong to let 'technical, intellectual processes' replace completely 'the old intuitive or primitive skills'

[558, p. 192]. Style, we have already seen, is a non-adherence to strictly logical expression. But it is still necessary for any definition of style at least to suggest a partly methodical approach to a text—not a pure dependence on one's own sensibility.

Riffaterre's approach is, therefore, of more practical use: 'Style is understood as the emphasis (expressive, affective, aesthetic) added to the information conveyed by the linguistic structure, without alteration of meaning. Which is to say that language expresses and style stresses.' [583, p. 155.] This is useful because it is not related to the old definition of style as conformity to established norms and values. Style is rather the bias, the attitude towards what is being communicated. As Ohmann puts it: 'Style is the hidden thoughts which accompany overt propositions.' [511, p. 408.] It is 'that which in a text is not a linguistic feature pure and simple'. [345, p. 379.] The 'pure and simple' element here is important, for, as we saw in the chapter on grammar, Ohmann offers a definition of style which depends on the modification of the most elementary forms an utterance may take. Consider too Riffaterre's statement: '. . . a Style is not the one or two elements chosen by the critic as a key to the rest: it is the combination of those elements with the rest . . . or even the original combination of quite ordinary linguistic elements. Not to admit this is to state that Voltaire has no individuality . . .' [590, p. 479].

This takes us some considerable distance away from the idea of style as being made up exclusively of striking elements like rhetorical devices, images and alliteration. It points to a definition of style as 'a selection [and a special combination] of non-distinctive features of language' (and here we think of Spitzer, Auerbach, Wimsatt) rather than as Dobrée's idea of style as the personality of the author [169, pp. 1 ff.] or 'the ultimate morality of the mind' Bloomfield considered it to be [v. 472, pp. 80–1].

Style handles and regroups elements which have everyday familiarity: '. . . the job of internal stylistics is . . . whilst confining itself to everyday language, to reveal the elements from which style springs, to show that the qualities which make it effective are deeply embedded in the most banal forms of the language.'

[37, p. 61.] It need not, in spite of what Hill implies, result from the combination of several sentences [308]. One of its basic features, therefore, as Milic has pointed out, is *choice* [v. 320, p. 8 and 436, p. 30]. We have seen how the style of some authors may be characterized by their use of some perfectly normal grammatical features: the subjunctive, the substantive [v. 273, p. 111]. Our everyday experience of style is, however, infinitely more complex and subtle than that. The idea of choice and the definitions from Riffaterre and Ohmann given above point to the closely related notion of alternative expression. It is that element involved when one talks about the possibility of changing the words or arranging them differently without a corresponding change in substance—something I am doing all the time as I correct the manuscript of this book [v. 509, p. 427]. Halliday develops this idea a little when he states that 'a text is meaningful not only in virtue of what it is but also in virtue of what it might have been' [282, p. 218]. A word very often used in this context is synonymy, which both Ullmann and Guiraud see as a key term [v. 704, p. 13; 273, p. 46]. Hough suggests that 'the differences between synonymous sentences may be called stylistic' [320, p. 7; v. 127].

These definitions are useful because they offer possibilities of practical application, as we shall see (otherwise they would be a waste of time). This is not to suggest that they are in any sense perfect, be it only because synonymy is in itself an impossible abstraction—if the mode of expression of an idea changes, the nature of the idea changes as well, at least in part. Moreover, the central notion of ambiguity suggests that to change the form of a message is to shift the impact of its connotations. At the same time, the kind of linguistic rewriting suggested by Ohmann, or Dupriez's consideration of alternatives in *L'Etude des Styles* is a very useful lead-in to the specific nature of a text's modes of expression, and is supplementary to a great deal of what we saw in earlier chapters.

Further definitions of style (again having practical value) may be seen in the chapter on counting and statistics. As is inevitable, they relate, too, in varying ways to the idea of departure or variation from an, at times, hypothetical norm. This is also true of Riffaterre's theories of style (which will be examined shortly) and of those of Ohmann, who suggests that '... the elusive intuition of *form* and *content* may turn out to be anchored in a distinction between the surface structures [the deviation] and the deep structures [the norm] of sentences' [510, p. 238]. Again there is considerable overlap with Zumthor's definition of style as 'formal variation of elements with an expressive function' [785, p. 27].

One question which inevitably arises is the extent to which general definitions of style, in the cases where they are at all useful, may be applied indiscriminately to different literary genres. One has only to think of Greimas's distinction between prose '(the form of content') and poetry ('the form of expression plus that of content') to realize how complicated this may become [257, p. 272]—all the more complicated and frustrating in this case because Greimas is characteristically interested in abstractions and does not give precise concrete examples to prove his point. Hjelmslev's notion of 'form of expression' does seem to relate to Levin's idea of 'couplings' which belongs essentially to the chapter on construction [403], and would tend to suggest that our preoccupation with the actual words of poetry will give orthodox stylistic value to elements which would have a purely communicative function in prose—and this is not without significance as will be seen when we look at Riffaterre's theories. Such ideas are an extension of the more commonly accepted notions that in poetry we may expect more frequently to encounter clear-cut stylistic features like imagery and rhetorical features. They also show that Ohmann's theories are limited: style is features as well as structures; as it is also linked to genre, the same element will affect us differently according to context.

This, in one sense, brings us back to problems of linguistics and style, to which I have perhaps devoted too much time already. Style is generally considered to be of necessity a linguistic phenomenon, and this necessarily creates varying degrees of emphasis, with the more linguistically-minded scholars like Charles Bruneau standing in contrast to people like Spitzer, Dámaso Alonso and Helmut Hatzfeld. [v. 345.] These latter are above all (and rightly so) concerned to avoid attaching importance to elements which are merely of linguistic interest. As Juilland points out: 'Linguistic methods can only define the style of one author by contrasting it with that of another and the pertinent elements would vary according to the different authors with whom a given author is compared.' [345, p. 377.] Literary stylistics, even when concerned with alternatives and synonymy, need not be comparative in this way. Moreover, the linguistic stylistician will often be interested in non-literary problems: the style of a scientific paper or everyday speech for example. This is a pure preoccupation with language [v. 158B and 4B]. Its opposite is Croce's notion that expression in literature is unrelated to linguistic formulae. Spitzer and the others mentioned above stand at a more realistic half-way house, taking the language of literature and seeing it in the emotional context which the notion of literary style implies. Description for them is an inevitable preliminary to interpretation and assessment, although again these three elements will greatly vary in emphasis from one critic to another. Style is thus seen as the nature of an experience in verbal terms. Which, once again, brings us back to ideas discussed more fully in *Meaning II*. In spite of the increased method and system which characterizes modern criticism, it might seem that Herbert Read is wrong to talk sadly about the 'total rejection of style as a criterion of literature' in the twentieth century [560, p. 31]. Notions of value have, it is true, receded somewhat but, as we shall see, stylistics today need not be as purely factual as he suggests. Textual analysis still relates in very large measure to the author's modes of sensibility and to the reader's.

Over and above definitions (which may well help to determine critical practice) there is the whole variety of general approaches to style: synchronic, diachronic, trope-biased, impressionistic, concentrating on imagery, tone and attitude, local idiosyncrasies or wider characteristics, and many more [v. 509, pp. 423–6]. These incidentally help us further to understand the area covered by the notion of style. But they are perhaps of greater value because they are more directly practical and may serve as a check list when approaching a text. Abstract theories, here as elsewhere in criticism, should be viewed with suspicion by anyone whose main aim is to understand an individual text. For example, McIntosh in an essay called *Some Thoughts on Style* divides his thoughts between theory and practice, his main theoretical pre-occupation being the idea of appropriateness, the gap between the appropriate and the adequate. These are very interesting notions. But our roused expectancy is sadly disappointed for, in the practical part, emphasis is placed upon the need to 'start with simple, examples of adequacy [p. 93]. This is, of course, precisely what a literary critic cannot do—he must take the material which the text offers and use examples which are representative of the text and not of any general theory of style. The nicest and neatest definitions often lead to disappointing practical results—one is forced to ignore too many elements to make them work.

I have already mentioned that the danger which must be avoided in stylistics is excessive compartmentalization. Stylistics is useful inasmuch as it can help to produce an objective account of a text, but this account may be much too fragmentary [v. 220, pp. vi-vii]. The orthodox stylistician cannot avoid starting with preconceived categories, which he examines in turn (if he is honest), the kind of rigidly and exhaustively systematized headings someone like Marouzeau will work out. [435; v. 155B.] The disadvantage is that they tell one what to expect. This leads to situations similar to those for which T. V. Benn criticizes Monique Parent's *Saint-John Perse et quelques devanciers*: 'many of the writer's critical remarks do not seem to derive from the experiments [in style] but from presuppositions and intuitions using the well-known vocabulary of appreciative criticism' [65, p. 126]. Such presuppositions are not very far from the abstract theories I mentioned a moment ago. The point I shall be trying to make in the course of this chapter is that stylistic description is less inadequate when it is specific and not related to over-formalized categories.

Having said this, it is perhaps necessary to suggest that such categories are *useful things to look out for and recognize if they crop up.* We should not dismiss out of hand such compendia as Morier's *Dictionnaire de Poétique et de Rhétorique* which is an exhaustive description of style terms looked at from an historical and an analytical point of view. Lausberg's *Handbuch der literarischen Rhetorik* in two volumes is very helpful too. Its aim is 'to facilitate the beginner's meaningful study of the phenomenological and historical aspects of literature' [p. 7], and it is all the more useful because it sets out to be no more than an aid to understanding. Rhetorical terms and source material are given detailed treatment, the indexing is good, as is the cross-referencing, and the period covered extends from antiquity to the present day. The only difficulty perhaps is that whatever the period, classical rhetoric supplies the terms, and, in spite of a recent revival of interest amongst advanced critics in rhetorical treatises of the past, I am not sure that it is wise to extend notions of classical rhetoric beyond about 1850 (dates are inevitably very crude indicators here). The *Rhétorique générale* produced by J. Dubois and others offsets this by studying figures of rhetoric as they are understood nowadays [v. too 160B].

These are useful reference books—they enable one to see, amongst other things, what traditional devices an author may be drawing on (and therefore what traditional attitudes he may be expressing).

This bias, which classifies stylistic elements as *genre* devices, is not accepted by everyone: 'The so-called "devices," really no more devices than a sentence is a device, express more specific forms of meaning, not so common to thinking that they cannot be avoided, like the sentence, but common enough to reappear frequently in certain types of thinking and hence characterize the thinking or the style.' [765, p. 372.] This is, however, mere hairsplitting: genre is rejected at the beginning to reappear in another guise at the end!

It must be admitted that rhetorical devices do exist and that they are a useful shorthand for certain phenomena in a text. But at least as early as 1925 it was pointed out that mere naming is a very superficial activity indeed, for one must take into account 'the similarity of a procedure in varying contexts, and the differentiation of a procedure according to the purpose to which it is put' [196, pp. 218–19]. In simpler terms, as Susanne Langer points out [378, pp. 280 ff.; see too 81, p. 60], the same literary device will tend to be polyvalent, its significance and value will vary from one context to another. This is true for such other devices as local colour or a discursive approach to a subject or free indirect style. An image in a poem will not have the same function as an image in a novel. Therefore, once the study of stylistic devices has made it possible to establish any traditional elements which may be present, it is necessary to see what the *specific* function of those devices may be in that particular text. This attitude is more firmly preached than it is practised—the simple identification of ready defined devices is too great a temptation, especially for the average academic, as every undergraduate knows: Hugo's antitheses will be pointed out as will Flaubert's liking for ternary enumeration, and that will be that.

Part of the reason for this lies in academics' characteristic reluctance to let their emotions participate in their thinking—everything must be shown to be neat and logical. Which is why the special poetic impact of La Fontaine, based as it is on a strikingly 'prosaic' handling of language, escapes so many of them [however, see 672]. Once again the necessarily subjective aspect of criticism must be stressed: 'There is no stylistic analysis which is not based on intuition' [10, p. 122], for 'it is impossible to separate the conceptual and the affective aspects of style' [10, p. 194]. This must be self-evident: stylistics is the expression of attitudes which are thus in a sense schematized. [v. 484 and 701.]

This schematization is not one where feelings lead necessarily to one particular device (hence the polyvalency of those devices) [v. 81, p. 82]—this would be too intentionalistic an approach. But the devices once used must be seen as a lead-in to an emotion: antithesis is the state where elements are significant because they are in strong opposition to each other. The opposition, the disagreement involved is as important as the ideas the different elements put across. Most style devices should be seen in this light: however worn out nowadays, apostrophe is a desire for direct contact, personification is a striving to give life to something inanimate.

The precise nature of this emotional involvement will depend to a very large extent on context. The need is to accept what the text offers and not to read in prejudiced anticipation. Critical open-mindedness (or naïveté, as Baudelaire called it) is an invaluable attitude to adopt here (as elsewhere). Even biased approaches may be loosened from too restrictive a grip: Josephine Miles and Christine Brooke-Rose lay emphasis not 'on the grammatical features themselves . . . but on certain attributes of the poems and devices in which the grammatical feature appear'. [128, p. 172.]

Such an attitude, which lets the text be as independent as possible and only points to externals which are, so to speak, dictated from within [v. 216, p. 20], is perhaps best expressed and developed by Michael Riffaterre, a critic who has established a solid reputation for himself in both the French- and English-speaking worlds for he writes in both English and French. His basic theories counter the difficulties outlined early in this chapter. They have not noticeably changed since the late fifties, and are perhaps best outlined in *Criteria for Style Analysis* and *Stylistic Context* [v. too 585]. There is an excellent study of Riffaterre's theories with full bibliographical details by A. Hardy in the September 1969 number of *Langue Française.*

Riffaterre (many of whose ideas are echoed in Barthes's *Le Degré Zéro de l'écriture*) rejects *a priori* classifications for they exclude organic description [582, pp. 128ff.]. Organic description as to a certain extent for Spitzer, is based, in part, on the notion that style is what the reader is aware of, what he notices—style is impact. The reader is an essential link who demonstrates by his response the existence of particular stylistic effects at a particular moment in time. To counter the dangers of excessive subjectivity here, Riffaterre puts forward the idea of the Average Reader or 'archilecteur' [583, p. 162], who, one must admit, plays a more important role in Riffaterre's theories than in his practical criticism. He suggests that analysis should be based on a consensus of opinion—he consults cultured colleagues (more 'cultured', one supposes, than those in I. A. Richards's *Practical Criticism*!) to find out what elements in a passage they are aware of. Thanks to the Average Reader, the analyst can observe too how stylistic devices remain effective or otherwise in the course of linguistic change—the text is thus described as it is at a particular moment in time and with minimum historical distortion.

Within this cunning subjective/objective context, it can be claimed that 'all elements in the text are stylistically significant (either as context or as contrasting elements)'. Literary effect, like the semantic impact of which it is an example, is much more a question of context than of separable features [703, pp. 48ff. and 216, pp. 10–11]. We accept an element as part of the general tone of a passage or we are struck by it because it does not fit in with that tone and is not therefore taken for granted [278, p. 92]. Our conscious response and our idea of what the style of a passage is will, therefore, come from the latter and this in turn implies that stylistic effect involves an element of surprise: 'The only procedure open to the encoder [i.e., the writer] when he wants to impose his own interpretation of his poem is to prevent the reader from inferring or predicting any important feature.' [583, p. 158.] The continuity of tone (the norm which the text develops) is suddenly broken by an element which is unpredictable [v. 583, p. 171]. This is so central to Riffaterre's approach that it would seem that for him features and effects which are expected are not stylistic: '. . . an hyperbole in an hyperbolic context will pass unnoticed' [583, p. 172].

Such an idea which defines style firmly *in exclusive relation-*

ship to a given context is an excellent guide for those who are anxious to avoid being sidetracked by elements which are not directly in that context, or by importing *a priori* notions—categorization can quite easily be done away with. At the same time the basic notion of surprise, or the unexpected, needs to be clarified, for it does not refer merely to unknown elements, or to elements which are necessarily not part of the conventions of a particular text—it simply posits the idea that the stylistic feature is the one which is *noticed*. Thus, it includes the expected and characteristic shift from *vous* to *tu* at the passionate height of a Racine tragedy: or the repetition of words, or the sharp changes in baroque style from literal to metaphoric statement or from one metaphor to another [v. 158, p. 346 and 352, p. 197], for the precise timing of such events may not be present in the reader's mind. In any case they cut violently across the conventions which the work so far has established (and the wider conventions of linguistic behaviour to which the audience is accustomed). Riffaterre's notion of the unexpected must allow us to include the poetic language of any poem as a stylistic feature, for the precise nature of that language is not foreseeable. The idea of 'convergence' too (the heaping up of stylistic features working together), although it creates a pattern of expectedness, has sufficient variation for it to be very significant stylistically.

The notion of the unexpected should, therefore, be taken quite literally and not excessively related to notions of shock—any interruption is included. The deviations which create stylistic impact on the reader may also be related to the two contrasting ideas of *context* ('micro' and 'macro') as Riffaterre defines them. Micro-context is the immediate surrounding area in which a stylistic device is to be found. Macro-context is the wider surrounding context. In plain words, micro-context would seem to be the context which makes unexpected contrast possible and is in direct contact with the stylistic device, whilst macro-context would relate to the wider processes which affect this contrast by strengthening or weakening it [v. 591], and therefore exists from the point where the reader becomes aware of some sort of consistent pattern [p. 213] necessarily including texts in the same tradition (although Riffaterre is insufficiently explicit about this) [v. 168, pp. 236–7].

Riffaterre thus sets up a theory where context, and wide context at that, is just as important as (because directly responsible for) the elements which make the impact. A study of any text demands that both be described—it is not enough to make a list of striking, flag-waving features: all the subtle changes in our expectation and the constant feelings of *difference* within the context of expected patterns must be considered if we are to describe the style of a passage adequately.

This does not necessarily imply total independence of the individual work of art—but given what has been said, Spitzer seems to miss the point when, in a criticism of Riffaterre's work [653B, p. 71], he claims that many features of expression in Gobineau are 'stylistic devices' only in the sense which Bally gave to that term, that is to say 'the style of the language' rather than individual expression—this disregards the subjective/objective process whereby style may be perceived. It does not, of course, take into account Riffaterre's later emphasis on cliché and neologism [v. 586, pp. 81 ff. and 585B, pp. 3 ff.] both of which impose themselves on the attention of the reader in distinctive ways dependent on context and historical period.

The dependence of the work of art cannot therefore be established by counting the number of clichés it contains—the more delicate problem of how these clichés function in the text must be considered too and what contrasts they achieve. Take for example Proust's sentence about Marcel's aunt:

> Et ce n'est pas cependant qu'elle n'aspirât à quelque plus grand changement [. . .] où la sensibilité, que le bonheur a fait taire *comme une harpe oisive, veut résonner sous une main brutale, et dût-elle en être brisée: où la volonté qui a si difficilement conquis le droit d'être livrée sans obstacle à ses désirs, voudrait jeter les rêves entre les mains d'événements impérieux fussent-ils cruels.*
> [*A la Recherche du Temps perdu*, Pléïade vol. I, pp. 115–16, my italics.]

Given that Proust's novel and the surrounding context here are not built up on clichés, those I have italicized are stylistic devices. They are a striking and very direct lead-in to the, at one and the same time, stereotyped and incongruous way Tante Léonie thinks and feels. How different, for example, from the impact of stereotyped expression in early Hugo (see his *Vierges de Verdun* in the *Odes et Ballades*). [v. too 783, pp. 77–8.]

Riffaterre's preoccupation is with linguistic features. It provides an admirable jumping-off point not only for poetry but also for the stylistic analysis of prose which, although such analysis may vary in importance from one age to another (the period since 1850 represents perhaps a peak), is always indispensable. One thinks of the ordering of ideas and words (and, therefore, the shifting emphases of character and emotion) in the complex sentences of Proust:

> Pendant bien des années, où pourtant, surtout avant son mariage, M. Swann, le fils, vint souvent les voir à Combray, ma grand'tante et mes grands-parents ne soupçonnèrent pas qu'il ne vivait plus du tout dans la même société qu'avait fréquentée sa famille et que sous l'espèce d'incognito que lui faisait chez nous ce nom de Swann, ils hébergeaient—avec la parfaite innocence d'honnêtes hôteliers qui ont chez eux, sans le savoir, un célèbre brigand—un des membres les plus élégants du Jockey-Club, ami préféré du comte de Paris et du prince de Galles, un des hommes les plus choyés de la haute société du Faubourg Saint-Germain.
>
> [*A la Recherche* . . . vol. I, pp. 17–18.]

The narrator's character constantly checks and qualifies (and therefore cuts across) the pattern as it develops. If this is to a large extent factual, it is a factuality which sprouts in various directions, and the most striking of these is the non-factual but somewhat incongruous analogy with the hotel keepers (all the more significant stylistically because of the sharp contrast set up with the normal tone of qualification in the sentence). One thinks too of the ironic bite of Flaubert (where all depends on positioning and contrast):

Que ne pouvait-elle s'accouder sur le balcon des chalets suisses ou enfermer sa tristesse dans un cottage écossais, avec un mari vêtu d'un habit de velours noir à longues basques, et qui porte des bottes molles, un chapeau pointu et des manchettes!

[*Madame Bovary*, Pléïade, p. 362.]

the incursion of 'tristesse' in the context of a search for ideal happiness is one pointer to our feelings of suspicion. Another is the detailed description which comes at the end of the sentence quoted: it is *too* detailed, the pattern set up goes on so long that it surprises—and with the help of the exclamation mark, this exaggerated pattern makes us implicitly critical of the emotions involved. Ullmann's admirable chapter (in *Style in the French Novel*) on the style of the Goncourts could also be extended in a similar direction. There is an infinity of further examples which might be given.

Riffaterre's ideas might well, moreover, be attached to elements which are not linguistic (the last quotation is ample proof of that): thus, the interruption of *any* pattern (sounds, incidents, character, etc.) becomes a significant element for an understanding of the whole. In this way we can get round one of the major problems brought up by Wayne C. Booth: '. . . though style is one of our main sources of insight into the author's norms, in carrying such strong overtones of the merely verbal, the word *style* excludes our sense of the author's skill [this is perhaps not a particularly relevant word at this stage for us] in his choice of character and episode and scene and idea' [81, p. 74]. We can avoid at the same time the kind of précis writing which often passes for criticism of works in prose: the preoccupation with the way patterns make and break makes paraphrase very difficult to justify. When I come to the chapters on structure and sequence, I hope it will be seen how these ideas may be even further developed. But already we can see that this demonstrates how right the Russian Formalists were to suggest that plot is just as much a formal element as, say, rhyme and that, for example, the hero is a device whereby the action of a novel may be unfolded [v. 205, p. 208]. So much for the idea that style is a purely linguistic element! Style, in the narrow sense, not being the *essential* activity of narrative prose (it should rather be described as pseudo-reality), although it is extremely important, such a widening of perspectives is essential [v. 555, pp. 280 ff.; 411, pp. 3 ff. and 81, pp. 83 ff.]; and healthy too, for, apart from anything else, it allows us to avoid isolating one phenomenon from another (which is always an obstacle as far as criticism is concerned). John Holloway points out that, with George Eliot, it is necessary to start with the broad outline of events and ideas expressed through human action, not with incidents, metaphors or snatches of conversation. [313, p. 113.] We can now see that Holloway's approach is still relevant to style although his distinction is perhaps excessive.

The points raised in the last few pages are important, I believe, but more practical examples would be useful. The difficulty is that there are so many of them that this chapter could very easily degenerate into a list. My aim, as always, is to keep well away from bibliographical exhaustion and to show the need to be as specific as possible in one's descriptions. This is why I devoted so much space to Riffaterre's theories: although often abstract, they are angled towards the need to make precise, practical statements about *any* text. How much closer it gets us to the reality of our experience as readers than the kind of deliberately schematic approach critics once tended to indulge in! One thinks of Dupuy's neat (and totally ridiculous) division of Hugo's life and works into four periods, four basic preoccupations and four main sources of inspiration [188]. How much safer too is Riffaterre's approach than the often vague comments in a book like Webber's *Contrary Music* or Groom's *Diction of Poetry from Spenser to Bridges*.

Rhetorical terms or notions of genre, as we have seen, need much closer examination in context if one is to understand, for example, the extent to which they are a means whereby thought, attitudes etc. are communicated, the extent to which they actually generate them and what precisely these thoughts and attitudes are. Hence the tendency in some critics [v. 351, pp. 41–74] to reject traditional literary history out of hand—or at least to be very suspicious of it—whilst Josephine Miles approaches period styles in a way which relies on the direct description of individual examples (the faults in her study stem, as we have seen, from inadequate sampling which makes period styles seem much more clear-cut than they actually are). Sayce too, although he is very much preoccupied with periodization, is keenly interested in the nature of individual style and most skilful at describing it [621]. And this is necessary, for the expression of very closely related themes at the same moment in history (i.e. at a time when the language is offering the same potential to all its users) will produce subtly yet widely varying modes of expression. This is true even in strongly traditional periods like the sixteenth century [731 passim], and powerfully striking when similar stylistic devices from different periods (for example the 'prosaic' tone often met in poems by La Fontaine and Verlaine) are compared. [See too 309, pp. 212 et seq. and 385.]

We must also be attentive (and this is linked with the last example) to the overall impact of a mode of expression which might be said superficially to 'lag behind' the sensibility it communicates. I am thinking specifically of Rousseau here. This aspect of his style has not been studied as far as I know, but it would be interesting to examine the extent to which the formal nature of eighteenth-century prose is changed when it is allied to a fully-fledged romantic sensibility. Or is the sensibility radically conditioned by (and therefore inseparable from) the language used? Only precise study (based in part on Riffaterre's approach) will tell us how individualistically different this is, say, from the shock tactics which nineteenth-century Romantics adopted systematically, for example, in their choice of analogies.

Whatever can be said about this kind of problem, one must come back to the central notion that style is a distinctive feature and should be examined as such. Some critics have even gone further than the points made above about Josephine Miles and

R. A. Sayce and objected to the notion of any typology of styles at all. Milic [469, pp. 442–50] offers a demonstration of the extent to which seventeenth-century styles cannot be classified: 'An individual's style is his habitual and consistent selection from the expressive resources available in his language'—this is not related to problems of quality. A writer tends to be unlike rather than like other writers. 'The notion of period styles underrates this tendency and implies a uniformity of expression which is wildly at variance with the facts.' [p. 448.] This again points to the danger or vagueness of talk about irregular or harmonious or precious styles. When the heroine of Margaret Drabble's *The Waterfall* talks about her baby's 'small local need' or the bed's 'warm evasion' [pp. 28–9] it is insufficient to talk about preciosity; rather we must talk about the impact of unusual and precisely descriptive combinations of words. In the second expression the combination is concrete-with-abstract, a sense impression and a moral attitude are brought together. In the first, the enriching ambiguities of the two adjectives most require our attention. A similar exactness of approach would be necessary to describe the preciosity (born of excessively detailed precision?) in a writer like Lautréamont: 'Ayez la bonté de regarder ma bouche . . . c'est que j'en contracte le tissu jusqu'à la dernière réduction.' [71, p. 199.] I have myself [750] tried to show in some detail that it is rather pointless to explain an author's corrections of his work in terms of grammatical correctness or elegance. They must be rather seen as a means whereby the author gets his work closer to the novel's overall themes and structures (whose problems I shall be looking at shortly).

Milic's remark, which I have just quoted, means also that such a phenomenon as imagery must be examined first and foremost from the point of view of its distinctiveness. When Mallarmé ends his *Toast funèbre* with:

> Le sépulcre sordide où gît tout ce qui nuit
> Et l'avare silence et la massive nuit.

—and when Hugo writes in *Le Hibou*:

> Et Dieu—s'il est un Dieu—fit à sa ressemblance
> L'universelle nuit et l'éternel silence.

it would clearly be wrong to ignore similarities of vocabulary in the last line, a logical overlap when the subject is death and eternity. But the very context shows to what extent the metaphors swing in different directions. Even out of context, the much greater degree of unexpectedness in Mallarmé's adjective/noun combination (and therefore their greater significance as Riffaterrian stylistic devices) offers a starting-point for a comparison which would bring out very real differences.

Comparison and contrast once again show themselves to be very useful in determining individual style. Another much rarer technique, but one which can be extremely revealing, is the pastiche—I am thinking especially of Proust's *Pastiches et Mélanges*, that delightful take-off of symbolist verse called *Les Déliquescences d'Adoré Floupette* [715] or the series entitled *A la Manière de* [561]. Some of these latter are so good that they have found their way into the collected works of the authors they are supposed to be pastiching! But most follow the usual pattern of exaggerating the characteristic traits of the original (the liking for ternary sentence ending or sustained analogy or exclamations) and thus making us more aware of them [v. too 476B]. Pastiche is, of course, highly subjective—Riffaterre might well criticize it because it creates micro- and macro-contexts which do not exist in the author pastiched—and the subtle combinations of the original will tend to disappear too. But whilst it is clearly an unsatisfactory *replacement* for the original, we must remember that it does not set out to be this: it is rather a critical tool than a rival. When it is available, it can be added to all the other descriptive techniques and principles I have mentioned.

The contrast here is between the writer's 'normal' style and an underlined version of that style. Other types of contrast exist and these too emphasize a distinctive style. One thinks of the 'gap' existing between the way a child's mind 'really' behaves (even in verbal transcription) and the highly 'sophisticated' and 'adult' way (these terms in inverted commas would require precise and constant refinement) Henry James represents it in *What Maisie Knew.* Closely related problems arise (so much so that comparison between the three books would be useful) in Joyce's *Portrait of the Artist as a Young Man* or Monique Vitig's *L'Opoponax.*

I have not mentioned practical procedures linked to Riffaterre's ideas mainly because I think that, like Empson's notion of ambiguity, they can be applied directly to almost any text as Riffaterre has shown in, for example, his analysis of Hugo's poem *Ecrit sur la Vitre d'une Fenêtre flamande* (*Les Rayons et Les Ombres*, XVIII) [587B]—they belong to that rare collection of theories which are of immediate and obvious practical value—examples are almost superfluous. Here, perhaps even more significantly, is a piece of analysis which is about fifteen years older than Riffaterre's early writings, and yet which shows what a rich practical vein may be exploited by following the varying impacts of a passage through, more or less word for word. The analysis relates to Shakespeare's 73rd Sonnet, and more specifically to the second half of the first quatrain:

> That time of year thou mayst in me behold
> When yellow leaves or none, or few do hang
> Upon those boughs which shake against the cold,
> Bare ruin'd choirs, where late the sweet birds sang . . .

'The fusion [of literal and metaphorical values] is brought about by Shakespeare's slurring up from *boughs* to *choirs* and then down again. He gets up to *choirs* with the adjectival sequence "bare ruin'd"; "bare" modifies primarily *boughs*, and it is only through the diplomatic mediation of "ruin'd", primarily the modifier of *choirs*, that *bare* becomes intimate with *choirs.* He gets down again to *boughs* with the pun on "*sweet birds*"; in the phrases's secondary, euphemistic sense, these are the choristers, but in its primary sense they are the quondam occupants of the now shivering boughs.' [v. 79, p. 120.] This is a most subtle analysis of the way the imagery shifts, expands and varies in its distance from literal values. It shows how effectively the style of a passage may be defined by close unprejudiced description of the features the text actually presents.

The need to be empirical is the main conclusion I should wish to draw on the idea of style. The shortness of this chapter and the vastness of the subject would make more detailed conclusions seem pretentious and unsubstantiated. No definition of style is really adequate in a practical sense—any comment we may care to make about the way an author handles the impact of language is stylistic. Style is, therefore, as already said, the other chapters of this book combined—plus the emotional content which arises when the reading individual meets the individual text. All we can do (and this is something of an understatement) is *describe* features we encounter, their combined function and the feelings they inspire in us.

CHAPTER SIX

COUNTING

I must tread carefully here, for this is holy ground. The specialists of electronic counting and superstatistics tend to cry blasphemy rather promptly and the danger of such a rebuke being directed at me is inevitably great, for this is a subject I hardly feel competent to discuss at any length or in any depth (which does at least mean that the average literary scholar will find what I say comprehensible).

There is another difficulty: this chapter does not really fit into the first (or the second) half of my study. It cuts across other chapters, necessitates a little repetition and concerns elements which might have been included elsewhere. Earlier chapters should be seen as background to this one. We have already met ideas such as counting, ratios, frequency etc. I have chosen to stress such elements (and others) further here because counting and statistics are not widely known or recognized activities in literary criticism—and, because they are linked with the huge development in computer studies, they concern a kind of information which even the most conservative scholars will more and more have to take into account in the future. When 'visual' forms of programming (similar to the way photocopying is done) become widespread, expansion will be astronomical.

The growth already involved is well illustrated by R. A. Wisbey's report on the first five years of the Literary and Linguistic Computing Centre in Cambridge [774]. This centre, although still somewhat modest in size, is growing rapidly as is the rather more orthodox tendency to draw on the services of large regional computer centres like Manchester or Edinburgh.

More and more scholars are making use of these institutions, thanks, largely, if my experience in Manchester is any indication, to the very real enthusiasm with which the staff of these institutions offer their help, advice and time.

The end-product of all this for the literary student is the steadily increasing volume of computerized and numerically biased material which is being produced and the significant regularity with which major symposia on the uses of computers in literary research are held nowadays. *The Times Literary Supplement* report on the 1970 Cambridge conference [410] and the forthcoming proceedings of the 1972 Edinburgh conference give detailed information on the importance and wide scope of these gatherings. There are, in addition, countless small meetings in various centres designed to inform scholars of the problems and techniques involved in statistical analysis.

The most striking area of development is clearly linked to the various uses of computers. But, for reasons which will become clear, I think it is necessary here to consider counting or statistics in a rather wider context. The basic principle involved is the same, in any case, and that is that a text may be reduced to a set of concrete, countable elements. Discourse is treated as an atomistic combination of measurable units rather than as a phenomenon to be described in overall, general terms. This is an extreme form of anti-impressionism [302, p. 85]. It seeks to replace individual subjective response by incontrovertible facts.

At this point perhaps it is already necessary to be cautious (although I shall save my main reservations for the second half of this chapter). We might remember Richard Sayce pinpointing the paradox that literary experience appears to transcend language and yet is communicated by linguistic means [620, p. 120]. We might also remember the deeply penetrating results produced by such relatively impressionistic critics as Leavis or Poulet.

And yet, whatever reservations we might develop, I think that when dealing with texts of manageable length (for a human being or a computer) it is worth while, as a preliminary to critical description, to gather material facts about them, counting the obviously countable elements (whether they are grammatical, phonetic or semantic) which will be mentioned in the coming pages. 'Once . . . a particular iterative feature has been isolated as being especially useful to the critical understanding of the whole, its merely numerical frequency of occurrence will have a certain interest and relevance.' [411, p. 85.]

It would even seem clear that certain types of textual analysis are in some measure inseparable from counting: vocabulary studies for example (which always seem thin if not based on an index or concordance [see *Meaning I*]). Moreover, statistical information about the vocabulary of a text will tend to stress its independent significance and not its historical value. There is a very valid hierarchy at work here too, for grammatical details will take second place to semantically biased notions of frequency.

It is thus difficult to resist the attractions of such new tendencies and the obvious countability of certain areas. With statistical studies, however, questions of method rather than empirical response are of supreme importance. We must know what we are looking for at the outset—we must therefore have defined it in advance and have worked out an adequate definition of what, say, a noun is, or a consonant, or a sentence. This is not as easy as it might seem—nouns may be verbally biased; there are such things as semi-consonants. Furthermore, if a computer is to be used, complex programming problems must be carefully worked out (how individual items are to be marked and classified and defined for the computer to be able to tabulate them on request). Manuals for this exist, like the one produced in May 1970 by the Edinburgh Computer Centre for the use of *Concord*, a programme which makes it possible to generate word counts and produce concordances. This particular programme may well be out of date (or the computer now superseded) but its function is a useful illustration.

Skilled knowledge is therefore required before a computer can be used. Moreover, standard programmes, although useful, are not enough, for there are the problems which relate to the feeding of any particular text to a computer and the specific kind of information a scholar will want to retrieve: if a computer can work superhumanly fast, it can only do what it has been programmed to do. Rhyme words, for example, will be indicated by the computer only if some sign is added to them during programming which shows them for what they are.

Once the information has been produced (manually or by machine) it has, like all other information, to be interpreted. The basis for interpretation here is more likely to be statistical theory than the history of a genre or of ideas. Such data cannot be interpreted crudely—mathematical theories like the calculation of probabilities must play a leading role. This is deep water for the number-blind humanist and poses difficulties not only as far as the establishment of data is concerned but also with reference to the evaluation of other people's work. And this, for the time being, is a crucial problem. It is clear that textual critics will more and more need to acquire a basic knowledge of programming and the appreciation of data. As Bailey points out [33, p. 219], the 'simple enumeration of relative frequency is insufficient'—sampling techniques as well as other statistical criteria are an indispensable support and filter.

In all this, familiarity with some basic studies would seem to be useful: Chandor's *Dictionary of computers*; D. Hayes's *Introduction to Computational Linguistics* for example; or, with a more literary bias, G. Udny Yule's *The Statistical Study of Literary Vocabulary*; J. Leed, ed., *The Computer and Literary Style*; J. Froger, *La Critique des textes et son automatisation;* E. A. Bowles, *Computers in Humanistic Research*; *Readings and Perspectives*; S. M. Parrish, *Computers and the Muse of Literature*; R. Wisbey, *The Computer and Literary Studies*; G. Herdan, *Language as choice and chance.*

Such writings point to the numerically definable stylistic aspects of a text which I shall be looking at more closely a little later. It may be said at this stage, however, that computers are also useful in the rapid collation of texts—establishing a version of a literary work with all the variants to be found in its different manuscript and printed editions. Computers can be invaluable too in producing selective or exhaustive bibliographies—a task which with the passage of time and the deluge of scholarly publication can now scarcely be done by hand.

But, mainly, specialists have been anxious to offer the numerical breakdown of a text, and in this the expansion has been very great, as can be seen from the long lists of *Literary Materials in Machine Readable Form* which have appeared with indications as to their location, length, availability and degree of completion since 1966 in *Computers and the Humanities* (another publication which enables one to take the pulse of recent developments in this field). Many of these texts may be drawn on for analysis by scholars from other universities—although I note that the academic mandarinate in some establishments is not prepared to make its materials generally available. This is very wasteful, given the phenomenal amount of computer programming a text requires.

At the moment, I suppose that, in spite of the problems involved, the average literary scholar is more preoccupied with the results obtained than with programming. And yet the process of programming is in itself a process of redefining the constituent parts of a literary text—of making objective what until now has been looked at with a great deal of subjectivity, or of making explicit what has so far been taken for granted.

Such a redefinition of what a literary text is is of fundamental importance—it takes us a stage beyond the idea that it can be reduced to countable elements. The end-product may be equally revolutionary: 'the effect of producing a machine-readable text has not simply returned us to the position occupied by the reader at the outset. It is rather . . . that the scholar, without surrendering his static printed book, has supplemented it with a dynamic text the evolution of which lies in his hands.' [773, p. 16.]

In addition, an important conclusion is that by looking at computer and statistical analyses, we shall see new ways of approaching a text which may be tried out even if one's knowledge of a text is minimal and even if no computer is available. In any case, it would seem clear that for a reasonably short text (a novel or even several novels) if the amount of information required is limited and the text is not going to be needed for further statistical study, it is just as easy to count manually (or better still, to get someone else to count for you) as to feed it into a computer. Guiraud's analysis of Valéry [270] is in this respect singularly revealing and should be read by all those who are interested in the subject.

The following pages point therefore to what computers can produce and have produced. They are also an attempt to underline more widely accessible techniques and definitions which may be generally unknown.

It might not be too rash to suggest that statistical information about a text will tend to be stylistic in nature (in so far, that is, as it is of literary value). This is inevitable since the most readily accessible *units* in a text are units of language rather than units of, say, plot or 'thought' (although these and similar elements may be programmed into a computer). A cursory glance through the main bibliographies of style [e.g. 295; 34] shows how often statistical information is used in definitions of style. Even more specialized bibliographies [35; 392 passim], in addition to such texts as the *T.L.S.* article on Computational Stylistics [673] show the importance this basis for style analysis has assumed [v. too 295 and 298].

In order for this to take place, it has been suggested that style must be seen as 'a selection of non-distinctive features of language' [v. 472, p. 80], for *all* elements in a discourse must be seen as stylistically valid, if statistics are to have any sense. Moreover individual style will tend to be the expression of unconscious rather than conscious selection [472, p. 82]. Once this is established, it is possible to suggest that 'the style of a discourse is the message carried by the frequency distributions and transitional probabilities [i.e. probable occurrences at a particular point in the discourse] of its linguistic features, especially as they differ from those of the same features in the language as a whole'. [v. 72, p. 42; v. too 204.]

The terms to add here to *choice* or *selection* are *frequency distribution* and *transitional probabilities.* Style is a question of relative (or abnormal) occurrence which makes expression striking in a particular context. To put it another way, a style is characterized by 'a frequency of features which is higher than that to be statistically expected and the distribution of elements which by repetition or combination underlines their presence' [v. 406]. Hence, the importance of word counts, statistical analyses of sentence structure, the length of words and the length of sentences used—all of which can point to the individuality of a person's style. [v. i.a. 437; 470; 230; 640; 384; 757.] It is clear from these and other studies that in order to establish such factors and make them statistically significant, samples of adequate length must be chosen—these will vary from a few hundred words when a single text is being considered to many hundreds of thousands when a whole period or genre style is being worked out. The samples must be representative too of the range and levels of styles present in the area studied. If attention is not paid to sampling problems results tend not to be representative enough. Although *relative* frequencies may be obtained for much shorter texts, no absolute statement can be made.

The key notions at play, whether we are dealing with relative or absolute notions, are, of course, our permanent companions deviation and the norm. As Riffaterre shows, style is the gap between what happens in discourse and what we expected.

This gap, it is suggested, may be measured [270, p. 16] by reference either to a general norm for the language at a particular period or, say, to an author's general style. The norms involved, in addition to the quantities mentioned above, will relate also to such questions as sound structure, stylistic levels, metaphor, and, from a linear point of view, the notion of the continuity and discontinuity of constituent elements from one passage to another [v. 108]. This therefore is another norm-based theory of style which may be added to those (of Ohmann and Riffaterre and others) dealt with elsewhere. An example of what may be involved can be seen in the thesis by J. Farrington Morris on

Thomas Hardy's style—a syntactical approach to the poetry [486], which I described in the chapter on *Grammar* [p. 59].

Burwick's approach which I have just mentioned is more mathematically biased and depends on a formula for a word sample representative of word/sentence relationship on the strength of a minimum extract of 10,000 words taking into account twelve basic functions of words. The significance of syntactic patterns and rhetorical figures is also measured. It is thus possible to establish the probability of occurrence of a given word or syntactic feature, and the probability of one word given another word (a very important consideration to which I shall return). Thus Burwick is able to point in Carlyle to a preference for subordinate modifications, the permanence of certain patterns, the sequence of different sentence types (Noun + Verb and Noun + Verb + Noun), the frequency of patterns which are not standard, the increase in use of verbal patterns, incremental techniques, parallelism and repetition—the rise then fall in alliteration, repetition and assonance. All this is, for good measure, set against the tendencies of late eighteenth-century Scottish rhetoricians [108]. Bennett's study of the *Statistical measurement of a stylistic trait in 'Julius Caesar' and 'As You Like It'* is similarly based on formulae for the evaluation of frequency (those of Yule, this time, whose book I mentioned earlier) in order to establish the variation in characteristics, their concentration or dispersion. The result of these calculations is to point to the *similarity* (not the same as the *identity*) of style in the two plays, given the same degree of repetitiveness in each.

Here the technique is to work exclusively within the norm created by the work itself. After which it is possible, in terms which remind one of structuralist theory, to define style, like J. B. Carroll, as 'predispositional sets which govern large classes of verbal response' [113]. These would be a kind of mental linguistic model which affects the writer's choice of the different forms of expression his discourse will take.

One word of caution, however, which statistical stylisticians have themselves expressed: all these findings point not to a particular fact at any particular moment in a text or to a fixed rigid habit, but rather to a tendency. They make up a general statement about a text or set of texts [v. 170B].

Statistical considerations should not mask the fact either that low probability occurrences are not necessarily the most significant in poetry—conventional events are of major significance in poetry [310, p. 118]. It is worth repeating therefore that the idea of the norm has to be made flexible, by using Guiraud's notion of theme words and key words for example [270, pp. 155ff.], or by looking on styles as different kinds of dialects, individual, social, genre and so forth [v. 770]. This has the advantage of breaking down any idea of a one-to-one opposition between individual text and general norm. The norm itself (unless the representative sources used to establish it are huge: a large slice of eighteenth-century literature or some such monstrosity) will tend to be a particular one too.

Norms and deviation will spring from and accentuate a preoccupation with distinguishing features. One unfortunate result of this has been an excessive concern with the attribution of anonymous texts. This is justifiable if one is anxious to 'establish' whether Paul wrote all his epistles himself, or who 'Junius' or the author of *La Tía fingida* was [v. 156, 199 and 200]. But there seem to be, rather tiresomely, more studies of this kind than there are significant who-wrote-its to solve. The waste of time is not total, however, for such studies, if their results are often devoid of interest, help to develop and refine a whole gamut of methods aimed at particularizing the style of individual authors. They will certainly have contributed for example to the development of ideas of style based on such elements as word class frequency distribution, units made up of three adjacent word classes, different patterns in three-word sequences or the frequency distribution of initial structures. [470.]

Overall, the basic principle will tend to remain the same at all times: 'If a sentence contains more of certain high frequency words in closer proximity to each other than in other sentences, then such a sentence is more representative of the subject-matter discussed than other sentences.' [v. 302, pp. 165–6.] For 'sentence' here it would, I think, be possible to read 'text'.

Furthermore, these principles may be turned in all sorts of directions, witness Ullmann's typology of language (i.e. style on the grand scale, or national styles) which depends so much on relative frequencies of such things as opaque and transparent words, particular and generic words, specific devices available for heightening emotive effect, synonymic patterns, polysemy, homonymy, and combinations of such elements [703, p. 257]. In turn, the notion at play is in no sense different from Monique Parent's lexical description of a Valéry poem [516, p. 103; v. *Meaning I*] or her study of Saint-John Perse which examines the statistical incidence of parts of speech and syntactical deviation [519].

It will have been apparent that very often the approach will be biased towards aspects of the articulation of the sentence rather than of ideas. Dolores M. Burton's study of *Aspects of word order in two plays of Shakespeare* [107, pp. 34–9] shows how severe this can be, for she uses a *grammatical* concordance to analyse *Richard II* and *Anthony and Cleopatra*—that is to say a concordance whose headings are all and only the structure and function words of a language (prepositions, conjunctions, pronouns, auxiliary verbs, determiners etc.). The inference here (and it is quite widespread) is that style may be characterized by reference to abstract and potentially semantic elements of language (to the ones just mentioned, might be added subordinate clauses, adverbs, definite articles and connectives and form words).

It is possible to add to the key terms already given: a phenomenon at work in the cases looked at so far is that of juxtaposition and combination: the collocation and correlation on the page or in a particular text of abstract as well as potentially semantic elements. As far as the latter are concerned, R.-L. Wagner's *Analyse des énoncés et des textes* [724, vol. II, pp. 95–121] considers the way the co-occurrences, correlations of vocabulary function, binding ideas and vocabulary into a unique combination which expresses the central preoccupation of the text. By highlighting different periods in a writer's career, the evolution of his style, imagery and ideas can also be pointed to. It is clear that computers may be used to produce a basis for such studies on a vast scale. They can also be used to underline departures from probability norms, which would otherwise not be apparent.

Juxtaposition and combination are also at play in a much more apparently abstract procedure, which is nevertheless one of the most interesting I have come across. This is the idea of verb/adjective ratios as a way of describing the degree of dynamism or expansive stasis in a passage. The basic operation being to take the number of verbs in a text and divide it by the number of adjectives. An article by F. Antosch, *The Diagnosis of Literary Style with Verb-Adjective ratios* explains the principle in some detail, and shows how it may point to a wide number of characteristics: factual works will have a lower VAR than more subjective ones; ballads have a higher VAR than reflective lyrics whose VAR is in turn higher than that of love lyrics. Thus subject-matter and genre define style. The dynamic impact of a text may be translated into concrete terms—and in a way which can be applied quite easily to texts. VAR has further uses: it may point to aspects of character (when establishing *levels* of character style, critics have looked at the distribution of such things as pronouns [494]); character thus turns out to be expressed by grammatical categories as well as moral attitudes or perhaps an interrelation of the two (although the fact that Faust's character is the same on this basis as Mephistopheles's and in *radical* contrast to that of Gretchen is clearly a fact which needs further refinement!) The development of a work, a style or a character can be indicated by shifts in the VAR too. Climax and emotion will have high VARs; a flat uneventful situation will produce a rather 'flat' VAR.

This kind of approach, which offers important supporting information to a whole range of critical analyses, contrasts technically with Wagner's approach and with the equally if not more useful one, critically speaking, outlined by Karl Kroeber in *Perils of Quantification* and developed in his subsequent book [370]. Kroeber establishes distinctions between four major nineteenth-century English novelists on the basis of the fact that the *frequency of words does not correlate to their necessary aesthetic significance.* It is important therefore to look at specific groups of words, vocabulary being determined by subject-matter. For the authors considered (Jane Austen, Charlotte Brontë, Dickens and George Eliot), Kroeber examines the number of references to the body and bodily movement. These are greater in the latter part of the century than at its beginning. Thus one specific aspect of word choice with very real significance can be tabulated and given meaning. Other tables relate to the comparative use of abstract nouns, 'psychic action' verbs, adjectives of measure, constructions introduced by 'how' and the use of words ending in '-ly', considerations one could without difficulty apply to one's day-to-day critical studies. Kroeber shows how it is possible to compare different novelists and to group them according to whether they use particular vocabulary or not. In his larger study, he produces 83 separate tables ranging from aspects I have already mentioned to the percentage of pages which begin chapters with an admixture of dialogues (40 per cent for Jane Austen, 30 per cent for the Brontës and George Eliot).

Not all words can be treated in this way: we must omit common ones whose frequency is to be expected, or which are not frequent enough in the text to be obsessive. Adjectives tend on their own to be semantically vague. But the main general principle which Kroeber demonstrates is the value of looking at *groups* of words defined semantically with reference to the areas of meaning one might expect in the genre examined. This increases the semantic significance and impact of statistics in a way which is of very great importance for the future.

Further elements can be brought into play by defining groups or co-occurrences in the light of degrees of distinctiveness, comparing relative frequency to a control list and especially by counting the occurrence of every word belonging to a group as an occurrence of the group [133]. This helps to clarify the significance of statistics for 'entities of considerable frequency are [thus] obtained and fluctuations due to low frequency or short text smooth themselves out' [133, p. 88].

The elements involved are, as has been suggested, much more unconscious than otherwise. This is why orthodox computational stylistics will tend to be especially interested (and this again points to the originality of Kroeber's approach) in the frequency of 'filler' words like the *a*, *all*, *an*, *and*, *any*, *or*, or in word and sentence length—although it is not felt necesary to analyse all criteria, for they overlap to a large degree [133, p. 88].

What is explicit however is that such things as conscious and deliberate rhetorical figures are not taken into account—they are not considered sufficiently individual or even typical of an age.

Conclusions to this kind of section are reasonably clear. Highly fleeting, subjective impressions may, through counting and tabulating techniques, be given concrete definition. It is now possible to suggest what is meant by a simple, direct, grand, majestic, jerky, vivid, rich style. Carroll's article on the *Vectors of Prose Style* offers tables on the basis of such notions arranged in antithetical pairs. What is involved here is not so much a question of objectivity ousting an essentially subjective experience. One's subjective response still comes first—quantification merely helps to clarify it. It is therefore possible to say that subjectivity and objectivity join hands. This is a great boon in the fight against slipshod impressionism.

Such a fact is generally true but nowhere more obviously than in the analysis and evaluation of sound as Ants Oras has shown. [v. 513, see *Sounds* p. 12].

Sound, as we know, may define semantic effect, a phenomenon which is obviously over-and-above the more plodding statistical study of, say, metric patterns and rhyme structures with a view to distinguishing between several poetic traditions—or Guiraud's suggestion that the phonetic structure of verse can be described by reference to the norm. I. Fónagy [211] is on the other hand doing something similar to Oras when he establishes a link between tender and aggressive poems on the one hand and bright and dark vowels on the other. [v. too 262.]

The most sensible approach, as with all critical method, must not however be exclusively preoccupied with one particular area. It would be wrong to study sound patterns without at the same time tabulating syntactical, word and sentence length tendencies and perhaps even relating these to concordance information. Combinations of such elements could perhaps be made even more significant if different stages of a work or works or a period were considered synoptically in this way.

The advantage of this is that the attraction of sterile patterning and abstract desiccated facts is resisted. The idea of literature as a humane experience is maintained because the elements of the discourse are seen implicitly as communicators of that discourse. Questions of personality (whether they relate to the writer or the critic or characters) are kept central, and thus 'quantitative and qualitative analysis . . . supplement each other' as R.-L. Wagner says they should [722], and as a critic like Empson frequently demonstrates.

But how far can counting be taken? To what extent do the various statistical methods provide one with a direct lead into the core of a literary work? I am aware that the rate of development in statistical stylistics and my naïveté about the subject are such that the point of view I am going to express can only be partially realistic. My only justification in writing about the subject at all (apart from the fact that I have tried out some of the more elementary methods with undergraduates—and they worked) is that I can offer a somewhat more objective if rather partial assessment, perhaps, than the true specialist. The computer experts are indeed often frighteningly indifferent to the end-product of their labours, as anyone who has attended a computer and literature symposium will know. They are also somewhat monotonous: from one article and conference paper to the next, one is mournfully struck by the repetition of the same basic principles (structuralists are similarly monotonous at times). Often too, a vast amount of labour is expended in stating the obvious. The result is, in one sense, the feeling that progress is not really being made (and the stagnation of computerized studies in the U.S.A., of all places!, has been noted)—if computers are becoming more and more refined the stylistic and other uses to which they may be put are not expanding at the same rate.

One may too feel disquiet about the central problem (for which a Jakobson may one day produce a satisfactory formula) of the extent to which countable elements are unfailingly pertinent to *literary* style (as distinct from any utterance).

There is no doubt in my mind that counting different features is useful because it is conducive to objectivity—but one must know to what purpose. And here even the results *aimed at* seem almost perverse. I admire Guiraud's study of Valéry greatly, but I am dissatisfied when he states that his 'conclusions have only a general value and may be refuted by reference to as many specific examples as one cares to cite'. [270, p. 17.] Perhaps the best solution is to avoid statistics as a *basis* for conclusions and see them merely as useful background or supporting information especially where individual works are concerned—and these must be a critic's central preoccupation. The norms or constants involved tend to be too vast for the precise statistical definition of small units to be possible. The statistician's rejection of conscious stylistic elements (rhetoric and the like) is a little disconcerting too for it would seem that these traditional aspects should not be rejected, but rather be evaluated according to the personal use the individual artist makes of them.

The needs of the critic would seem to be against the typology of styles, whereas computers and most statistics aim at wide generalizations—except where relatively short texts are involved —and this in spite of the fact that 'a writer tends to be unlike rather than like other writers' [469, p. 448]. Statistics will tend not to be related to close textual criticism therefore or at most to be valid as a background, a norm to set against the individual passage. Clearly this must not take place to the exclusion of other essential features: quality as opposed to quantity. The former is extremely difficult to quantify [704, p. 31]. The emotional core of a poem (its key image perhaps), the decisive events in a novel, may come up once and be associated with not to be repeated vocabulary and rhythms. Highly frequent elements or stereotyped situations may on the other hand be of minor significance. Impact is difficult, if not impossible, to assess [773, p. 10]. We are thus tempted to conclude with Kroeber that very often the 'quantitative analysis of literature destroys in the very process of analysis the literary qualities it seeks to describe' [369, p. 205]. Kroeber offers ways of avoiding these pitfalls as we have seen and this allows him to bear in mind, for example, the passage from Jane Austen which achieves results by means contrary to the author's normal procedures or to attempt to relate the time structure of a novel to its vocabulary. The all-important process of relating apparently non-literary elements to theme is thus carried through. But it is not sure that more than very crude information can be produced in this way.

The other danger is that quantification prejudges the issue. The free orthodox critic if he is working well surveys and notes his personal and unbiased response to an individual text—the only conditioner is his previous reading, and the influence of this may well be modified by what he has in hand. But with quantification, it is imperative to know *in advance* the categories under which the various elements will be classified—and such categories will very largely tend to be conventional and pre-established features rather crudely defined.

One should not therefore be surprised that it has so rarely been possible to link up qualitative and quantitative aspects as Wagner exhorts us to do. And yet, Cohen is not wrong to stress the fact that poetic language is deviation from a *qualitative* and not exclusively linguistic norm [141, p. 10]. We must seriously consider the widely voiced fear 'that the computer will cause humane studies to substitute counting for thought, procedure for understanding, linearity for complexity' [773, p. 10].

We must even remember that in its own specialized domain,

statistics will tend to produce dubious results. It cannot for example establish the boundary between the normal and the variant [402, pp. 279–80]. There is always a largish twilight area to contend with. The shift from one country to another and from one period or genre to another further confuses the issue—what is normally verbal in one language may tend to be expressed nominally in another [v. 718].

Deviation is a complex semantic problem as well as or even more than a grammatical one. A rich semantic bias to counting is possible as we have already seen in this chapter. Thematic studies are therefore possible, and for this we should be grateful. But even counting which leaves such a door open leads also to a break away from the text as text (i.e. as both a linear and structural experience). Statistics or the listing of collocations turns the text into a set of abstractions. One cannot but be suspicious of the statistical concentration on 'fillers', whilst those elements which visibly separate a Rimbaud from a Balzac are neglected. More traditional methods of textual analysis will tend to quote more readily and at greater length (computerized collocations are notoriously short and therefore a simplification [v. 724, vol. II, p. 157]). The *feel* of the work is thus not lost in an orthodox study. We keep the work human, and I for one am not particularly impressed by Jakobson's attempts to curb such an heretical tendency '... the terminological confusion of "literary studies" with criticism tempts the student of literature to replace the description of the intrinsic values of a literary work by a subjective censorious verdict... no manifesto, foisting a critic's own tastes and opinions on creative literature may act as a substitute for an objective scholarly analysis of verbal art' [335, pp. 297–8]. The biased sensibility of author and reader cannot be exterminated in this way, for a text does not exist without them. A text cannot be looked at in an exclusively objective way. As Jean Onimus says [512, p. 26; v. pp. 67–9], 'literature is more concerned with experience than with facts'. Statistics must be in danger of missing the mark here and, worse still, making us feel that there is no mark to hit. 'Nous avons beau compter les pas de la déesse, en noter la fréquence et la longueur *moyenne*, nous n'en tirons pas le secret de sa grâce instantanée.'* [709, p. 42.] Statistics cannot explain anything—they cannot say why the complexities of any particular writer make him majestic or terse or what have you, and we often know instinctively about such qualities. The need for at least controlled impressionism remains. Statistics may act as support. Providing of course that the initial criteria on which it is founded do not lead to a distorting of the facts. One is a little concerned to read that the complexities of preparing a text for the computer may encourage a scholar 'to ignore less obvious features of his text which otherwise he would be happy to preserve' [773, p. 13]. One is also startled to notice the extent to which texts are chosen for treatment, especially by the more statistically minded who could theoretically solve major programming problems, because of their simplicity [v. 745, pp. 213–20].

This paring down is perhaps not surprising given the relatively limited number of operations a computer can be made to perform—it cannot even be taught to recognize grammatical categories [v. 671, p. 822]. But it does justify extreme caution in handling data thus provided.

Another source of disquiet is underlined by the fact that machine translation has been more or less abandoned for the time being. This inability to recognize anything other than the most simple semantic constants in the complex situation presented by any sentence or any literary context means further (and this is perhaps the central defect in statistical analysis) that the unpredictable on which literature thrives, the unforeseen impact or device, will be ignored. Thus computers and stylistics based on statistics will tend to keep clear of the idea of ambiguity and cut out of their searches and findings a central phenomenon of literary experience (that any element in a text will tend with varying degrees of emphasis to be at one and the same time

* Note: 'It is of no avail to count the steps of the goddess [poetry], to note their regularity and their *average* length—that will not give us the secret of her instant charm.'

literal and metaphorical). When this is pointed out experts tend to retort that you can't expect their machines to do everything. But the defect here is so crucial that it cannot really be ignored in this way. Non-mechanical and non-mathematical analysis retain their pre-eminent importance.

The same problems arise inevitably with respect to imagery, that supreme exploitation of ambiguity. Empson suggests correctly that Caroline Spurgeon is wrong to lump together descriptive metaphors and normative ones [203, p. 175]. This shows that counting procedures may be useful with reference to co-occurrences and correlations but that connotations must be tackled by a non-electronic brain. The complex impact even of individual words in varying contexts, the thematic suggestiveness of the individual words in varying contexts, the thematic suggestiveness of the individual scene in a novel cannot otherwise be assessed. Levels of style and emotivity too indicate that prejudging is out of the question: 'the minute gradations of tone and texture, the delicate sense of situation . . . the detection of an underlying sense of structure confirms the rôle of the human observer' [773, p. 26].

The conclusions are, I think obvious and brief: computers can provide us with vast and diversified quantities of facts which would otherwise not be humanly available. Statistics from whatever source objectify what would otherwise be impressionistic. But once such data has been obtained, the task of integrating them into a wider and more sensitive appreciation of the text (to which all sorts of methods and approaches will contribute) has still to be undertaken.

PART II

G

CHAPTER SEVEN

CONSTRUCTION

This chapter and the one which follows it are not a straight continuation of what we have been looking at so far. They are an attempt at a radically different approach. Instead of more or less categorized analysis, my aim is now to look at the way a realistic synthesis, a coherent and far-reaching statement about a literary work may be arrived at. I have already suggested several times in passing that this is indispensable. I now want to approach the problem systematically.

I should have liked to use the general heading *structure* rather than *construction*, but the word *structure*, like *theme* (which I shall have to risk using later on), is so loaded, so much a part of modern pseudo-technical critical jargon, that I have decided to avoid it except in particular cases where it seems indispensable.

This restriction is in a sense ridiculous, for the idea and even the term are far from new, even if they have assumed massive importance over the past fifty years. Wellek, in his *History of Modern Criticism* [vol. I, pp. 2–3], has shown how the notion developed towards the end of the eighteenth century, when the objective canons of literature were giving way to the idea of a literary work as an organic individual production, something with its own rules.

A literary work is now seen therefore as a kind of closed shop, something which, unlike normal discourse and experience, may be defined primarily by the fact that it is finite [411, p. 56]. Such a definition (which would seem to be true) makes the literary (or any other) work a unit—logically therefore we should attempt to describe it *in terms of its unity.*

This definition and this conclusion may be reached by other routes: the notion for example that a literary work of art is an organization of experience. We should therefore consider too the kind of coherence this presupposes.

It is clear that the need to look for unity and coherence has been strengthened and universalized by tendencies in modern literature: '. . . the common reader when confronted with such novels [as *Ulysses*, *The Waves*, *The Sound and the Fury*] is compelled to use faculties of perception and interpretation, of analysis and synthesis that we generally assign to the literary critic. [This process of putting the story together means that the reader will] tend to find spatial patterns in these novels.' [293, pp. 98–9.] The habit is catching—conventional novels will come to attract a more 'spatial' approach. And there is nothing strange about that: already Henry James in his *Art of Fiction* stresses the ideas of unity and the search for form [340, pp. 81 and 88] so cogently that departures from such an attitude must seem foolish, like this one on George Eliot: '. . . *Middlemarch* is not ideally done; it is set down just as it arose in the mind of the author without any arrangement [or] . . . previous consideration of the form, everything being left to the confusion of life' [in 293, p. 90]. This by the way stands in full opposition to George Eliot's own very conscious preoccupation with unity [293, pp. 93–4].

Unity may be simply described as the means whereby an author kills a multiplicity of birds with one stone: 'I cannot . . . conceive in any novel worth discussing at all of a passage of description which is not in its intention [the modern critic might prefer to talk about *function*] narrative, a passage of dialogue that is not in its intention descriptive . . . A novel is a living thing . . . in each of the parts there is something of each of the other parts.' [340, pp. 87–8.] All elements thus live in close relation to each other, and this to a large extent makes them significant. For this reason Dámaso Alonso can suggest that poetry especially is 'rather [the] creation [of significant forms] than [the] exploration [of reality]' [10, pp. 22–32]. This, Jean Ricardou has suggested, is also true of the novel: 'Far from using writing in order to present a vision of the world, imaginative writing makes use of a concept of the world with its inner workings to produce a universe which obeys the specific laws of writing' [567, p. 25], which is a bit contorted but sufficiently banal to be acceptable. One is reminded of Wellek and Warren's remark that 'art imposes some kind of framework which takes the statement of the work outside reality' [744, p. 14].

Such ideas are reasonably straightforward. They may be complicated by trying to make them fit something like Pepys's Diary where day-to-day reality very definitely imposes itself on the construction of the work, and where selection is much more difficult. Here perhaps (and in many other cases) the half-way house approach suggested by Baudelaire would be more appropriate (bringing in another definition is useful too for it shows that no single one is ever definitive). '[Pure art according to the modern mind is] a suggestive magic in which both subject and object, the world outside the artist and the artist himself are combined' [59, p. 119].

All this fits in with a notion of literature which obeys 'the basic human need to impose an order on the chaos of reality' [332, p. 1205]. Critics have to see in what way (and to what extent of course) this coherence is achieved. Making do with isolated features, whether they be stylistic features or short extracts, will not do. Attacking Jules Lemaitre's isolationist analysis of a passage of Nerval, Proust says that 'the sentence must be put back where it was, illuminated in its own particular way' [547, p. 185]. It is the idea of links and cohesion which must be at the forefront of our minds therefore. We have seen the way images will bind a work together. Images are however not isolated phenomena: they belong to a texture both verbal and psychological which is either not permanently metaphorical or which is symbolical in ways which we do not traditionally recognize as being linked to imagery (these alternatives are not mutually exclusive—they are rather a question of critical emphasis). Imagery is thus part of syntax, rhythm, and apparently literal vocabulary. To ignore this general notion of interdependence is to make nonsense of the efforts of a writer like Mallarmé who spent days, as he says himself, harmonizing the different parts of a sonnet [430, vol. I, p.

32]. Any analysis is fragmentation of course, but we must attempt, in ways indicated in past chapters and in the coming pages, to search for unifying principles.

For some people, there must always be some gap between the true unity of a work and that which is described 'externally': for the French New Critics 'varied phenomena interlace and converge provided of course they are made to converge' [176, p. 64]. What is clear is that as reading is a subjective experience our choice of the material on the basis of which the work's unity is established will inevitably be biased [v. 415, p. 19]—but this should not imply a refusal to be as comprehensive as possible or any sort of *a priori* thinking, and it should follow perhaps the exhaustive, descriptive approach adopted by Monique Parent [516]. The unity described may still be that forcefully indicated by the work itself: 'Each work has its own particular form . . . critical procedures can never be fixed if one accepts the need to leave the initiative with the work itself.' [607, p. 106.] The work, as I have suggested, being finite, creates its own norms, and in many senses it is more important to study the way these norms are manipulated than to consider the extent to which they are deviations from 'common practice'.

The search is therefore for some sort of pattern—not just in esoteric works (especially post-romantic ones) which may not be otherwise described, but also, and just as importantly, in 'straightforward' ones—for here patterns allow one to see the work in depth and not merely as a story: 'Whatever our integrated organic response may be, it is a response not to cumulative little verbal stimuli . . . but a response to a strongly articulated *virtual experience*, one dominant stimulus.' [378, pp. 214–15.] We are searching for that 'consistency of impression' which C. Day Lewis talks about [407, p. 75], and which Dámaso Alonso calls the 'total image', which is not a sum of a work's parts although it is built up on them [10, p. 40; v. too 594, p. 92]. For Dámaso Alonso however this 'intuition of the work' is not expressible critically. The rest of this chapter should show that this is not totally correct.

We should not forget either the possibility of searching for a unity which might well go beyond the individual work and embrace the whole of a writer's production. As Claudel says, 'every artist comes into the world in order to say one thing, one little thing. That is what we must find, grouping all the rest around it' [v. 481, p. 171]. Or we may even feel a need to define unities which go beyond the individual writer. For Northrop Frye the 'aim of literary criticism is to find an intelligible order in the inexhaustible field of literature' [318, p. 8].

The notion of unity will therefore tend to vary. But whether we are dealing with Frye's approach, Grammont's attempts to parallel poetic words and their sounds [252, p. 195], the preoccupation with key words or the kind of dominant combinations found in Nadal and mentioned in the first chapter (etc. etc.) the basic principle is the same. It is very close to the field theory [v. *Meaning I*, pp. 77 ff.] which fits in with the idea that the total impact is greater than the sum of the parts.

Our search for cohesion in a work should be pursued in spite of the feeling (experienced for example in poems by Rimbaud or Dylan Thomas or in the opening passages of *The Waste Land*) that the poem is in some sense disintegrated. This may merely mean that *the poem's unity* (as is often the case with the writers mentioned above) *relates to an experience of disintegration*: images fly in all directions because this corresponds to the logic of the poem [v. 407, p. 117]. Even with a poem like Baudelaire's *Le Cygne* there is a shifting 'illogical' structure of associations (Andromache/the rebuilding of Paris/a swan which has escaped from its cage/a negress/shipwrecked sailors) which, although dominated by the theme of exile, represents an essential part of the experiences of the poem. Once again the idea that poetry is basically a continuity (like any other work of literature) is shown to be fundamental.

Indeed the word *pattern* which I have used several times so far might be felt to be inadequate. Stephen Booth suggests that we are faced with a multiplicity of patterns rather than one 'to which all others must be argued into auxiliary positions' [79, pp. 82–3].

A Shakespeare sonnet has 'coexistent schemes of organization'. This is a departure from attitudes already quoted. It contrasts strongly with, say D. Van Ghent's declaration that the novel is a world in which a 'vast number of traits all organized in sub-ordinate systems, . . . function under the governance of a single meaningful idea' [712, pp. 6–7]. I do not intend to come down on one side or the other, in the main because I think that the right theory will depend on the work in question and its degree of complexity. Marvell's *To His Coy Mistress* may well be nearer to Susanne Langer's conception of things (see p. 178 above) than for example *Le Cygne*. Shifting patterns will come too from a poem with a refrain, like Hugo's thirteenth Ballade because of the constantly varied relationship between the idea of the refrain and the preceding stanza. Similar points may be made about the function of rhythm in poetry [v. 564]. Typical recurrent devices, for which we are constantly searching, belong equally to single and multiple patterns. Meaning by association is achieved in both cases.

In the case of the novel, such meaning may well depend on parallel (not the same but similar) behaviour or gradation or antithesis [685, p. 128]. One thinks of Catherine Anne Porter's book *Ship of Fools* with its large number of groups of characters. One thinks of the way in Flaubert's *Education sentimentale* Frédéric and Louise Roque offer contrasting patterns of behaviour [634, pp. 427–36], as do Emma Bovary and Homais in Flaubert's earlier novel or Casaubon and Will Ladislaw in *Middlemarch* [293, p. 117]. Characters indeed are defined by their interrelationships (that is to say implied contrast and parallel) as much as by any direct description the novel may contain: Rastignac in *Le Père Goriot* exists to a large extent because of his links with Vautrin, Goriot, Delphine, Anastasie and the like. Even this is not enough, for there is a real danger of considering character in isolation as Philip Hobsbaum has pointed out [309, pp. 73 ff.]. Barbara Hardy tackles the problem by realizing how difficult it is 'to abstract strictly formal features like development or contrast or symmetry from such things as plot and character and language' [289, p. 1]. Henry James's attitude was evidently a very rich and forward-looking one. It makes possible the kind of analysis offered by Clemen who shows that characters like Iago and Othello are distinguished by the kind of imagery they use—Iago's is static and flat, Othello's opulent, swelling and dynamic. In *The Tempest*, earthy and concrete imagery serves to balance out the supernatural [136, pp. 123 and 187].

Similarly, unity (in a novel especially) may be approached by examining that phenomenon known as point of view already briefly mentioned in *Meaning II*—'the author's independent moral relation to the subject' as Tolstoy calls it [v. 8, p. 131]. This is an area which has been very thoroughly studied in Wayne C. Booth's *Rhetoric of Fiction* [see too 538, pp. 237–8, 246]. Todorov [685, pp. 141–3] has tabulated the different relationships which can be said to exist between narrator (who is not necessarily the same as the author) and tale: (1) the narrator may be better informed than the characters; (2) narrator and characters may be equally well informed; (3) the narrator may be less well informed than the characters; (4) the same event may be looked at from a variety of points of view; (5) appearance and reality may be contrasted. The amount of detail and the nature of the detail given will vary widely according to the category of tale involved. Bias creates a particular kind of unity. The extent to which the story seems to tell itself (as in Robbe-Grillet), the degree of authorial intervention (the extreme cases here are perhaps Sterne and Thackeray) will have a very profound effect on the way the whole of the work is organized. The presence or absence of narrator is clearly part of the scheme of things and not something imposed as an afterthought. It is a central organizing principle and needs to be carefully defined. The reading of a novel like *La Peste* with its hidden narrator drives this home very clearly—as does Conrad's *Nostromo* with its varieties of points of view intensifying and even defining the whirl of variously centred action which makes up the plot. Examples are inexhaustible, for each work offers a different adaptation of basic procedures. But the most telling and therefore the ones which most require patient and detailed study, are clearly those which, like *Le Rouge et le*

Noir or *Moby Dick*, offer in different ways a shifting view of events and characters or, like *The Brothers Karamazov*, suddenly impose silence about the meaning and causes of a central event (the death of old Karamazov).

Another way of looking at this problem is to consider not the presence of the narrator but that of the reader. As Ian Watt suggests [728, p. 327] 'stream of consciousness [writing which purports to be a direct representation of a character's thoughts as they occur to him] pretends that the reader does not exist . . . [it is] the extreme limit of subjective realism'. Free indirect style offers a variation of this, the reader both present and excluded. The variations are of course infinite: Bateson and Shahevitch show how, in Katherine Mansfield's *The Fly*, direct description merges into reported speech [58]. One might suggest that the impact of an action-biased work will be radically different from that of a description-biased one. This is shown by a comparison of *Le Rouge et le Noir* and *A la Recherche du Temps Perdu* (or if you prefer *Humphrey Clinker* and *The Portrait of a Lady*), the novel which defines existence as movement and the one which sees life as expansion from a series of points of contemplation. This could be seen as life represented by the notion of the straight line or as a series of circles. Thus changes in technique will make the work more complex in its meaning and therefore in its unity. At a late stage in *The Portrait of a Lady* there is a radical shift from Isabel Archer's point of view to that of Rosier and then to that of Ralph Touchett (see chapters 36 and 37). This leads to an exploration in depth from a very unusual angle of Isabel's disillusionment, a totally external approach (for Rosier is a scarcely met and very minor character and Ralph's position has always been ambiguous). Then we return to Isabel's own point of view—but now the complexity of interpretations and parallels is greatly increased (for, in addition, the whole question of Pansy's future adds to the parallel and contrasting views of marriage so far encountered).

The same category of narrative will of course produce radically different impacts, and other factors must be taken into consideration. The careful progression of first person narrative in *David Copperfield* does not belong to the same world as the wandering, socially and literarily iconoclastic point of view set out in *Catcher in the Rye.* (Which incidentally rejects Dickens's approach in the first paragraph!)

All depends to a great extent on the logical cohesion which the work creates—the way it presents norms of experience which to some extent replace those with which we are familiar in everyday life. I am thinking here of the way an author may (perhaps as a central element in his work) manipulate notions of time: this is not just a question of flashbacks (time in an 'unnatural' order), it may well, as is the case in *Ulysses*, a work by Claude Simon or even a novel like Aragon's *La Semaine Sainte*, remove the notion of the passage of time as a significant factor.

The rejection of familiar reality may well be a unifying feature in our experience of the novel—we are once again being invited, because of our surprise, to view the work as something other than a mere sequence. This fits in not only with modern critical tendencies, but also, it would seem with a basic human need: 'The intelligence can perceive with clarity only that which is discontinuous. Our intelligence can grasp with clarity only that which is immobile.'* In this way, Wilson Knight can justifiably say that 'a Shakespearian tragedy is set spatially as well as temporally in the mind. By this I mean that throughout the play there is a set of correspondences which relate to each other independently of the time sequence which is the story.' [v. 292, p. 157.] Notions and the experience of time clearly play a large part here, for as Harvey has suggested [293, p. 108] 'any disparity between the narrative and the reader's chronology will tend to provoke the reader to a spatial reading'. Thus, 'if its limitations are to be counteracted, criticism must range in all directions, but in order to range over the work in all directions it must neglect what makes that work a creative progression, an irreversible movement towards the establishment of a particular order: that

* Note: Bergson, *L'Evolution créatrice*, p. 155; quoted in the *Dictionnaire Robert* under 'se représenter'.

the work contains an affirmation which becomes progressively more distinct, with a goal in view which is only comprehensible when related to temporal movement, is what in our analysis we must disregard' [71, pp. 274–5]. This is an aggressive statement, the practical and theoretical implications of which will be seen in the next section. For we must now shift from the simple notion of unity and cohesion to the more exacting, if only partially relevant, one of structure.

In order to explain structuralism satisfactorily, it would I suppose be necessary to point to the whole linguistic background on which it rests. I am thinking mainly of Saussure and his notions of synchronic study, opposition, and the distinction between those scarcely translatable terms *langage*, *langue*, and *parole.* These last two are especially relevant (*le langage* relates to all forms of communication, verbal or otherwise). Saussure, in his *Cours de linguistique générale*, sees *la langue* as the abstract idea of language, the principles on which communication in a particular language is based. *La parole* is the individual actualization of these principles. It is however much more difficult to describe than *la langue* and for this reason the linguist proper will be most concerned with the latter [302, p. 71]. For the critic the situation is slightly different. He will tend to consider the *langue/parole* relationship in a semi-metaphorical way. He will feel that under *la parole* we should see a literary passage as it finally emerges, as the actualization of criteria existing at the (more abstract) level of the total work or in a wider, less tangible, abstraction (genres etc.), both of which may be seen to equate to *la langue*. We are dealing therefore with differing degrees of explicitness, but ones which are only important and significant because they are interrelated.

This is at the same time an explanation of Saussure's theory of opposition: sounds in a language are meaningful only inasmuch as they combine and contrast with other sounds—a structuralist critic will assert that the same is true of the different segments (verbal or otherwise) of a literary work.

In refusing to give any priority to notions of development, Saussure gave the lead to those critics (we have just seen Blanchot's statement on the matter) who consider that a work should be viewed as a synchronic whole. Different elements of a work are like linguistic categories which may be very well defined by the company they keep: a noun is a word which follows *the*, *any*, an adjective . . .; only a restricted number of word classes could complete a sentence beginning 'I saw him at . . .'—and so on [403, pp. 21–2]. What I said before about interconnections now becomes more explicit. Literary works, it may be advanced, are built up on the kind of links which are directly related (even if they are not linguistic themselves) to the foregrounding of similarities which goes on in a sentence like 'He washed the dishes and scrubbed the floor . . .' with its noun-parallels-noun and verb-parallels-verb construction.

All these ideas are excellently analysed by Todorov [v. 183], although he tends to take 'structure' as having scientific value [685, p. 125] whereas for me it does not have the rigidity of truly scientific terminology. It is what William Righter calls 'an insight' [594, p. 115].

With Saussure's principles in mind, the aim of structuralist critics is to describe a work not as meaning but rather as a *system for producing meaning* [51, pp. 255–7]: 'It is much more the attention paid to the organization of signifiers (i.e. meaning-producing elements) which provide a basis for the true criticism of meaning, than the discovery of the thing they signify and the links it has with the signifier.' [48, p. 368; v. 302, p. 233.] The important idea of a *system* is therefore clear. The tendency (which we have already seen) to use grammatical terms metaphorically for the different aspects of the work's articulation will also be clear.

Of course there are theories which tend to be less harsh than those of Barthes or Blanchot. Genette for instance, does not dispense with the signified but sees both signifier and signified as levels on which the system of forms which makes up the work will articulate reality. Both events and the words used to describe them should be taken into account when assessing a work's meaning.

The importance attached to meaning (as distinct from meaning-making patterns) here would seem to be a healthy pointer to the need to avoid excessive abstraction. At the same time both attitudes stress the notion of the work as an organization rather than the idea of the work as an object.

What is avoided is the idea that the work may in any way be seen as a fixed and unequivocal thing. For me, any theory which discounted the idea of ambiguity would be useless. As it is, the notion of structure means that when one passes from the *langue* level to its realization (words often used will be *actualization* or *generation*) in *parole*, all sorts of variables are possible—*multiple values are created from a basic unformulated pattern.* Thus Doubrovsky can claim that 'the work of literature is no more endowed with a single meaning than human nature is' [176, pp. 24–5]. And Riffaterre can describe style as a constantly repeated set of deviations from the norm of the work. Variables and constants are thus just as pertinent here as in linguistically biased semantics. Synonymy is another example of this.

Surprise is therefore in no way eliminated. Stavroguine's suicide in *The Possessed*, totally unexpected though it may be at the level of plot, is quite compatible with a structuralist interpretation of the novel. So is the unforeseen and the unforeseeable which characterizes so much of Conrad. This is because 'the literary work is a very special semantic system whose purpose is to give meanings rather than one particular meaning to the world' [51, p. 256]. Therefore if our 'reading should be biased towards the definition of a system' we should remember 'there are many possible systems' [176, p. 82]. We should avoid being 'committed to a rigid system of constraints and necessities' [176, pp. 82–3].

A certain suppleness of approach must always be maintained in spite of this—characters in a novel, for example should be seen as both a function and an end in themselves [293, p. 155]. Ambiguity and structure cohabit more easily too when it is realized that the signifier and the thing signified need not necessarily have a purely linguistic function. Alongside the analyses of a Harris which relate to such structures as the parts of a sentence, there is the method of a Lévi-Strauss for whom the sentence is treated holistically as a semantic unit [302, pp. 69–70]. Nor is Barthes in any sense preoccupied with purely linguistic features, but rather with the nature and function of signs, and these may deal with things completely unrelated to literature like fashion or wrestling [see 46; 53; 50] for, clearly, signs (i.e. functions indicating meaning) crop up with great complexity in a huge variety of situations. They may be only partially verbal as in drama which is 'a highly developed semiological object with six or seven sets of information of a variable kind being produced at any one particular time' [46, pp. 258–9]: stage presentation, the distancing of audience and performer as well as the words spoken all condition our response. We must be aware of them all and of their interrelationships if we are to discuss what the play signifies. Conversely, signs may be totally non-verbal, like traffic lights which vary in meaning according to sequence and combination (red and amber together are very different in meaning from either colour alone).

It is perhaps such facts which make one wonder whether structural considerations might not have helped Susanne Langer to develop more cogently her ideas on unifying motifs and on the way symbols of feeling or experience may be used to define a work of art. Empson's studies of words (and perhaps even his typology of ambiguity) could have benefited from such notions too.

Meaning in the narrow sense need not necessarily be the only basic consideration of structuralism. Indeed Hendricks [302, pp. 74–5] has pointed out that meaning was for a time replaced by Harris and other scholars as a criterion of linguistic analysis (which often gives a lead to literary analysis) by 'distribution': the sum of all environments in which an element occurs. For the novel this could offer distinct possibilities. One could for example examine the circumstances in which a particular scene will tend to recur. Such a phenomenon is particularly striking in Zola: both

L'Assommoir and *La Bête Humaine* begin with a character waiting alone in a room for someone else to return; trials of strength scenes are also frequent in such works as *La Terre*, *Germinal* and *L'Assommoir*.

All of these phenomena are closely related in their various ways to the idea of the generative system (as in Ohmann's notion of the links between the idea of style and generative grammar). The link between generation and distribution becomes apparent when we read Todorov's suggestion that a narrative like *Les Liaisons dangereuses* may be made up of ten or so stable-structured 'micro-narratives' [685, p. 129; see too 687]. To detail them is therefore to state the *langue* which produces the *parole* of the finished work (for the micro-narratives *taken individually* have no more significance than the scenes in Zola which I have just mentioned).

The structural approach will tend to give equal value to all elements in the work: 'every part of the poetic message is a sign in relation to the others' [785, p. 34]. This means that all the different aspects of a work offer an equally sure lead into its deeper unity. Spitzer puts this usefully (in spite of the question-begging beginning): '. . . any good observation, when sufficiently deepened, infallibly leads to the centre of the work of art. There are no preferential vantage points (such as the ideas or the structure of the poem) with which we are obliged to start.' [652, p. 198; v. too 273, p. 71.]

One important result of this is that it is now very difficult to talk about digression or irrelevance, for *everything in a work of art is to the point.* Its structure is made up of everything it contains. 'Digression' in an author like Balzac or Sterne is therefore an element by which the structure of a work may be defined. If an author moves away from a preoccupation with a sequence of events or ideas and prefers a process of expansion, this is because the experience offered by the work is closely related to the notion of expansion. Unity thus ceases to be related to value and becomes rather a fact which must exist and which we must strive to find. Everything must be linked to function. Lubbock's approach is particularly unhelpful therefore when he regrets greater neatness of form in *War and Peace* or states that, 'We know of novels which everybody admits to be badly constructed but which are so full of life that it does not appear to matter.' [415, p. 10.] Not because it is no longer the done thing to evaluate the cohesion of a work of art, but rather because an exclusive preoccupation with this kind of evaluation will tend to blind us to the true nature of the work *as it is*. If we want really to understand the impact of *War and Peace* the sections on historical theory are just as important an element as the details of Natasha's life and loves. Similarly the tendency to present literature in the form of extracts or abridged versions (à la *Classiques Larousse* or *Readers' Digest*) is a particularly destructive one—which into the bargain deprives one of the chance to evaluate structure! As Barthes says, therefore, 'all the different parts of a narration are functional' [46B, p. 7]—a work is a 'functional set of figures' [42, p. 249].

Taking all this into account, and especially bearing the notion of ambiguity in mind, it is possible to say that a structuralist approach has the effect of giving all elements in a work symbolical, metaphorical or representative value [637, p. 10], for they have a significance greater than themselves, they point at one and the same time to themselves and to the wider tendencies in the work which they exemplify. Repetitions of similar phenomena at different levels, once recognized, point to fundamental structure. Context and sign mutually interact, the one echoing the other. Yet again, structural equivalence will imply semantic equivalence. This has been explicitly stated in English-speaking countries since at least 1923: '. . . when a context has affected us in the past, the recurrence of merely a part of the context will cause us to re-act in the way in which we re-acted before' [507, p. 139].

One notion of structure and system which needs to be gone into further is the idea of a work or of literature in general being held together by a language peculiar to it. This is part of the theory of *literarity* which has preoccupied linguistically and semantically biased scholars for some time—the attempt to define those factors which make literary expression what it is. Marcello Pagnini claims that 'literarity is not to be found in the signifiers but in linguistic structures'. [515, p. 169.] This may be somewhat restrictive, but it does point again to the notion of system. It offers an extension of the established fact that literary language is finite (because it belongs to a finite structure). It must therefore be different from everyday language which is by definition imprecise, indefinite and shapeless—whereas with literary language everything is form, sign and value [173, p. 105]. Earlier chapters have shown that, because we are dealing with a system, the rules to which literary language is subjected are less concerned with the way expression is conform to reality than with the system of signs which the author has worked out for himself. Signs cease thus to be the arbitrary things they normally are. The signifier and the thing signified merge.

This can be applied to the individual work, but it can too be studied generally as Jean Cohen has brilliantly shown in his *Structure du Langage poétique.* Cohen points to deviation as a basic *unifying* phenomenon in poetic language. Normal linguistic procedures at all levels in poetry are for him the dissociation of generally linked elements [141, p. 194; v. to 391, pp. 139–40]. But this is clarified by S. R. Levin's insistence [402, p. 278] that deviations in poetic form are not those which can be properly related to linguistics as it is normally understood for they relate to the impact of rhythm, rhyme and the like on such things as syntax and emphasis.

Another idea frequently linked to the structure of poetic language (*and again related to deviation*) is redundancy—i.e. expression which in normal discourse would appear to be superfluous as in the opening lines of Eliot's *Ash Wednesday*:

> Because I do not hope to turn again
> Because I do not hope
> Because I do not hope to turn
> Desiring this man's gift and that man's scope. . . .

If someone spoke to us in conversation like that we should I suppose surreptitiously make for the door—in Eliot on the other hand repetition takes on the consistency of the despair expressed.

The emphasis so far has been on poetry. But even when talking about linguistic structures, we need only be aware of the *kind* of system involved to accept the idea that structures of some sort may be equally relevant to prose, which sets up a denotative system whereas poetry relates to a connotative one [v. 265, p. 41 and 710, pp. 150–2]. The notion of system however remains in both cases—though it is clear that in prose we might expect a rejection of things like redundancy and greater links between language and the non-linguistic aspect of literarity. Another term can thus be added to our list, that of competence (which may however be encountered with a meaning similar to that of *la langue*): not just the fact that each element fits into the basic scheme of the text, but the *way* it fits [v. 371].

Some modern critics, as we have seen, seem to be a little obsessed with linguistics, but this does have the value of a corrective. I. A. Richards makes timely criticism of people's 'tendency to read meaning into poems at random, regardless of linguistic limits' which would seem to be synonymous with 'linguistic structures' [578, p. 335]. And the dangers of this are amply demonstrated in the author's *Practical Criticism.*

Such a warning points to the variable critical value of Jakobson's work, although other influences have been at play here too. His collaboration with the anthropologist Lévi-Strauss is an indication of this, and in their joint paper on Baudelaire's *Les Chats* they claim that 'in poetic works the linguistician perceives structures which are strikingly analogous to those which the ethnologist reveals by studying myths' [339, p. 5]. Jakobson has shown his approval too of the value of phenomenology. But he would seem to be interested essentially in defining literary and especially poetic language, and for this, one of his basic statements is that 'any sequence of semantic units will tend to set up an equation.

Any element in the sequence is [implicitly] a comparison' [334, p. 238]. Poetic language makes such a process stronger by exploiting the phonological, syntactical and semantic components of an utterance. We have already seen the echoes a word like 'teaching' may evoke [v. *Sounds* p. 22]. Jakobson has shown how such phenomena may be taken into account, in his article on the Baudelaire poem I have just mentioned and in his study with Lawrence Jones on Shakespeare's sonnet 129 [338; v. also 576] in the course of which every conceivable kind of linguistic interrelationship (grammatical, phonetic, semantic, lexical) and its conditioning by the sonnet scheme is considered, each one seeming to be founded on the key ideas of parallel and contrast: lines which contain nouns and lines which do not, the position of caesura breaks ('centrifugal' and 'centripetal' lines), the degree to which rhyme words can be pigeon-holed grammatically, parallel constructions and phonological patterns (either echoes or similar sound-types, e.g. diphthongs).

Jakobson is setting up here the basic notion of equivalence (very close to what Levin calls *coupling*) on which the unity of the work may be founded. Perhaps it would be even more illuminating if he made use of transformational theories as Levin has tended to do in his *Linguistic Structures in Poetry*, for this would seem to make notions of equivalence easier to grasp and in practical criticism less exclusively based on a dry listing of examples. More detailed reference to the *langue* of a poem would make a description of its actualized *parole* more explicit and, I think, significant. The analysis would too be more overtly literary: 'If the key activity for the linguistician is the analysis of deep structures, it would appear that the stylistician works rather at the level of transformational rules and that his area of activity relates to surface structures, that area in which the utterance of the work develops.' [372, p. 89.]

There are of course dangers in all this: 'the most significant words [for exegesis] will not necessarily occur in equivalent syntactic positions (even if the sentences are normalised by means of grammatical transformations)' [303, p. 6]. The higher unity of poetic language which Levin sees as being defined by couplings is thus something which has to be handled with great care. For example, important words point to significant syntax or sound, and not vice versa. Collocational effects are indeed of great importance in a poem. However they should not make us forget that words have some constant value of meaning which will strike us whatever the context may be. Furthermore, as Charles Rosen points out, 'the subsidiary non-canonic phonetic patterns in harmony with the principal ones, are partially gratuitous, can never fulfil the criterion of relevance. Their interaction with the semantic structure can never be complete; [we are dealing with] arabesques of phonetic and semantic patterns that imply a meaning and yet elude interpretation.' Charles Rosen suggests that this is why Jakobson's (and Lévi-Strauss's) analysis of *Les Chats* is better than the study of 'Th' expence of spirit' [602, p. 38].

Jakobson is therefore referring to a very complex situation when he claims that 'the poetic function projects the principle of equivalence from the axis of selection into the axis of combination' [335, p. 302]—which means that words, sentence structures and the like are chosen with a view to making them 'fit' in as many ways as possible (i.e. grammatically, lexically, phonologically etc.) with the other elements of the work in which they are found. Selection would merely relate to the communication of a message, which, one supposes, could produce a very similar effect if different words were used: 'I'm going now' could quite easily be replaced by 'I'm off now'. Combination is very different: it would be impossible to rewrite the following lines without severely damaging the linguistic structure and therefore the essential impact of its message (even if things like rhyme and metre were maintained):

> I wonder by my troth, what thou, and I
> Did, till we loved? were we not wean'd till then?
> But suck'd on country pleasures, childishly?
> Or snorted we in the seven sleepers den?
> T'was so; but this, all pleasures fancies be.

> If ever any beauty I did see,
> Which I desir'd, and got, t'was but a dreame of thee.
> (Donne: *The Good Morrow.*)

The example chosen is a deliberately 'prosaic' one—but the systematic combination of prose structures and verse patterns makes for a linguistic unity, and this in itself (not to mention alliteration or the compression of l. 5) will tend to make the utterance unique in the total sense of the word.

We have already seen that grammatical categories may form a dangerous basis for criticism. We also know that not all linguistic structures are critically significant [584]. A lot of what I have said about Jakobson could be attacked on that score. This is in spite of the fact that Jakobson insists on the subliminal effect of the structures he describes: we are not aware of the effect upon us of elements which undoubtedly exist. The trouble here of course is that if we are not aware that something is happening to us, it may not in fact be happening to us, or may be of such little impact as not to warrant the phenomenal labours which went into the production of Jakobson's thirty-two page study.

What is useful about Jakobson's approach, for the critic if not for the linguistician, is perhaps less the at times dubious practical results he himself has published than the stimulus to very careful examination of interrelationships and the definition of poetic language (equivalence, combination especially) which he bases it on. In the finite world of the poem we can thus postulate that patterning and cohesion will be meaningful (although we might do well not to separate patterns too far from the meaning of the words involved), and that *pattern is in a sense meaning*—to describe it is thus the same as describing one aspect of the poem's significance. Indeed, I am not sure that Jakobson's reference to the 'nearly unexplored question of [the] interrelationship between message and context' [v. 399, p. 159] might not be something of a red herring. Martinet points out that style, 'the choice of a linguistic unit is not solely the result of the attempt to express, in simple and direct terms, one aspect or another of the experience to be communicated, but relates also to the kind of effects which will be produced by the presence side by side of that particular unit and others which are already there or which are about to appear' [438, p. 1288].

The most intense form of such a phenomenon is often imagery, but this is far from being always the case, and other elements do at times take over its function and may, as I have already suggested, take on metaphorical value: 'as a rule, in poems which have no imagery it is the "grammatical figure" which replaces tropes' [337, p. 26]. Character, event, point of view and the like will perform a similar function in works of prose. Here of course we are shifting to a non-linguistic area (another example of the fact that linguistics is in no sense a thing apart), and this involves a very healthy blurring of categories. We can easily link it with such statements as: 'a sentence in literature is not made up of a series of words added together. It implies a predilection for certain kinds of words: short . . . or long, rare or . . . common —sonorous, striking or deliberately dull, precise or vague—and between these words there will be harmony or dissonance.' [155, pp. vii–viii.] As this can be taken either literally or metaphorically we can thus turn our backs on more rigid grammatical (or any other categorizing) formulae, and point to wider, more supple notions of structuration.

These elements work in a way which can be compared to the predetermination involved in the choice of a cliché-dominated rhetorical medium (cf. Hugo's 'murs entourés de cohortes sanglantes' and 'la hache à vos regards se cachant sous les fleurs' in *Les Vierges de Verdun*) or the suggestion put forward by Jean Ricardou (which will be relevant for what I have to say later on in this chapter about semiotics and archetypes) that 'a given piece of writing is shaped far more than we realize by the "productive potential" of the language itself. The writer frequently takes his orders from phonic or graphic coincidences like puns or anagrams or from metaphors which perform as "generators" only when the second term of a comparison is allowed to switch the writer from one set of rails to another.'

[566 and 502, pp. 1055–65; v. too Riffaterre's notions of micro- and macro-contexts.] Rhetorical (or indeed any stylistic) constants and those mentioned by Ricardou [187, p. 14] would seem to make nonsense of Winifred Nowottny's suggestion that 'above the level of the sentence, the structure of the language itself does not constrain a speaker's choice of the best way to arrange his discourse' [504, p. 73]. Jakobson's analyses show Nowottny to be wrong too. Even characteristic vocabulary determines linguistic structure above the level of the sentence itself. So does the basic poetic process of image-building [v. 459, p. 10], for we have seen in Christine Brooke-Rose and Josephine Miles that imagery is grammatically as well as semantically definable (not that these two characteristics should be separated) [504, p. 50].

Linguistic approaches thus appear as a global notion and not as a series of fragmented elements. It is a notion which must coexist with non-linguistic phenomena (or better still be another aspect of those same phenomena) as an explanation of what literariness implies.

A further dimension can be added to the idea of structure through a definition more specifically based on semantic rather than grammatical criteria (again inadequate in itself because partial). In recent years that branch of semantics called semiotics or semiology (the theory of signs concerned therefore with meaning (linguistic or otherwise) as a structural pattern, or with patterns which generate meaning) has busied itself with literature to an increasing degree. This can be seen by looking at such periodicals as *Semiotica* and *Tel Quel.* Inevitably perhaps (and mercifully) the preoccupation here has been with prose works (though it is clear that some similar studies of fixed poetic forms like the sixteenth-century sonnet could also be fruitful). There seems too to be a distinct tendency for this field to be more restricted to continental (and especially French) scholars, whereas poetic analysis of an objectively structuralist kind is perhaps more highly developed in North America and in Great Britain.

Once again a value of this approach is that it breaks away from excessive standard linguistic categorization and shifts the emphasis to the idea that the text to be analysed may be considered as a unit in itself.

Of course it is possible to reduce the structure of prose works to a series of stereotypes, as W. Hildick has done in *Thirteen Types of Narrative*, which is a useful study of the way a particular set of events may be angled. But whilst we should beware of old wine in new bottles (a favourite critical pastime) it could be stressed that the semiologist would tend to look also at *basic patterns of events* and to be much more rigorous in the theories on which his findings are based.

He might even claim to be scientific but I personally would once again be a little sceptical here: is it possible to be scientific about the inevitable emotional content of an individual text or even about genre patterns—or conversely to exclude that emotional content? The danger here is that a text may be emptied of its reality. To this the semiologist would offer two answers: first that it is the notion of textuality (or once again literarity) which is at a premium or even that 'for the semiologist literature does not exist . . . it is [merely] a special kind of semiotic activity' [368, p. 92]. It is legitimate to ask how 'a special kind of activity' can be anything other than a thing apart: but I think these ideas should be seen as typical Gallic aggressiveness (or galloping Cartesianism—even from a Bulgarian critic) rather than as an excuse for us to fault the rest of what the scholars involved have undertaken.

Semiotics is defined by Julia Kristeva (the high priestess of the movement) as an 'elaboration of models' [366]—models in this sense being comparable to those formulae worked out to define economic processes by indicating symbolically the different components which go to make up that process. Thus a pattern A—B—C (= birth, marriage, death) in a straight biography with variants A^2, B^2 to express the birth and marriage of dependents and D (breakdown of marriage) could lead to a simple model A^1—B^1—A^2—D—B^2!—C to express the main components of the story. For Julia Kristeva [366, p. 424] 'the object is built up on the basis of the model; it does not exist before it has been "presented" by the model'. The work depends for its meaning on our awareness of the 'model' which constitutes its essence. It would be more exact to suggest that narrative and model are constituted simultaneously—but this is not the genre approach which semiologists too rigidly adopt. The work is seen as a system of signs of various kinds of meaningful stimuli, and there is no fundamental gap here between Barthes's approach and that of Julia Kristeva, except perhaps that Barthes has a much less arid and narrow and therefore much more pertinently literary approach to his topics. Both however, like Bremond, see narrative as a kind of logical process, where decisions as to its different components and developments depend on the logic of the work itself [256, p. 157]. For Greimas, quoted here, narrative structures should tally to a large degree with linguistic ones, although (like Barthes) he acknowledges (and one might note in passing the search for overall definitions) that 'narrativity may relate to non-verbal forms such as the cinema, dreams or painting. So the models established are distinct from linguistic structures and exist before they do.' [256, p. 158.] Of course close links between the two may finally be underlined by suggesting that the linguistic structures will be determined by the pre-existing ones (an acceptable idea, I suppose, providing narrative structures take tone into account). But on the same page Greimas asserts that meaning is indifferent to the possible modes of its expression, and here one feels that Greimas's thinking (and Julia Kristeva's) parts company with that of any self-respecting literary scholar or critic —a text *must* have more individuality than that.

It should be stressed that there is no complete agreement on the way symbolic formulae and models are expressed. This does not make for the easy understanding of a type of thinking with which most literary scholars are not familiar. The kind of terminology used will vary too. The main point to remember, whether one is dealing with a supple critic like Barthes or hard-liners like Kristeva, is therefore, for practical purposes, that a literary work can be reduced schematically to blocks of significant motifs. And the basic idea behind this is once again that of transformation or generation. As Julia Kristeva says in her own inimitable style, 'to handle a narrative as a transformation means that a model (the transformation) is applied to a meaningful phenomenon (the narrative)' [366, p. 422]. This, although a little circuitous, points to a technique which can be useful when a prose passage or a narrative poem is being looked at. On the basis of the model the work may be said to generate its different elements. The work is a 'system which generates deep forms' [455, p. 20]. Julia Kristeva calls this generative pattern the genotext, and claims that '. . . discourse in the novel is quite easily subsumed by transformational analysis as is perhaps the case with any representation, any phantasma' [366, p. 440]. She goes on to make a specific distinction between this and poetic discourse: 'The situation is quite different when one is dealing with a text which dispenses with representation and becomes the inscription of its own production. [*sic*! meaning presumably when form and content merge so completely that one is interested in the words as an end in themselves.] This is true, in our culture, of Mallarmé, Lautréamont and Roussel. The productivity here, inasmuch as it permeates THROUGH representation (and meaning), may no longer be expressed through transformational analysis.' [366, p. 440.] I am not sure that these contortions go much further than repeating the familiar idea that form and content in modern poetry (taken as an extreme abstract idea) are often inseparable.

As far as straightforward prose is concerned we are close too to the long-standing Bloomfieldian idea that the reasons for a particular form of behaviour may be traced to internal and external influences and *are therefore predictable* (this is not refined enough however to take into account the ambiguity inherent in literary transforms). Hence the self-explanatory notions of 'competence' and 'performance', the Chomskian equivalent of *langue* and *parole* which one encounters so often in modern French critical writing—the notion that any particular element in the text actualizes the semiological model established to define that text.

All this is somewhat abstract—but there is a reason for it which should make literary critics a little suspicious: the scholars working in this field are excessively preoccupied with theory and with the typically French insistence on founding a *school* of thought (and therefore to some inevitable extent with a stereotyped way of looking at things). The studies I have quoted abound with repetition of first principles and praise of Saussure. There is also a monotonous regularity with which the same examples are cited over and over again (*Les Liaisons dangereuses* for Todorov; a somewhat obscure fifteenth-century novel, *Jehan de Saintré*, in the case of Julia Kristeva).

The aim is clearly to establish general principles, not to explore a multiplicity of works (it is also of course disturbing that the general principles tend not to be established on the basis of a multiplicity of works). The lead for these new approaches comes significantly not from purely literary investigations but from those more closely related to fringe areas—one thinks especially of the structuralist studies of the folk-tale undertaken in the 1920s by Propp [v. 670] and of course Lévi-Strauss's monumental researches into primitive mythology and behaviour. The preoccupation with an underlying pattern is justifiable and inevitable here. It is not surprising therefore to find Greimas in turn talking about the general structure of narrative on the basis of widely varying versions of folk-tales [260].

There are however structuralist/semiological studies of individual works: those of *L'Etranger* by J.-C. Coquet in *Langue Française*, September 1969, of Claude Simon's *Routes des Flandres* in Ricardou's *Problèmes du Nouveau Roman*. Interestingly, Todorov suggests in *La Grammaire du récit* that Boccaccio's *Decameron* may be reduced to two basic story-types: one recounting punishment avoided, or equilibrium which gives way to a lack of balance, the other recounting a conversion where an initial lack of balance gives way to balance.

Clearly, it is useful to schematize these motifs symbolically, with letters and/or numbers to represent the constituent elements. But it would be (for me at least) less confusing if some sort of standardization were possible. I am worried too by the excessive simplification which occurs from time to time. Superficial works like crime novels fall prey to zealous (but unimaginative and tasteless) pattern-hunters. At the Cluny colloquium, delegates were presented with the basic elements of the crime story [141B]: break in balance (the crime), the Search, the Chase, the first being situated outside the main body of the story, the other two being fixed although of variable importance—thus, a pattern may be worked out B^1—S—C—B^2. This kind of study tends to produce results which seem to be both unsurprising (unless you have never read a detective story, in which case they matter even less) and debasing, for the formula produced could apply to the crudest as well as to the most refined examples. One has the feeling that it would be impossible to try to account for any major work of real complexity in this way—schematization may not leave much room for ambiguity. The basic pattern of *Goldfinger* does not really provide a stepping-stone for the understanding of *Middlemarch*.

We are thus dealing with an analytical method which may at times be as clumsy and vague as the old-fashioned literary history classification which French New Critics take such pleasure in castigating.

It does not seem very satisfactory either to claim that 'a structural interpretation of literature may utilize categories which appear abstract because they are equivalent to phonemes in their law of combination' [292, p. 153]. The abstraction remains. And it is an abstraction which is rendered even more dubious by the process of *normalization* whereby patterns are established: 'In order to study the structure of plot we must first set out the plot in the form of a résumé in which every separate action coresponds to a clause.' [686, p. 120; v. too 302, pp. 77 ff.] This kind of emasculating process occurs whether we are dealing with structural analysis proper ('concern for a system of differences') or content analysis which is 'concerned with frequencies rather than the internal relations of categories' [302, p. 84]. Some structural approaches are more subtly controlled than that: Lévi-Strauss clearly applies a strong sense of the contextual determination of meaning [302, p. 85]. But all too often we are presented with the kind of study offered by Annie Ubersfeld on the structure of the elder Dumas's plays [695]. Her first deed is to eliminate all consideration of sentences and vocabulary! Structuralism under these conditions becomes as potentially narrow and restricted as the grammatical or phonological approaches looked at before.

Of course, it is useful to know basic patterns, for there are works which are so tradition-bound that their description through pre-established structural models would seem to be almost totally adequate. Witness Adam de la Halle who indulges in 'prefabricated combinations whose elements as such may scarcely be dissociated. The linguistic and stylistic means which he brings into play are less like the keys of an instrument . . . than like a set of different keyboards which correspond to different registers of expression. . . .' [782, pp. 77–8.] The kind of operative norms which Julia Kristeva describes in *Jehan de Saintré* are interesting too: 'Any anecdotic value is . . . eliminated: the novel has life and death as its two main axial poles and is nothing more than the notation of deviations (surprises) which do not destroy the solidarity of the life–death thematic ring which binds the whole together. The text has a thematic axis: a play between two exclusive oppositions whose nomination changes [*sic*; one supposes Madame Kristeva means 'which do not always have the same name'] (vice/virtue; love/hate: praise/blame . . .) but which always runs along the same semic axis (positive/negative).' [366, pp. 431–2.] Ambiguity is not ignored here either—the importance of deception, strangers, hermaphrodites: 'the trajectory of the novel would be impossible without that non-disjunctive function, THE DOUBLE, which programmes the novel from the beginning' [366, p. 432]. All of which enables her to suggest differences between the epic and the novel [p. 435] . . .

One does at times have the feeling that semiotic studies may ultimately provide important information concerning literary meaning. The texts which are studied with that in mind are however not always illuminated in a significant way for the critic even if he can wade his way through the often unnecessarily pretentious jargon. Transformational models, as Julia Kristeva points out [366, p. 436], bring out synthetic considerations 'which lead semiotics towards the problem of the production of meaning and not only towards the description of a given state of meaning' (i.e., a particular text). The emphasis is very definitely on meaning as a process rather than literary meaning as a source of elucidation of an individual literary work. The significant difference in impact and relevance between Ohmann's generative grammar approach to style and semiotic analysis is perhaps clear.*

A further potential advantage of semiotic techniques would seem to relate to the new idea of genres which they appear to offer: 'thus the *parole* which is a poem achieves itself as a poetic structure not merely by satisfying the norms of a *langue* but as much and perhaps more by its satisfaction of norms current for aesthetic structure in general in its period and place . . .' [374, p. 95]. This is the intermediary level of any text which comes before any specific realization of the work's potential [638, p. 324]. It is much more biased towards the idea of the interrelationships between different texts than say the American New Criticism in the thirties and forties. Inasmuch as the preoccupation, for the French, is with *prose* works, this is at least partly justified. As a branch of those studies which include typology, common practice, stereotypes, clichés etc. it should be treated with circumspection (in case it becomes a dictatorial end in itself) but it would be foolish to dismiss it out of hand.

As is always the case, we must reconcile the work's specificity

* Note: One element I have not so far mentioned is the notion of intertextuality—the way external elements (tradition and social factors, literary influences etc.) change once they are integrated into a new work [v. 367, p. 312]. I shall go a little more deeply into this when I mention Goldmann's approach to literary structure.

and the tradition to which it incontrovertibly belongs. French structuralist semiology is to my mind over-preoccupied with the latter. The 'hidden and secret form underlying the explicit one' [602, p. 34] must primarily be an elucidation of the *individual* work.

Partly for this reason, I find it a relief to shift from such a potentially arid, fragmented and purely descriptive naming of parts not all of which is critically relevant to methods which take into account the resonance of a work: the fact that it is essentially a human experience (a deliberately wide expression) and that any critical work which does not take this fact into account must be missing the point.

This need not encourage a loose impressionistic approach—it can quite easily be systematic without, in any sense, being dehumanized. The basic aim is that expressed by Thomas Aron at the beginning of a brilliant comparison of Racine's *Bérénice* and Thomas Corneille's *Ariane* [18]: to see how the true meaning of words and structures may be looked at. And of course, this is only possible if they are related to central phenomena *which make them* significant. These I would like (perhaps rashly) to call *themes*: characteristic attitudes and phenomena which constantly recur in various forms throughout a particular work, which point to the truly binding unity of the experience which the work communicates and through which *everything* can be justified. Zumthor calls themes a 'centre of interest which in the finished work is revealed in the form of a relatively rigid scheme of expression thanks to which an "object" is actualized through one of the objects in the book. The theme constitutes what might be called a field of expression, in the same way as one talks of semantic fields . . . The theme is not an ideal entity. It comes to life through a multiplicity of factors of expression, some of which are closely attached to it, whereas others only come in at irregular intervals to "amplify" it . . . [these would be better called] "motifs" . . .—their function is to give the theme existence in the verbal reality of the work. The theme of the amorous plea [in medieval literature] is [thus] communicated to us through the motifs of hope, fear, desire, service and prayer; the theme of the unhappily married woman through the motifs of the husband's hate, the absence of love or the secret friend.' [782, p. 76; v. too 208 and 225B.] This is useful providing once again one sees the motifs as elements which characterize one work and not exclusively a particular type of work.

The notion of theme is of supreme importance, to my mind, because, even more than the model-biased structuralist approach I have just been looking at, it avoids the fragmentation techniques (character/style/imagery/description/humour/social background/ideas and so on) which so many journalists and academics (and worst of all, academic journalists) feel to be adequate.

Thematic criticism can be either *conceptual* or *emotive*. It may deal with the concrete notions of a more or less intellectual nature such as ambition, jealousy, the unusual and the kind of notions referred to above—or it may be more specifically concerned with the unity of the work as a kind of 'sensation'. I intend to look at the conceptual themes first.

It is of course possible and no doubt useful to list the great conceptual themes in literature (because they are the fundamental keynotes of our experience): illusion and reality, power, communication, experience and maturity. But these labels by themselves are too vast to exemplify a particular piece of writing with any precision—the theme of prostitution (metaphorical rather than literal) can be applied to works as vastly different as *Illusions perdues*, *L'Education sentimentale* and *David Copperfield*! This kind of imprecision is a fault which mars Percy Lubbock's book, Barbara Hardy's otherwise penetrating study of George Eliot and even Wayne C. Booth's *Rhetoric of Fiction*. Fox's study of Villon's poetry makes a similar mistake with thematic headings like 'the beauty of women', 'love', 'devotion' etc.—which could equally well be applied to Victor Hugo, Dante, any troubadour one cares to mention, or D. G. Rossetti.

Conceptual thematic analysis is not necessarily more peculiar to prose than to verse—we should rid ourselves of this kind of prejudice. Eliot's *Four Quartets* are an experience of the *idea* of time which can be very precisely related to such phenomena as motionlessness:

> At the still point of the turning earth. . . .

or to that of simultaneity:

> In my beginning is my end. . . .

or to transience:

> O dark, dark, dark. They all go into the dark,
> The vacant interstellar spaces, the vacant into the vacant,
> The captains, merchant bankers, eminent men of letters . . .

and hope in the face of this. And these themes can be shown to have a stylistic dimension too. By repetition, the passage from *Burnt Norton* V ll. 137–59, quoted at the beginning of this book, constantly creates the sense of unity and permanence which the passage is preoccupied with [v. too 225B]. In the same way, the image patterns of a Shakespeare play may well point to intellectual concepts. The function of these at one level is in no way different from, say, the general keynote of economic, social and even individual decrepitude, allied very often to a mysterious journey, which is a striking feature of some novels by Julien Gracq (*Le Rivage des Syrtes* or *La Route*). Flaubert's *Salammbô*, much more than being an adventure story (with love interest . . .) about warring mercenaries in third-century B.C. Carthage, hangs together, it has been suggested, around the notion of immobility: a movement getting nowhere, achieving nothing, opposing factors locked in paralysed opposition [v. 186]—although I personally feel that its thematic unity is much more centrally related to the idea of cruelty and its attendant implications: individuals both isolated and the agents of isolation, self-centredness, individuals' inability to communicate except by destroying each other (not unrelated to immobility)—these are recurrent patterns made explicit and given density in a work where scenes of destruction and torture are very frequent.

Deep motive elements and the explicit ones of plot thus interrelate in a way which proves the validity of both. Fragmentation is thus avoided—an especially important consideration when one is dealing with a complex author. Proust, for example, is anything but brought to life by the kind of précis cum genesis study which Germaine Brée offers in *The Art of Criticism* [85]. Because, in part, Proust seems to be such a diffuse, digressive writer, any analysis of *A la Recherche du temps perdu* should preferably start with its permanent theme of distortion: the constantly recurrent uncertainty about the reality of things, Marcel's mistake about the room in which he thought he was sleeping, the unrealistic artist's impressions of Venice, aunt Léonie's imaginings, the obsessive snobbery of so many characters. Experience in Proust is a constant falsification, as Genette shows through the image of the palimpsest, the constant erasion of one idea or impression or event in favour of some other: 'feelings, memories and even forgotten things slide across from one character to another' [239, pp. 66–7] —it is a 'destructive movement which questions and casts doubt upon an emotional presence every moment of which seems in itself to be quite permanent' [239, pp. 52–3]. Such dominant motifs as distortion or erasion must be seen as coherent illumination for the fact that Proust's novel is about remembering—the act of reconstructing what is only partly retrievable, bringing things back from elsewhere or fitting them willy-nilly into a scheme of things. The passages directly concerned with memory (the madeleine episode or Marcel trying desperately to remember Mme d'Arpajon's name) and the meditations which spring from these incidents thus belong to a noticeably wider context (to which for example Charlus's antics to hide his true nature belong equally well). And of course the theme of distortion has another dimension inasmuch as Proust's novel is about writing a novel, the reshaping of material with a view to imposing coherence upon it, and therefore the danger that the searched-for reality might be lost in the process. The more superficial and obvious idea of memory would not allow us to explore the coherence of the novel to this extent. The fusion in Proust of art's intemporality and justifiably rich distortion and life's temporality and dangerous deformation can only be achieved at a particular level. At the level of real life human behaviour, the distortions of art are unacceptable because they falsify. They can be acceptable only when they become the *coherence* and therefore the true substance of the work.

Theme in this way becomes the flexible factor which gives each apparently disparate element its significance for the work as a whole.

A similar approach to Jane Austen's *Emma* would show how the notions of self-centredness and domination rank as key terms, together with insecurity. *The Portrait of a Lady* turns round the notion of compatibility, not just in Isabel Archer's marriage, nor even in merely human relationships—the book basically explores the extent to which the various elements of experience and reality actually fit. In contrary fashion, Conrad's *Heart of Darkness* is very much preoccupied with inconclusiveness and unsatisfactory 'restraint' as Guetti calls it [264, pp. 46 ff.]—the coherence of the book is the incoherence which reality seems to offer to the supposed story-teller Marlow—moral darkness and emptiness add depth to the central theme.

The works looked at here, with the possible exception of *A la Recherche du temps perdu*, are quite readily circumscribable, and even Proust has an area of preoccupation which, as we have seen, can be pinned down without too much difficulty.

There are, however, massive works of art, which demand our attention although they are at times disorganized—they do not appear to follow the rules. One thinks especially of a novel like *War and Peace.* It is not the multiplicity of its different plots which is disconcerting (*Gil Blas* is like that too) but rather the seemingly very disparate areas of interest it covers: historical theory, real events and characters as well as the extremely varied private lives and interests of fictitious people. I wonder whether it is adequate therefore to make do with an examination of the 'larger structural patterns which Tolstoy employed' and to relate them to such undoubtedly useful but excessively vague themes as the distance between the real and the artificial life, the superiority in this of intuition over logic, the heart over the head and the importance of cosmic submissiveness (either to history, nature or God) [v. 280, pp. 18–22]. These elements are important and to a certain extent they allow us to see general significance in particular events—but the truly dominant, cohesive themes of time, change and stability, restoration and rebirth would seem to be inadequately defined by them.

However difficult the solution, the problem is clear—and it can be raised with any kind or quality of literary work: to be critically preoccupied with the isolated elements of a text only inasmuch as they point to a more fundamental underlying definition of the reality which the work is communicating and creating. This means that, although we may be impressed with the documentary value of novels by Balzac, Zola, George Eliot or Dreiser, we must, if we are properly to assess them as expressions of reality, see the kind of reality they are defining—not just facts therefore, not just facts for facts' sake, but the world as something tangible, measurable and definable and hence (in a sense which many twentieth-century writers will abandon completely) dominatable and deterministic. Flashbacks are thus not a means of questioning the past as in Proust, but of showing the present to be *a logical result of that past* [v. 164, pp. 88–98]. Factuality as a theme (which would need refinement to make it applicable to the individuality of the writers mentioned) defines our reaction to other apparently unrelated elements.

A technique which has perhaps been insufficiently used is, once one has a thorough knowledge of a novel or a play, to examine in detail the way it begins. The elements given early on in a work very tightly condition our way of reacting to everything that is to come: modes, contexts and 'angles' of behaviour at this stage produce standards, a sounding-board against which our reactions to the rest of the work will be set. Notions of uncertainty and instability, leading to the key theme of incompatibility, occur at the very beginning of *The Portrait of a Lady.* In the opening pages of Flaubert's *Education sentimentale*, for example, a certain number of tendencies are set in motion and underscored which will constantly recur: in the bustle of leaving and the way characters shift from one idea to another, the notion of incoherence and dispersion is very clear—there is a real sense of passivity here too; in the conversations where characters appear to be following their own thoughts and not to be interested in those of other people, self-centred isolation and the inability to communicate offer typical themes—characters are clearly too intent on hiding their feelings from others. They are intent too (in ironic contradiction with their incoherence) on imposing a view of things, an interpretation of the world which corresponds to their prejudiced notions, their *idées reçues*. This all boils down to the feeling that from the beginning Flaubert is presenting us with human beings who systematically distort themselves and reality—in a world which has no true objective reality—an 'absurd' world in fact (in the twentieth-century philosophical sense of the term), as the subsequent events show.

Examination of a Balzac novel like *Illusions perdues* produces a radically different point of view. Different notions of coherence are involved: the coherence of Balzac's world is a general fact, the coherence of *L'Education sentimentale* is peculiar to that work at that time and is the result of a detailed presentation. Close inspection shows the themes of *Illusions perdues* to be highly individualistic. In the opening pages, we must reconcile Old Séchard's conservatism, David's researches into paper-making and Lucien's impending departure for Paris. This leads to the conclusion (again borne out by these characters' adventures throughout the novel) that *Illusions perdues* is fundamentally about new areas of experience (whereas, in marked contrast, *Eugénie Grandet* is about the notion of surprise) [749].

As is usual therefore, the kind of theme involved will tend to take on 'moral' overtones—just as lexical constants in a Baudelaire poem (*gouffre*, *noir*, *glacé*, *horreur* . . .) cannot be seen as purely abstract, non-moral elements [v. 274, 382 and my chapter 3]. In *Le Rouge et le Noir*, Stendhal establishes a central tension between truth and falsity, the real and the feigned [v. 748], binding characters as widely disparate as Mme de Rênal and Julien Sorel's father (in an opening passage) and showing that Julien himself in all his fluctuating hypocrisy is in no sense an isolated figure—he is part of a world which in the first paragraphs of the novel shows a characteristic shift from a pleasant exterior ('La petite ville de Verrières passe pour l'une des plus jolies de la Franche-Comté. . .') to a much more grimacing and antithetical truth: 'A peine entre-t-on dans la ville que l'on est étourdi par le fracas d'une machine bruyante et terrible en apparence . . .'

The study of expository techniques need not be restricted to the novel. Clemen, in *Shakespeare's Dramatic Art*, studies the opening scenes of *A Midsummer Night's Dream* and *Macbeth.* Here too patterns are set up for which each character, each event will offer a recognizable transformation. This is what Todorov points out in his analysis of *Les Liaisons dangereuses* [685, pp. 131–3] when he underlines recurrent motifs of planning, obstacles, flight and help.

There are, of course, drawbacks to this kind of approach if one is not particularly careful: there is a risk that 'by tearing passages out of their context one may miss important connections and come to view the material in an artificial vacuum' [704, p. 261]. Thematics should, on the contrary, explicitly replace the passage examined in the context of the whole work, as I hope the above analyses have shown in some small way, and as is masterfully demonstrated in Auerbach's *Mimesis* (based as it is on the analysis of a large number of extracts). The effect must be to show the peculiar distinctiveness (in literature at large) and particular relevance (to the work) of each passage. This is why the same event in different contexts will never have the same impact. The reception at the beginning of *Illusion perdues* is radically different in significance from the Vaubyessard ball in *Madame Bovary* or the Dambreuses' parties in *L'Education sentimentale.*

The impact of apparently similar themes will be similarly varied. Indeed, a comparative approach can be very useful. The individuality of, say, *Illusions perdues*, *David Copperfield* and

Middlemarch is clearly brought out by the way the theme of fulfilment is treated in each novel. The central notion will have to be radically redefined in each case.

Non-conceptual thematic analysis is the one considered nowadays to be real thematics—it deals, as I have suggested, with much more intangible notions such as atmosphere and mood. It is not even very easy to define (definition being formulated in this case after the practice got under way) [v. 663, p. 34]. Very often it is close to the idea of conceptual themes: '. . . the theme is a much more complicated thing than the word [; it is a] combination which works in relation to the context, both the successive contexts of the work and the metaphorical context which is the totality of the work itself. A theme only takes on importance in the organized network of relationships which are both linguistic and experiential . . . Of course once that kind of metaphorical necessity has been established [by the critic] one must try to find it in the [contextual] necessity of the work [with its succession of relationships]. This kind of structural convergence and verification is absolutely essential.' [v. 538, pp. 309–10.] Thus meaning is not in details: 'what is meaningful is the link between one fact and another and, if possible, several other facts, [ibid., p. 10]. For example, 'the word "star" has thematic value in Mallarmé, but what makes it thematic in Mallarmé is something quite different, it is the way the star manifests itself, shooting up, spreading out, the result of some other event and finally manifesting itself as an ultimate fortuity' [538, p. 309]. Definitions may, however, be more specifically concerned with 'atmospheric' analysis: 'Theme, the key notion of modern criticism, is simply the emotional coloration of any human experience in the sense that it brings into play the fundamental relationships of existence, that is to say the special way in which every man lives out his links with the world, with others and with God.' [176, p. 103.]

For this kind of critic, literature offers evidence of a state of mind, a state of receptivity even, as much as something actually realized. The sensibility of the writer and the way it expresses itself are the critic's main preoccupations. The gap between American New Criticism and French *nouveaux critiques* is therefore very marked here.

Hence Proust's fight against traditional criticism and his attempt in his study of Nerval to define the feel and not the meaning of sensation [547, p. 183]. Hence, too, the kind of analysis one could make of a writer like Camus with his preoccupation with the wind, sea and sun—just as determinant for meaning as the ideas expressed (and of course inseparable from them). Meursault lives essentially through the senses; the victims of the plague are oppressed and obsessed by the stifling heat: this is the true nature of their experience [v. 674, pp. 79–81].

These examples are perhaps rather loose and may offer an insufficient definition of the work as a whole (which true structural studies *must* undertake). This is also the case with the chapters devoted to literature in Matoré's *L'Espace humain* [pp. 205–36] where the presence or absence of time, gaps in the narrative, colours and heat and the nature of the physical impact of objects are used to give thematic meaning to novelists like Proust, Robbe-Grillet or Camus. In the latter, for example, there are three groups of colours in decreasing order of importance: black/white (or a light colour), red and brown. In *L'Etranger*, the whole structure of experience would seem to hinge on the degree of violence of colours and light involved. Light too is apparently a major expressive element in Gracq's *Le Rivage des Syrtes* (although I personally do not feel that this can be significant unless it is related to the dominant theme of decrepitude (which is both conceptual and emotional) mentioned above). Matoré's main aim in any case is to define ways of perceiving peculiar to a period (in contemporary literature colour is described mainly by reference to light or in relation to physiological experience [444, p. 222]) rather than to an individual work.

More precise analyses suit our purpose, I think. These could be said to include the kind of atmospheric (and not purely intellectual) tensions explored in poetry under the heading of paradox [v. 96, pp. 1–16, 17–39, 124–38; 302; 226]. But the important work involved here is that of critics like Poulet, Starobinski, J.-P. Richard. Because they are preoccupied with thematic study, they are interested in significant forms: *signifiant* rather than *signifié* [v. 48, pp. 268–9]. These critics do not cover all aspects of the technique involved. One thinks of Jean Rousset who, in studies like those on *Madame Bovary* or *Salammbô*, sees experience in terms of spatial relationships: looking down on a scene or a difference in height repeatedly separating two characters [605, 606]. One thinks too of Leavis, who, well before Rousset, talked about upwards and downwards movements in Keats [387]. Movement as a definition of experience is similarly present in a poem like Hugo's *Pente de la Rêverie* where the horizontal progression of time often contrasts with the vertical movement as the poet plunges more deeply into his experience (although here we are not so far from Poulet's approach, as we shall see).

Poulet, J.-P. Richard and others do not present a united phalanx either. Ricardou's justifiable criticism of Richard is only partially applicable to Poulet for example: 'In Richard the *textual* side of imaginative work is hardly visible. He gives the impression that the logic of imaginative writing is independent of the text which produces it . . . Whereas for some of us, the most important thing is not so much the world of [the writer's] imagination as the workings of the texts which give substance to that world.' [538, pp. 226–7.] The movement of the mind involved can be analysed in a variety of ways. Poulet is less supple than J.-P. Richard inasmuch as he systematically relates his reading of a large number of authors to a restricted number of concepts, *time* especially, but also space and circularity [v. 534]. These are approached with a distinctly metaphysical bias. The concepts do not merely relate to characteristic sequence (whether it be 'confused' or 'normal') —and yet his analyses of particular literary figures are in another sense most precise and relevant. In his study of Balzac [534, vol. II] (which with those devoted to Hugo, Mallarmé and Proust, is perhaps the finest example of his skills), he begins with the characters' central feeling of ambition and shows how this projects the individual mentally forward in time, the past existing only as a lead up to the future, and outwards in space: the individual invades the world. It seems that the world is devoid of obstacles; distances can be covered in a flash—so much so that time and space are abolished: 'to desire is to possess' (at least in the imagination). The phenomenon is also typified by a multiplicity of simultaneous desires and aspirations—a painful experience when real time and space take over again. The experience of time is twofold: inflexible futurity and continuity for the reader, and a present difficult to define for the characters in whom present, past and future may be confused. Often time is replaced by unique moments of high intensity but this eventually leads to the sense of time 'bursting in once again like a torrent'—a delirium of passion and therefore of the imagination. Once again reality is abolished. The experience of characters is thus saturated with the experience of time and related space as emotional forces.

It should be pointed out that Poulet does tend to indulge in generalizations on the basis of somewhat restricted examples, and this means that one should always relate his analysis to his examples (Balzac, the portrayer of ambition and not the author of *Le Lys dans la Vallée*) and not to all aspects of the writer from whom they are drawn. However the *relative* suppleness of his techniques becomes very clear when one compares the Balzac study to the way he tackles Hugo [534, vol. II]. The Hugo poem (and the one mainly referred to is the first one of *La Légende des Siècles: la Vision d'où est sorti ce livre* although *La Pente de la Rêverie* is also relevant here) begins in an indeterminate place with confused, moving masses which expand and become more distinct, although at first with no semblance of order. The main impression is one of constant piling up, proliferation and expansion. This relates to time too, for it is another aspect of space: the confusion of the past impinges on the present. Such is Hugo's awareness of things and even of his thought: a huge mass flowing over him—all general and individual experience merging into time. As to the links between dream, imagination and perception, the characteristic dilation of the real is paralleled by that of the dream world. All is intermeshed, all becomes hollow, porous, permeable. The poet's vain attempts seem to be directed, 'in the emptiness of thought', towards fighting the proliferation and 'condensing a misty core of imagery in order to make it into reality, the whole of reality' which is ultimately equated with God. Such an experience cannot but be one suffused with terror. Experience which seems to be directionless, delirious, thus takes on a positive significance—provided it is described in a way which refuses to extract ideas from it (a favourite academic game) and sees it as a state and movement of perception, the poet's gaze subjected to and struggling with the pullulation of an internal and external world. This particularizes the nature of a specific number of Hugo poems.

Poulet's sensitivity and powers of expression offer tremendously penetrating accounts of a wide variety of writers, or rather of the emotional 'area' in which those writers move. Defects, inevitably, are not lacking: partiality, the tendency not even to consider individual works as a whole and to take anything as grist for one particular mill (Poulet's study of Flaubert owes more to the early drafts of *Madame Bovary* than to the finished work!). We may, at times, be tempted to feel that the true deep structure achieved by Poulet's method is rather that of his own essays than of the works he happens to be studying.

This may help to explain why another critic's analysis of Hugo based on similar principles can, at one and the same time, be equally acceptable and radically different. I am thinking particularly of Riffaterre's studies [v. 593 and 588] where notions of terror, spectral visitations and the concrete expression of abstractions are given pre-eminence.

Poulet's bias is perhaps justified, for in the eyes of critics like him, as I have already suggested, the true reality of the work can only exist in the mind of the beholder [176, pp. 70 ff.]. This is an attitude which Poulet seems to have come over to in recent years. His preface to the second volume of the *Etudes sur le temps humain*, if I read it correctly, rejects the notion of the subjective existence of literary form; his essay *Phénoménologie de la Conscience critique* states quite categorically on the other hand [p.

17] that 'a book only exists because someone is reading it', another demonstration of the inseparability of form and content.

In view of all these considerations, it is clear that distinctions between poetry and prose will tend to break down. Indeed, Poulet does not seem to distinguish between them at all: there is no *essential* difference between the study of Hugo and that of Balzac. Perhaps this justifies even further my feeling that adequate description of a literary work should try to take into account such apparently intangible but (if literature has anything to do with life) definitely central aspects of a literary work—for *literature can only be 'significant'*, as Cleanth Brooks points out [91, p. 194], *by being an experience* rather than by being any mere statement about experience or any mere abstraction of experience.

Thus it is useful here to mention Stephen Booth's demonstration that the essential 'climate' of *Hamlet* may be defined as *patterns of frustration*: 'throughout the play, the audience gets information or sees action it once wanted only after a new interest has superseded the old' [80, p. 143]. The information given is less important as such therefore (or at least not important merely as facts) than its timing and the frustrated impatience it instils in the audience. A pattern of (ultimately resolved) stresses is essential to our experience of the play [v. 91, p. 186] or any work of art for that matter—its definition is thus equally essential.

The danger in non-conceptual thematic analysis is of course vagueness and impressionism—this is just as dangerous as the dead-end erudition, the stereotyped abstractions and the threadbare ideas which make up too much university teaching. Both of these kinds of 'analysis' are more easily or lazily achieved than the precise delicacy required to express the unique affective quality of an individual work. Poulet shows how this may be done—as does Jean-Pierre Richard in, for example, his study of the flat, toneless atmosphere ('fadeur') in Verlaine [568]. But we do not, I think, need to have their writing skills, or to subscribe to Poulet's contention that criticism is a work of art parallel to the work criticized [536, p. 25], to attempt to define the atmosphere of a work, its fluctuations and tensions in non-conceptual terms.

Barthes, whose attempts at stylistic rivalry with Poulet are in the main unfortunate and who is too often given to pretentious jargon, nevertheless offers us an interesting example of the way atmospheric definition can be achieved in his *Michelet par lui-même*. Here he shows Michelet to be expressing himself within an organized network of obsessions made up of such curiously associated elements as smoothness, history as a plant, water as a fish, the world as a female, dry death, death as sleep and death as the sun. Jean-Pierre Richard's definition of Sainte-Beuve is very similar [572, pp. 205 ff.]. Expression in Sainte-Beuve would seem to be dominated by notions of liquidness, the poverty of things, their scrawny unhealthiness, muffled noises, mistiness and perfume.

The material, factual, physical tangibility of the book is replaced, therefore, for these scholars by a central *awareness* [v. 536, p. 26]. It is the nature of this awareness (*in* the work but brought to unique reality by the awareness of the critic himself) which one must seek to track down. The links with phenomenology are clear—as is seen in the title of Poulet's essay. They are also seen in Poulet's statement at the beginning of the second volume of *Etudes sur le temps humain*, that all thought is thought about something, and that [v. 536] all thought is thought by someone. The awareness of the critic is founded on the fact that this awareness 'behaves like that of someone other than himself' [536, p. 23].

Again variations will occur from one critic to another. On the one hand, we have Sartre's approach in *Qu'est-ce que la littérature?*, on the other, Starabinski who, for Poulet, is too intellectual, whilst Marcel Raymond is too subjective, although like Jean Rousset he aims through structural analysis to use the study of literary objects in a perhaps more conceptualizable way to reach the subjective principle which dominates them. J.-P. Richard, on the other hand, like Jacques Rivière (a much earlier critic) and Starobinski, undertakes 'a form of criticism which is initially intuitive of the "thought" behind the work before objectively noting the forms through which that thought is fixed and developed' [536, pp. 28 ff.].

Yet another and rather more amusing form of thematic criticism (part conceptual, part emotive) is offered by Jean-Paul Weber who firmly believes that individual traumatic experiences in childhood are centrally determinant for the thematic structure of future works. Hence the clocks which Weber resurrects in the works of Vigny and the fires in Victor Hugo (the central presence of which specialists would hardly suspect) [v. 732 and 733]. The theories are advanced here with the naïve certainty of a nineteenth-century scientist and on the basis of frighteningly truncated readings.

Weber serves perhaps to highlight the danger of excessive subjectivity which I have already mentioned. A work does have objective features whose impact is at least partly the same for all and which may therefore be described. J.-P. Richard's statement that he is practising 'not a stylistics of form but a stylistics of theme' [538, p. 307] gives arms to someone like Jean Ricardou quoted earlier—especially as Richard's major study of Mallarmé is singularly lacking in systematic quotation (quotations and references being mainly relegated to a position of secondary importance at the back of the volume [573]).

The thematic approach can here be seen to fall into two main tendencies: *polythematicism* where, even if a main line of research (as in Poulet) is maintained, the criteria are very wide, revaluation is radical with every new author studied and the multiplicity of components which go to make up the theme is underlined; or *monothematicism* where the attempt is to tie an artist down to one basic principle: not just the clocks Weber universalizes in Vigny, but the 'fadeur' which J.-P. Richard examines in Verlaine's *Fêtes galantes* and *Chansons sans paroles* [568].

With both types of approach, we are dealing with elements which are not merely to be noted as non-rational motifs but which are also to be seen in characteristic recurrence as having *metaphorical* value. As with all techniques of structural analysis, no part has purely literal value but rather expresses the wider impact of the whole. The trick in the opening pages of Stendal's *Chartreuse de Parme* of topics being taken up and dropped before they have been fully treated is, in a sense, a metaphor for the inconclusiveness which characterizes the novel as a whole (Fabrice who sees the battle of Waterloo through the back door; the terse way the novel fizzles out). The boundary between individual tropes (the natural prey of the listers, classifiers and tabulators of this world) thus disappears. This would be very important even if non-conceptual thematics were to achieve nothing else.

We have seen that theme and structure studies can relate to the not negligible problem of genre. These are, of course, not the only possible approach. One thinks, for example, of the categories of the novel according to Lukács: abstract idealism (*Don Quijote*), psychological (*Oblomov* and *L'Education sentimentale*), educative (*Wilhelm Meister*) [417; v. 247]. But they are perhaps too wide in scope—they are also highly debatable, for if one is going to classify it as anything, *L'Education sentimentale* must be seen as an ironic (or even anti-) *Bildungsroman*, and therefore stand with *Wilhelm Meister*.

Other approaches take into account norm figures—those which are 'predictable in terms of a norm', like Dickens's heroes and heroines—but not, as Northrop Frye would have us believe, inconceivable in modern literature (*Herzog* and *The First Circle* are there to prove it) [v. 228, p. 70]. Norm figures are the archetypes we can expect to find in the categories Lukács explores and defines: young or at least ambitious men and women in a *Bildungsroman*, characters out of touch with a reality they have not yet sufficient maturity to grasp, trying to interpret it according to their own abstractions. Such norms, according to Frye, may set up a logic not inherent in the story [228, p. 56] but rather 'an impatient sense of absolutism' (they may, for example, be strongly manipulated towards a happy ending), and this, in Dickens, might be related to the New Comedy tradition of Plautus, Ben Jonson and Molière and to the characteristic situation involved in the clash of two societies. The heroes and heroines are thus according to Frye neither real characters (whatever that may mean) nor caricatures—they are rather 'humors', endowed with an overriding characteristic [p. 56]. Balzac's characters might fit into such a scheme too.

Again the dangers in this are as apparent as its uses. It can so easily tip over into the kind of subject imposed in desperation on unimaginative M.A. candidates: the rogue in medieval Portuguese literature, love and marriage in seventeeth-century French comedy, the devil from then till now. Not useless subjects in themselves but a very pit and trap to the unwary and the undersupervised.

Great subjects are important, as I have already said: they point to deep and important patterns of human experience and behaviour. The study of archetypes is therefore most useful and in no sense in opposition to close textual examination—providing, of course, they are not seen as a departicularizing end in themselves but as preliminary constituent elements.

These may well not be purely literary in origin—they may be related to general human make-up and psychology. Indeed one of the theories put forward by Jungian psychology is that beneath the variations of conscious human behaviour there is a collective unconscious, myths and situations common to all men, whose literary expression is revealed through archetypal contexts and attitudes. This is a fascinating area which I do not really feel competent to discuss, especially as far as its basic premises are concerned: does this collective unconscious really exist or has Jung made it all up? The work of Northrop Frye and the *Symposium* number on myths [496] would tend to demonstrate that the indispensable and deep human value of a literary text is borne out by such phenomena—and their identifiable recurrence is some proof of their existence.

Perhaps the best introduction to this kind of study is the work which put it on the map: Maud Bodkin's *Archetypal Patterns in Poetry*. The author makes her aims quite clear in the opening pages: '... in poetry ... we may identify themes having a particular form or pattern which persists from age to age, and which corresponds to a pattern or configuration of emotional tendencies in the minds of those who are stirred by the theme.' [75, p. 4.] It is an emotional approach rather than one which demands critical judgement [p. 29], for emotional forces are important in the selection or the fashioning of the material of a poem [p. 40]. Archetypes are important inasmuch as the individual is linked with humanity at large [p. 8].

Maud Bodkin examines a number of texts using chapter and page headings like 'the image of woman', 'the devil, the hero and God', 'poetry and dream'. She suggests that such elements as the father king (in *Lear*), the idea of rebirth (in *The Ancient Mariner*) or the heavenly journey (in Dante or Virgil) are deep-seated patterns of experience which we recognize instinctively (although unconsciously) and to which we respond powerfully.

Freud's huge breakthrough in our understanding of human personality and motivation led to a profound rethinking about literature in all sorts of directions and not merely in connection with the archetypes I have just mentioned. Such a phenomenon is of great importance of course provided the work of literature is not turned into a case history of purely therapeutic value (the exponents of which I am ignoring here—they tend to date from the early years of psychoanalysis anyway). A good account of psychoanalytical criticism is given in Hyman's *The Armed Vision* [v. too 754]. Psychology now replaces for the critic yesterday's 'knowledge of the human heart' [176, p. 114]. Again there are archetypal implications but they are not necessarily as with Maud Bodkin at the level of actual expression—they may be the drives and tensions *behind* the work.

Gaston Bachelard (who has shown the rich potential of psychological criticism) can, it is true, write: 'when the poet invents those great images which reveal the intimate nature of the world, is he not remembering something?' [31, p. 94]—which sounds very much like Maud Bodkin. But his more characteristic preoccupation would seem to relate to an idea of poetry in which the major role is accorded to the subconscious, involuntary expression and the way things reverberate in the minds of the creator and the reader.

The nature of Bachelard's studies can be seen in the titles of his books: *Air and Dreams*, *Water and Dreams*, *A Candle's Flame* etc. In each case, the preoccupation is with the emotional, associative impact of elemental phenomena on an individual sensibility. They are the archetypes of the imagination and may be seen in examples drawn from literary texts—not, it should be noted (and again this reminds us of Maud Bodkin, or even Poulet), the systematic analysis of a rounded literary work. Bachelard puts himself into a state of non-rational receptiveness which considers something other than the structure of the poem. We are dealing here with a different kind of unity: that of the phenomena emanating from an isolated image (sometimes quoted second-hand) or even the isolated word. This is because Bachelard is, as he says, first and foremost, 'a dreamer about words' [31, pp. 1–4]. He is a man who nourishes and transforms their initial impact, for his imagination, like that of the poet, consists in 'the ability to deform the images which one initially perceives, and especially the ability to free us from those initial images and change them' [28, p. 7]. Hence the proliferation of responses which Bachelard traces from a central point —a controlled dream state, not merely something which is described passively but rather something actively developed.

The results of this are literary in the most original way for although it is text-based, it leads to an examination of the relations between literature and a wider phenomenology of the imagination. Bachelard (whose criticism depends so much on the sensitivity and articulateness of its exponent) tells us many original and important things about the emotional depth involved in our experience of literature, of words (for he is much more preoccupied with the verbality of literature than Poulet or even perhaps Jean-Pierre Richard would seem to be. For these two, the movements of the sensibility and even pre-verbal states of mind are of primary significance).

Psychoanalytical techniques can be more concerned with the impact of individual works than this, of course. The work may be defined as a psychological entity: 'inasmuch as the structures referred to here are not sociological but psychic, they will have to be described in psychoanalytical terms', as Barthes undertakes to do in *Sur Racine* [v. 176, p. 12].

More than Barthes, of course, Charles Mauron has shown himself to be a major exponent of textual analysis based on psychoanalytical studies in France. In the words of a *Times Literary Supplement* reviewer, Mauron 'starts from the principle, or assumption, that every author has a "social ego", that part which deals with the outside world, and a "creative ego", the self which evolves patterns of phantasms to mask, or cope with, the strain of living'. The work of art which results from this thus becomes 'an inner drama which is as constant as it is multifarious' ... 'an obsessive schema to which the individual writer keeps returning in his attempt to keep his psychological balance'. This is 'not scientifically verifiable', it is based on 'assumptions' and 'intuition' [168B]. Man is, therefore, in his superficial manifestations totally divorced from his works (the opposite of what Sainte-Beuve would have thought) just as our behaviour is not a direct expression of the drives which occasion it. This does not exclude, in Mauron's case, the use of biographical data to set up his hypothesis about the work: 'In a man's writings are to be found not only the constants of his mind but also the variables of his existence. Everything must be taken into account.' [450, p. 13.] Thus in his *Psychanalyse de Mallarmé*, he attaches great importance to the early death of the poet's sister (and finds 'evidence' of the trauma caused in several poems). This is purely speculative, as is frequently the case with Mauron: his studies are peppered with expressions like 'in all probability', 'there is a strong chance that' and 'evidently'. But I am not sure that this really matters. Criticism is not an exact science at any time—a working hypothesis is not aimed at discovering the absolute Truth but rather at underlining an acceptable coherence—and in both this study and in *Mallarmé l'obscur* Mauron is able to point to networks of recurrent imagery which are very important for the understanding of such a difficult author: the angel-musician, hair-flames, the setting sun, the triumph of love and death. The 'Truth' here lies in the fact that however debatable one might find the initial hypothesis, the elements established as a result are really there. It is interesting to read that in Mallarmé 'idealised apparitions are always given musical connotations'—one thinks of the sonnet 'en -yx', *Apparition*, *Sainte*, *La Pénultième est morte*. The work viewed as a psychic phenomenon in its own right thus takes on a very real literary pertinence (even if we perhaps learn very little about psychoanalysis in the process).

Psychoanalytical criticism is in no sense restricted to France of course. It has been a steadily rolling American bandwagon for some time, as Hyman shows. It has been an excuse for the worst kinds of humbug, inevitably. But at the same time, it has produced extremely useful results. For example, Hyman quotes the way E. A. Armstrong [17; v. 328, p. 176] takes the death-eye-socket-mouth-vault-womb image chain which Caroline Spurgeon had found so central to the poetry of Shakespeare's plays and points to the fact that we are dealing with a chain of 'hollow' symbols extending between birth and death.

The kind of approach which makes use of psychoanalysis (or any other source of possible explanation) when necessary strikes me as being much more useful, and unlike any blinkered, one-track minded, ideology-based thinking, much less in danger of distorting the truth, than an absolutist approach.

The mind (collective or individual) is not the only source of archetypes. At a more conscious level, the structure of a text may be considered to be an extension or a résumé of structures in society at a particular time and existing independently of the literary work.

The social context aspect of criticism is a growing area of study. This fact is not independent of the wider realization that literature, like anything else which one's sensibility comes into contact with, is made up of systems of signs (meaningful stimuli) and these (as Barthes shows in his *Mythologies* and his *Essais critiques*) are in no way exclusive to literature (although art may manipulate them more systematically). There is, too, the idea that the literary work may be the *parole* of which society (which can perhaps never be defined as a wholly concrete entity) is in a sense the *langue.*

In a loose sense, the second part of my chapter on *Meaning* brought up these ideas. Lukács's *Theory of the Novel*, with its classification according to civilization types, offers a variant of this. It is a very valuable and penetrating line to adopt—witness Girard's statement about the novel: 'The debasement of the world of the novel is caused by a more or less acute ontological sickness which is paralleled within the sphere of the novel by an increase in metaphysical aspiration, that is to say, of debased aspiration.' [v. 247, p. 19.] The whole pattern of behaviour of so many romantic heroes from Musset's 'enfant du siècle' to Dorothea Brooke, and of the society they inhabit, is deeply illuminated by this statement, which, of course, has wide non-literary significance too.

But, as is to be expected, more rigid analyses are quite conceivable and these are exemplified by the work of Lucien Goldmann in such studies as *Pour une sociologie du roman* and *Le Dieu caché.* Although he does not seem anywhere to define the term, the search is for a very real structure (and not merely for the notation of motifs). The attempt is to 'dissolve the literary work in [a wider culture]' and leads to the '*logos* common to all the synchronic manifestations of a culture and a society'—a kind of positivism without causality [663, p. 38]. The structure of the work is therefore perhaps not so much the extension or the expression of social structures but rather part of them [532, pp. 1465–6]. Thus Goldmann can himself, rather clumsily but comprehensibly, talk about 'the historical and social character of the objective meaning of the emotional and intellectual life of an individual'. [247, p. 208.] The study of literature, according to this view, is, therefore, in a sense, a genetic one but it is considered, at the same time, to be essentially structuralist. In this instance, the structures are a coherent part of the social group (seventeenth-century Jesuits or nineteenth-century bourgeois) to which the work belongs [v. 247, p. 23 and 176, p. 131]. These socio-literary structures are of supreme importance: 'any group of works by one particular individual is not in itself a meaningful structure' [246, p. 109]. The creative individual in this context is thus less important (as is to be expected in Marxist thinking) than the social group. The novel is the expression of a 'coherent mental structure which corresponds to what is called a "world view". Such a structure could only be worked out by a group; the individual is merely [!] able to take this structure to a very high level of coherence and transpose it on to the level of the imaginary creation of conceptual thought.' [247, p. 28.] Or again: 'The genius expresses the group, but it is the group which is the milieu in which cultural creativity takes place, especially that kind of creativity which produces a world view.' [176, p. 130.] The work is, thus, complete as a social phenomenon. The world view is an operative concept which intelligibly links the individual and the group. It is the 'set of aspirations, feelings and ideas which links the members of a group (which most frequently is a social class) and contrasts them with other groups' [176, p. 130]. What is important is the fact that for Goldmann 'individual existence is not inserted into the framework foreign to it as a means of clarifying that existence but rather that the external framework is inserted into an individual existence in order to see how the infinite multiplicity of meanings which a given objective situation makes available acquires significance through the human activity which commits itself to that situation' [176, pp. 155–6]. Literary form thus becomes 'the transposition on to a literary plane of daily life in a consumer-biased individualist society' [247, p. 24].

Goldmann's work is on the fringes of textual criticism proper. I have made brief mention of it mainly because it completes the notion of structure with which this chapter is concerned. His is, in no sense, an isolated example, either. J. Ehrmann sees anthropological archetypes in the notions of exchange which make up the thematic structure of Corneille's *Cinna* [v. 195, p. 180]. E. M. Zimmermann says of Proust that 'society is not an external reality which [he] observes sociologically as a side-issue to the basic preoccupations of his novel, it is merely the enlarged reflection of human beings in their contacts with others, like someone about whom one person might know one thing, someone else something else, depending on the time of his life when they met, but who cannot be entirely comprehended [779, p. 439].

Julia Kristeva comes very near to Goldmann too when in explaining the structure of the French novel in the fifteenth century, she sees it as 'the result of a transformation of several other structures: scholasticism, courtly poetry, urban oral literature (advertising), the carnival. The transformational method leads us to situate social structure with a social entity considered as a textual entity' [366, p. 443]. C. L. Barber, in *Shakespeare's Festive Comedy*, talks, with reference to the plays, of a saturnalian pattern through local mediation (May Games etc.), beyond which may be discerned a social pattern as permanent as society [292, p. 151].

The technique is not without its defects. These are apparent in my last reference and become quite clear in Starobinski's suggestion that 'social' structuralism does not take into account the permanent fluctuations to which society is subjected [v. 663, p. 38]—not to mention the fact (looking at a quite different aspect) that criticism which cuts out stylistic considerations altogether is tending to make the text examined something less than literature.

The idea of construction, unity, structure (call it what you will) is as essential to literature, and therefore to criticism, as ambiguity. If we search for the way features recur and parallel or contrast with each other (whether they be linguistic or behavioural), we are certain to be examining in the most direct and fundamental manner what the work really means.

This does not, however, mean that structural ideas cannot be taken too far. The last example given above illustrates one danger. It is not that the critic should be encouraged to confuse art and life in any simplistic manner—this is indeed Doubrovsky's mistake when he says that 'the weakness of structuralist analysis is that it thinks that it can account, through a combination of operational formulae and signs, for the tangible movement of real existence and lulls itself into thinking that in the last resort human experience may be comprehended scientifically whereas only dialectical comprehension is adequate' [176, p. 18]. This seems to miss the point and to ignore the fact that structuralism is a means of expressing the cohesion of a work of art and that this cohesion is distinct from everyday life. Or, to put it differently, a novel is 'a complex structure which is in its totality constructive of meaning rather than . . . an imitation of life' [474, p. 201].

Once this has been said, it is still necessary to look at the other side of things and to work out to what extent *sequential* analysis can at least be a useful support to the nowadays more popular notion of structure.

Perhaps as good a starting-point as any is to look at the other shortcomings of 'structure'.

CHAPTER EIGHT

SEQUENCE

Dissatisfaction with a structural approach will tend to centre on results achieved. We may tax structure with superficiality and unoriginality—it is a form of analysis which only reaches infrastructures, the least original aspect of a work, and its most static [512, p. 170]. This is borne out by the fact that semiological studies and the like are principally concerned with very straightforward, not to say downright simple, texts: detective stories, *Jehan de Saintré* (Julia Kristeva), Boccaccio (Todorov—in addition to the formally simple *Liaisons dangereuses*)—all of which must have taken some finding, given the natural bent of most modern critics. I find the repetitive references to these texts just a little suspicious.

The desire to generalize and establish laws at all costs (or the fear of being too specific) is certainly not critically laudable (whatever the linguistic or semantic bonuses may be). Characteristically, Barthes's description of narrative mechanisms [46B] is too general to be of specific, practical value. We may, therefore, be mistrustful of aims and results when we read that 'structural studies are not interested in the work of literature itself. They are anxious to define the properties of that special form of expression which is the literary form of expression. Every work is then considered merely to be the manifestation of a much more abstract, general structure, of which it only constitutes one possible realisation.' [688, p. 102.]

One of the problems here is that we may well be left with a series of patterns which the individual work only partly fills. It is as if we were to say that a sonnet was a fourteen line poem and nothing more.

I think Valéry is mistaken when he states that '... fine works are the children of their form which is born before them' [707, vol. II; v. vol. I, pp. 658, 1244, 1504]. Once again the specific semantic properties of a particular work are being ignored. Propp in his study of the folk tale has been shown to do the very same thing [670, p. 808], and Propp's influence on structural literary criticism is well known.

The trap the structuralist approach sets and springs lies in the idea that we should constantly be preoccupied with similarity. And yet Leavis demonstrates the importance of difference when he compares descriptions of Cleopatra in *Anthony and Cleopatra* and *All for Love* [385]—a point fortified and extended by Philip Hobsbaum who brings in the source passage from Plutarch [309]. Structural technique tends, when faced with such phenomena, to be less interested in form and the ordering of information than is acceptable.

Obviously, I am not trying to denigrate structuralism. I am merely trying to suggest the value of the kind of balanced attitude put across by W. J. Harvey: '[Structuralism] has undeniably thrown much light on many novels and has made impossible the retreat to certain older fashioned inanities, but it has also tended to petrify into a mechanical routine which substitutes a skill in handling formal properties for a full and responsible reaction to the total work.' [293, p. 99.] This kind of bloodless impersonality, as Harvey points out [p. 153], can be just as much of a distortion as more conventional approaches.

Moreover, structure, like (perhaps even more than) anything else, is exposed to over-selection and the elimination of material which does not fit into the law-giving pattern. Jean-Pierre Richard's mere handful of quotations in a 600-page study of Mallarmé is unsatisfactory for that reason, as I have said [v. too 664]—there is no attempt at systematic analysis of individual poems. And yet, if they are to appear without bias, critics must take relevance and apparent digression into account—this is what the total impact of a work involves, and it is not out of the structuralist's reach provided he can avoid the temptation to cut corners. Coherence in a work is not necessarily so neat and simple as some (Weber is an extreme example) would wish.

There is perhaps a distinction to be made between the total impact of a work and its coherence—the first to some degree being an 'objective' element, the second will relate to questions of the work's logic and, ultimately, value (as will be seen in my concluding chapter). I am not convinced, however, that structural considerations have yet reached the stage when apparent superfluities and digressions can be indicated and satisfactorily described. It may be some time before we get beyond the tendency David Lodge mentions whereby structural critics distort a text by highlighting unrepresentative elements [411, p. 80]. This, in spite of scientific pretentions, creates a structure which is that of the critic's mind or personality. Such hidden subjectivity is as dangerous as the indiscriminate listing of structural elements which have nothing to do with literature [584, pp. 202 ff.].

Jakobson (whom this criticism concerns, as we have seen) tends also to put abstract formulae and patterns first—binary correspondences, rhyme and rhythm patterns [v. too 343]. Even word patterns are seen initially as patterns and not as words with their centrally important emotional impact.

In the looser studies of unity, like the analysis of key words, the tendency to be over-selective and prejudiced is still frequent, as David Lodge suggests [411, p. 149]. The work is thus turned into the untiring repetition of a kind of cliché. This, like all the rest, cannot be seen as true semantic criticism of the kind established and exemplified by Richards, Empson and Cleanth Brooks. Perhaps because non-semantic patterns (especially in a foreign language) are much easier to establish, down-to-earth, specific, line-by-line meaning tends to be avoided on a large scale in favour of genre-biased embryonic patterns.

I am, of course, being a little unfair, for advances in structuralist techniques will surely eradicate many growing pains. But for some time to come, practical critics will have to be cautious. If we have reached a stage when the novel as well as poetry can be studied (because structure can now be worked out by reference to things other than imagery), the gap between form and the content realized in that form is still there and will perhaps always be there: 'It is easy enough to see the implicit meaning hidden within the exterior shell once the methodology has been learned, harder to decide why the inner sense should have taken just this form.' [602, p. 35.]

One can thus see the justification for Jean Onimus's assertion that connotations rather than structures are what literature is really about [512, p. 102]—which points fairly and squarely to the indispensable importance of individual and specific meaning.

And this in turn brings us back to the too often forgotten fact that literature is about, or a reflexion of, human beings. Anyone who, like Greimas, can study the structural semantics of Bernanos without giving a single quotation or offering a single specific allusion is not providing information useful to the critic [259]. This is another reason why so-called purely objective studies break down: '[A work of art] is not only a structure to be analysed descriptively, as the Russian and Czech formalists assume. It is a totality of values which do not adhere to the structure but constitute its very nature. All attempts to drain value from literature have failed and will fail because its very essence is value.' [739, pp. 51–2.] For *value* here it would be very easy to substitute *emotion*, the association between our own experience and that which the work is describing to us. I think the links between literature and reality (a complex problem which I looked at in the chapter on meaning) thus further strengthen the need to avoid an exclusively structuralist approach. Things in a literary work are not purely functional—character, for example, is a function *and* an end in itself which must interest us for itself. We are dealing with humanity and not merely with pieces on a chess-board [293, p. 152 and 744, pp. 212 ff.]. The characteristic merit of Philip Rahv's article (which I have found so useful) [555] is that it reminds us that the novel is closely related to life (poetry too, it might be added)—a fact which shows us how narrow and desiccated some twentieth-century 'criticism' has become. Rahv quotes Trilling who, having noted that, for many critics, money in Dostoievsky has taken on symbolic value, comments: 'as if no-one ever needed . . . spent . . . gambled . . . squandered the stuff—as if to think of it as an actuality were subliterary' [555, p. 286 Note]. The point being that 'whatever symbolic value we may discover in the story is incremental to its actuality . . . it is more gratuitous than necessary' [p. 288].

To shift from an exclusively structuralist standpoint is therefore to bring back the perfectly acceptable notion that a novel is a story or a poem is about feelings (or may even be a story too). It is to realize that literature is both the reproduction of reality and (by the organization of that mimesis into greater coherence) the creation of meaning [v. 474, p. 213].

Lubbock is therefore not wrong because he insists on the imitative quality of literature, but rather because he makes light of questions of cohesion by saying such things as 'we know of novels which everybody admits to be badly constructed but so full of life that it does not appear to matter' [415, p. 10], and ignores what has been called 'the intrinsic conflict between the imaginary and the real' [476, p. 28]. Such a tension does not exclude moral, human considerations, as Leavis demonstrates when (in a way, it will be noticed, not unconnected with a structuralist view-point) he talks about Maggie Tulliver whose immaturity is unsatisfactorily shown because 'to understand immaturity would be to "place" it, with however subtle an implication, by relating it to mature experience. But when George Eliot touches on these given intensities of Maggie's inner life the vibration comes directly and simply from the novelist, precluding the presence of a maturer intelligence than Maggie's own.' [386, p. 54.] Here, too briefly quoted, is the essential combination of analytic and moral criticism which we should all aim at and which excessive preoccupation with structure so often impedes.

The isolationism of structure can quite easily be broken by realizing that structure cannot really exist without its apparent opposite, sequence. This fact, indeed, underlies many structuralist statements: '. . . equivalence in sound projected into the *sequence* as its constituent principle . . .' [335, p. 368, my italics]. This is Jakobson. Todorov cannot avoid using the idea of episodes as a key term in his thought [686, pp. 94–5]. Kuentz for his part finds himself talking about the syntax of the text [371, p. 9].

All this implies not stasis but movement—one thing coming after another. It is possible to say that an individual work is comparable to a transformational grammar, but this can only be meaningful if one remembers that this 'grammar' has been created *as the work goes along.*

Moreover, as my quotation (v. p. 193 above) from Charles Rosen hints, it is a primary principle that if recurrence, equivalence and the like are fundamental structural notions, *nothing is really recurrent in literature.* Not even a refrain. The pattern may be the same, but the new episode, image, phenomenon, which confirms that pattern, *is something different*, an addition not a mere confirmation. If Constant's *Adolphe* is about the nature of the self from the first page onwards, the way this phenomenon is explored varies and develops continually. We are similarly more struck by the new meanings and information appearing in a poem than by the fact that rhyme schemes, metre and even syntax may be constant.

Texts cannot thus be seen purely as a space, a state. The different elements of a work are to some extent separable—as when we quite legitimately illustrate experience in our own lives by a quotation or some other kind of allusion.

Any work reveals constant shifts in emphasis and association which structuralism cannot account for. The link between characters at any moment, in say *Anna Karenina* or *The Golden Notebook*, is never reproduced at an earlier or later stage. For one thing, we either know less or more about them.

Because of this general fact we should perhaps realize that style must be defined sequentially as well as spatially. If 'all elements in an utterance are stylistically pertinent . . . the succession of contrasts sets up a discontinuity in that utterance' [287, p. 92].

And so, discontinuity and permutation are key-words too. When Riffaterre says that 'several different images can be seen as variants of a single semantic structure' [584, pp. 232–3], *the emphasis must be placed as much on variation as on similarity.* In

Les Beaux quartiers, there is a point [16B, p. 139] where Aragon uses a series of disjointed comparisons: stepping-stones like broken Pompeian columns, siesta-time like artificial night in a film, the sun weighing like a knee on the main character's head, plane trees like men stripped of their flesh. These comparisons hang together because they point to the character's shifting disorganized state of mind—but, because they are so very striking, they nevertheless offer a linear experience of the disjointed, of fragmentation.

Even when fragmentation is not characteristic of a particular sequence (and such a phenomenon is rare), the sequential nature of an experience should be carefully described. This is not at all old-fashioned. In addition to the modern examples already given, one could cite a critic like Poulet whose work is dotted with such expressions as 'from that point onwards', 'thereafter, once again, everything changes', 'this whirling universe thus appears now . . .', 'suddenly' [534, vol. II, pp. 214 ff.].

The axis of Poulet's studies is the reader's experience as a work unfolds before him. The links, at this level, with Riffaterre's notions of style and his theories of surprise and expectation are clear. It relates both to verbal and non-verbal elements which are inseparable from sequence rather than from structure.* The text creates its own norms, as we have seen, and these norms are flexed, flouted or modified by the series of events the text is made up of. Of course the establishment of norms and their contrasting use go on simultaneously: the expository section of a novel is never totally clear-cut. New information is constantly provided by the plot. The implication is nevertheless that style is the result of constantly renewed deviations—and these can only be caused by the linear aspect of a work, whether we are talking about the introduction of a new character, the way an event develops or the shift from 'literal' expression to imagery. Meaning in literature must relate both to simultaneity *and* to opposition, and opposition is impossible without progression.

* Note: At the same time it should be realized that the text as a set of expected recurrences points to the inseparability of structure and sequence.

Sequence, it is clear, makes the ambiguity of the work possible. The system of a work does not constitute its meaning, progression does that. It is the only way we can approach the tension resulting from 'the provision of contradictory elements out of which a new synthesis can be made', for writers 'arouse our expectations, postpone the satisfaction of those expectations and finally make all well after, it may be, a period of almost total disintegration of the . . . structure' [668, p. 1364]. I have borrowed this description from a music critic, although I know analogies with other arts are always dangerous, for the conditions and nature of expression vary widely from one art form to another. But here the nature of sequential experience is revealed in a particularly pure way and clarifies the process in the referentially more confusing sphere of literature.

We can now perhaps more easily understand what is involved in Todorov's already quoted statement that narration is a series of micro-narratives—a more 'narrational' definition of what Riffaterre generalizes into the stylistic idea of contrast-based micro- and macro-contexts [591, p. 209] and which may be presented as a more or less *anti*-structural device. Style is a phenomenon which continuously constitutes itself—and the process of 'constitution' is as important as the overall picture.

This is a further reason why transformational grammar, useful though it may be, cannot provide a complete description of style: in addition to its inability to cope with anything non-syntactical (tropes, rhythm, repetition, alliteration, substance, event), it can only treat style as a purely static element.

So much for generalities. I want now to look at the particular applications of sequential analysis.

To begin with, I think that prose and especially narrative prose has most need of it. Here words are used much more as counters than in poetry. They have a fixed relationship with the outside world. They are therefore less interesting and less deliberately ambiguous in themselves. More important still, they are related to a story, a plot which unfolds progressively. There is nothing simplistic about this, for the form of a novel is 'not . . . a single form, but . . . a moving stream of impressions paid out of the volume in a slender thread as we turn the pages' [415, p. 14]. The experience of the conventional novel is a temporal one (and that of the non-conventional one too, for we contrast it instinctively with what we expect), with a permanently shifting centre of interest (the passage being read). 'The rest of the novel organises itself with varying degrees of immediacy around that temporary center.' [476, pp. 23–4.] The relation between different parts of a novel is fluid and they must be taken in order, therefore [v. 508, p. 109].

This is especially true because of the way the events described relate to a time scheme centred on a hypothetical present. As we saw in the chapter on meaning, everything leads up to the standpoint from which the narration takes place. In this, the novel contrasts with drama (which also requires considerable emphasis on sequence): 'Drama, although it implies past action (the "situation") moves, not towards the present, as narrative does, but towards something beyond [the future]; it deals essentially with commitments and consequences.' [378, p. 307.] Past, present and future thus bear upon each other—motivation is inseparable from them. And such a chronology is to be added to the more simple order in which the reader (or hearer) is presented with information.

To describe this kind of process is not easy—indeed I feel the more orthodox the novel involved is, the more delicate the critic's task will be. Perhaps this is one secret reason why Leavis decided to neglect the Daniel Deronda strand of narrative in George Eliot's novel, and to concentrate exclusively on the experience and character of the heroine [386]. I would even simplify further and suggest that sequence is one of the most difficult things adequately to analyse. The need to take time sequence into account is always in danger of encouraging a lurch either into the description of unrelated elements or into that other undergraduate time-waster: telling the story. This all too often boils down to offering a truncated and biased version of something the author has done much better already. It can only lead to the faulty conclusion that the need to emphasize linearity means that there is nothing else worth looking at—that the book is therefore mediocre.

This is countered by the more useful method of simply pointing to the sequence of events in a work and contrasting them with 'real' chronology (i.e. the time order in which events took place). Yet again, this is easier for an avant-garde novel than for a conventional one, for the 'modifications' in the latter will be more subtly significant than in, say, Robbe-Grillet or even Joyce (where sequence is shifted so much from our normal experience, by a disrupted order of events or by unacknowledged flashback, that one cannot tell which episode 'really' comes before which). Modification in the conventional and in the avant-garde novels must both be given detailed examination, however. The metaphysical implications involved are evident: Balzac's use of flashback has clearly deterministic implications just as Robbe-Grillet's demolition of chronology (except for the order in which events are recounted, and that drab necessity, syntax) implies a world without objective, or objectal, meaning.

Jean Verrier, in a series of lectures given at Manchester University in 1970, suggested further methods. It is useful, for example, to relate the duration of events or episodes to the number of pages allotted to them. This helps, in the case of Balzac, to demonstrate the static structure of *Eugénie Grandet*, concentrated as it is on two short three-day periods with a huge time gap linked to the second of these—whereas *Le Père Goriot* fits into a period of a month subdivided into three sets of days in the following manner: 3 days (80 pages) + 6 days (95 pages) + 8 days (177 pages), pointing to a very real effect of expansion and dynamism, a forward drive further stressed by the almost obsessive repetition (fifteen times!) of 'the following day'. Any literary work can be tackled in this way. The duration of events, related to the number of pages involved (added to the way normal chronology is modified), allows one very precisely to define the time experience, the evaluation of time, which the novel communicates—and this is a very profound part of the novel's meaning.

This kind of phenomenon need not be seen in isolation. It can be closely linked to other crucial aspects such as point of view (the *present* from which events are surveyed may be that of an impersonal or of an involved narrator).

Sequential techniques do not thus merely offer an *available* approach; they are in many cases an *indispensable* means of analysis. Katherine Mansfield's *The Fly* [v. 58 and 147], cannot really be understood if it is not approached sequentially. This is the only way in which, for example, the increasingly ambiguous implications of the boss's character, which are at the core of the story, may be understood.

The same is true of Camus's *L'Etranger*, which recounts Meursault's (and our) gradual realization of his position in relation to society, and which too by its use of the perfect tense (in the original French) gives direct expression to the notion of one thing coming (more or less coherently) after another and of the isolation of events [v. too 159B]. Camus's earlier novel *La Mort heureuse* is significantly biased towards events in a specially meaningful sequence: the search for happiness through love, travel, community life, solitude and nature and finally perhaps in death.

I suggested in the last chapter that a study of expository techniques would help to establish the norms and criteria which make a work tick. Once again this has strongly linear implications, for it points forwards or back, sees the work as a progression and examines the importance of the opening pages as a preparation for or a conclusion to that progression.

This has implications which do not only impinge on plot. The vocabulary of a novel, for example, need not point to a static situation. There is even a need to differentiate between the vocabulary at various stages in a work, the different points, say, in a character's development. [v. 724, vol. II, p. 116.] Kroeber points to the time structure to which Jane Austen's *Emma* must be related [369]. It is also possible in this way to define the progressive (Dickens, Tolstoy) or cyclic (Proust, Virginia Woolf) nature of works studied, for new preoccupations and experiences will tend to bring a semantic and grammatical shift in the kinds of words used—obsessional states will keep vocabulary much more static. If one goes so far as to *start* with vocabulary, an objective assessment of these phenomena is possible, as Mitterand demonstrates in his study of 'face' and 'visage' in *Thérèse Raquin* [477, pp. 27–8].

These examples show that 'pure' linearity and its nature will vary considerably according to the type of novel involved. *Tom Jones* and even more so Giono's *Le Hussard sur le Toit* (so different in this from its 'preparatory' version *Angélo*) are very linear and need to be described accordingly. This is also true of Dostoievsky, but the reasons are different, for now one is concerned with the way the author underlines the striking instability and mobility of characters who are often describable not in terms of prediction (who would have expected Stavroguine to commit suicide?) but in terms of what they actually do (only then does their potential become apparent). Flaubert's characters on the other hand conform much more to the conditioning and to the reflexes established in his novels' opening pages. The variations between descriptive or meditative novels like those of Henry James or Proust and 'active' novels like *Le Rouge et le Noir*, *The Grapes of Wrath* or *The Secret Agent* will again call for varied emphasis on sequence. This may lead to the interesting conclusions Northrop Frye comes to in connection with Dickens: that the plots are imbued with a logic not inherent in the story but rather with 'an impatient sense of absolutism' [228, p. 52]. But whatever one's *conclusions* may be, an initial premise must always be that no type of novel can ever be adequately studied from a purely non-sequential point of view.

I would even suggest that this is true of poetry too—any poetry. And this in spite of the fact that, so much more than prose poetry explores the affective associations of words; that, as N. Frye says, it is centripetal whilst prose is centrifugal [2, p. 122]; that all sorts of interrelated similarities are imposed on verse whilst prose tends to be a sequence of semantic differences [141, p. 97]. Linearity is always present. I have given some reasons for this in the early part of the chapter. Basically, a poem offers a changing body of information. But we can go further than that. Even at the level of sound, we can say that if echoes and parallels are important, Cohen is wrong to infer that they do not shift and evolve as the poem progresses. We need only think of Shakespeare's sonnet No. 33 of which Stephen Booth has said that it offers 'a good example of the contraction and expansion of phonetic particles operating in conjunction with other manifestations of unity and division' [79, p. 88; see *Sounds* p. 9]:

Full many a glorious morning have I seen
Flatter the mountain-tops with sovereign eye,
Kissing with golden face the meadows green,
Gilding pale streams with heavenly alchymy;
Anon permit the basest clouds to ride,
With ugly rack on his celestial face,
And from the forlorn world his visage hide,
Stealing unseen to west with this disgrace:
Even so my sun one early morn did shine,
With all triumphant splendour on my brow;
But out! alack! he was but one hour mine,
The region cloud hath mask'd him from me now.
  Yet him for this my love no whit disdaineth,
  Suns of the world may stain, when heaven's sun staineth.

Syntactical patterns similarly communicate a sense of expansion [79, p. 98]. The whole process is that of motion—the motion of the mind. And this may well be encouraged by rhythmic patterns whether it be the steady incantatory beat of a Baudelaire poem or the surprising line and word divisions in e. e. cummings.

At the level of ideas, sequence is obvious. But this may be true even of themes: Donne's Holy Sonnets VII is built up of short-lived thematic patterns, and this makes meaning and sound echoes harder to link [440, p. 61]. The poem is therefore the expression and the experience of a forward drive in thought.

This is yet more striking in a narrative or semi-narrative poem like so many of those that Hugo wrote. The contrasts between dynamic movement and stasis, driving violence and calm in a poem such as *Mazeppa* exploits this very fact—whilst *La Pente de la rêverie* exploits the same technique in reverse: the calm present is overwhelmed by the incursion of the past, the future and eternity.

Line-by-line commentary would seem to be essential if these motifs are to become apparent in criticism. It is only in this way that we can point to the patterns of connection and division, continuity and change [79, p. 83] which go to make up any discourse and which are especially complex in poetry. Stephen Booth can thus describe the thrust of Shakespeare's sonnets, the ease with which shifts and connections are made and the sonnet's decreasing complexity as it progresses towards the explicatory lines of the close [pp. 145ff.].

This is how Stephen Booth describes sonnet 33: 'The unit of the poem was first the quatrain, then the octave and sestet and now twelve lines and a couplet. As the reader moves through the poem he has constantly to widen his vision, and, ... he is constantly changing his idea of the relationship of one part of the poem to another. Each formal division is greater than the one before and each new section relates itself to all of what went before so that each division acts to obliterate the one that precedes it.' [p. 41.] Such an experience of the poem is still temporal, and must be so, even on the fiftieth reading, even when the poem is known by heart. It puts across too the idea that the poem with its shifts and changes offers not information about the mutability of the human condition but rather participation in an actual experience of mutability [p. 59]. As he goes through the first eight lines of Shakespeare's sonnet 94, 'the reader's essential experience ... is the experience of his own mind in flux' [p. 165].

The number of examples from Stephen Booth's remarkable study could be multiplied even further—but I have given more than enough to show that sequential analysis can produce brilliantly original and penetrating results. Cleanth Brooks demonstrates this in his analysis of Keats's *Ode to a Grecian Urn* [92]. Here again we are dealing with a poem which ends with an intellectual statement. The build up to and the justification of the conclusion are of primary importance. With long poems like *Paradise Lost* or with closely integrated cycles of poetry like *Les*

Fleurs du Mal, analysis may hinge also on the significance of the order in which the episodes are set: the constant swing between hope and despair, beauty and morality, being contrasted in *Les Fleurs du Mal* with the sequence which describes an experience of escape into art, love, the big city, alcohol, vice, blasphemy and death.

One might have the impression that sequential analysis of poetry is especially or even solely effective with *intellectual* poems. This is not so. The sequential study of esoteric verse (the natural hunting-ground of the structuralist) can be very profitable indeed and need never be the blundering attempt to reduce such verse to clear prose which is often mistaken for criticism. It is useful to remember that for Valéry 'the poem's sole function is to build up to its own conclusion' [480, p. 183]. Here is a sonnet by Mallarmé:

Ses purs ongles très haut dédiant leur onyx,
L'Angoisse, ce minuit, soutient, lampadaphore,
Maint rêve vespéral brûlé par le Phénix
Que ne recueille pas de cinéraire amphore.

Sur les crédences, au salon vide: nul ptyx,
Aboli bibelot d'inanité sonore
(Car le maître est allé puiser des pleurs au Styx
Avec ce seul objet dont le Néant s'honore.)

Mais proche la croisée au nord vacant, un or
Agonise selon peut-être le décor
Des licornes ruant du feu contre une nixe,

Elle, défunte nue en le miroir, encor
Que, dans l'oubli fermé par le cadre, se fixe
De scintillations sitôt le septuor.

The constants of loss, death, decline and absence are stressed throughout the poem by such words as 'brûlé', 'ne recueille pas', 'cinéraire amphore', 'salon vide', 'nul ptyx', 'aboli bibelot', 'allé'

'Styx', 'le Néant', 'agonise', défunte nue', 'l'oubli'. Even the reference to unicorns can be seen as the evocation of a *non-existent* animal. Rhyme endings remain constant throughout too. But over and above this, the poem offers an experience of movement and change: the sense of loss increases in the early stages of the poem; the darkness of the opening lines gives way after a pause in the second quatrain first to golden and fiery light and then finally to a bright, sparkling one. The movement would seem to be a qualified shift away from the pessimism of the quatrains. That a change is taking place is further indicated by the presence of that, for this poem, most important word, *mais.* Contrast between quatrains and tercets is insisted upon—initial motionlessness is replaced in the tercets by the violent movement of 'ruant' and the associations in 'scintillations'. None of this makes the poem any less esoteric (in the sense of clarifying it). It does however point to fundamental aspects of what our experience of the poem entails. The essential procedure with a poem like this is to find out what differences (*any* kind of differences) there are between its various stages and describe them in detail (far greater detail than I have set out here). This offers a straightforward method which avoids any distortion of the material. It implies an exhaustive approach, but one which bears the fundamental and meaningful movement of the poem in mind.

Variations of this technique are not hard to find—again applicable to 'difficult' poetry. Two recent studies [482 and 129] offer highly detailed analyses of poems by Apollinaire (*Mai* and *Rosemonde*). The basis of the critical technique involved is one of progressive reading—an experience which, as in Stephen Booth's study, unfolds as the poem develops. It would seem potentially to be just as successful with modern, esoteric poetry as with Shakespeare. And the reason for this is quite clear: even the most 'obscure' poem sets up a logic which is as 'horizontal' and linear as it is 'vertical'. Poetry which is meaningless in the normal sense of the term—surrealist poetry for example—can be shown to hang together (and therefore have significance) not only because, as we have seen, the syntax is reasonably regular, but also and perhaps especially because, as the poem develops, one image will tend to spawn another [v. 587].

It could of course be objected that these elements often relate just as much to the constants of structure as to the progressive nature of sequence. And this would be correct—it would underline the conclusion which has been several times apparent in this chapter: that it is a mistake explicitly to separate structure from sequence, for they are almost invariably inseparable and in no sense antithetical to one another. Blanchot's statement, quoted in the last chapter [pp. 183–4], is unfortunate and perverse. It pushes the Romantic notions of organic form to the point where words and events in literature are denied everything but recurrent significance. Moreover it is extremely difficult, as Harvey points out, 'to abstract strictly formal features like development or contrast or symmetry from such things as plot and character and language' [293, p. 1]. Analysis of the constants in a work must bear in mind such things as gradation by which potentialities become real experience and *langue* becomes *parole*. If the shift from *vous* to *tu* can be more or less counted on in seventeenth-century French drama, the precise context of the event in our emotional experience of the drama is renewed every time we go through it. The pattern involved will tend always to be a dynamic one, and this dynamism must be described—otherwise the increasing complexity which a literary work demonstrates as it progresses will not be accounted for. In a *Bildungsroman* the progress through the early stages of life is at one and the same time an expected pattern and a temporal feature the details of which are in no sense any more predictable than the core images in mature Shakespearean tragedy.

Both the successive contexts and the metaphorical contexts of a work must be borne in mind [v. 538, pp. 309–10]: a passage's literal as well as its representative value.

And yet having said all this, and in spite of my anti-structuralist asperities, I would not hesitate to suggest that the emphasis, the procedure which more than any other allows one to grasp a work in all (or in spite of all) its phenomenally complex fluctuations and changes is the one which sets out to define the work's unity. Linear analysis can so easily become a fragmenting process unless something like structural preoccupations are there to ensure that the essential interrelationships in a work are recognized. When one is short of time (in teaching for example or in an examination) the aspect of a work to which one must devote most attention would seem reasonably clear.

CHAPTER NINE

CONCLUSIONS

Criticism is a filtering process. We subject a book to a series of checks which enable us to define its true nature. These checks are, briefly, the subject of each of the preceding chapters: I have worked from the ideas of sound, grammar, individual words and statistics through wider notions of meaning and style to the yet wider and more fundamental questions of the way in which the work may be seen as a pattern, a unity and how important the actual sequence of events and details may be considered to be.

The fact which I have stressed continually is that each one of these filters is not self-sufficient—they overlap and combine: although the second part of my study raises the most important problems it is largely dependent on Part I. We might consider that the chapters taken independently relate to scholarship; grouped together they relate to criticism. My preoccupation has been with criticism, and good criticism gives most weight to the techniques which seem to be of primary importance in the work studied: it examines sound patterns in Dreiser *only* if they are demonstrably relevant to a better understanding of that particular novelist. Thus the degree to which one particular filter will be of use will vary enormously from text to text—grammatical structures will *tend* to be more important in verse whilst less verbal processes of meaning will more closely relate to prose. But this is no hard and fast rule—in the last analysis the individual text must tell us where critical emphasis should lie: grammatical analysis is very useful both for the understanding of Pope's intellectual trenchancy and Proust's subtle probing of feeling and sense.

The conclusions from this are reasonably obvious: the definition of a work's individuality or the refinement of our ideas about literary genres might well be achieved by precise reference to the critical techniques we make use of when we study them. Abstract definitions thus disappear for good—and good riddance. If we consider the massive mixing of genres today or the still accelerating growth of writing which is a varying combination of fact and fiction, it becomes clear that for the twentieth-century reader even the distinction between literature and non-literature is generally tedious. For the modern critic it is positively dangerous: it could inhibit him in his prime duty which is to make use of *any* tools of analysis which the text may require. Critical practice must in other words take precedence over critical theory (which when applied is so often disappointing): the filters I have mentioned allow one to examine phenomena from a multiplicity of points of view without losing sight of the tangible elements which the text alone can offer. Words are both referential signs and objects which may be patterned. The artist's point of view becomes something we can put our finger on: it may relate to the relative importance of pronouns or the sequence in which events are recounted. It may have to do with a preference for verbs over adjectives. It has little to do with criticism about criticism about criticism. I am saying explicitly therefore that whilst I cannot follow the kind of old-fashioned ideas which equate style with absolute notions of correction or elegance, at the same time I cannot accept the way French New (but by now somewhat ageing) Critics are obsessed by literariness and other general or generic definitions. Textual criticism is a practical affair. As far as my present preoccupations are concerned, I am not sure that it is satisfactory for Doubrovsky to claim that French 'New Criticism is less worthwhile for the answers it suggests (which are always debatable) than for the essential and hitherto unknown questions it poses' [176, p. 17]. This may well lead to purely philosophical speculation although the attempt these critics have made to express themselves as precisely as possible is no doubt a notable advance (when it does not lead to unwarranted preciosity).

We must keep our feet on the ground. We must base any statements we make on a multiplicity of examples firmly related to their context. Therefore the initial need in the study of a text is to describe it in some considerable detail (using my chapter headings as a check list). This is not an end in itself (as, say, Jakobson might have us believe) but it is an essential preliminary. The value of pointing to elements of which the reader cannot possibly be aware is dubious—but it is better to discard a fact as irrelevant than not to point to it at all. Individual common sense is the only guide as to how exhaustive a description should be and what bias it should have—just as common sense alone can tell us how relevant 'non-textual' details like social history and biography are.

Given the importance of description, the critic must, as I have already suggested, adopt a certain *naïveté*: he must be able to accept what the text offers without prejudice and then make a description of what is there. All too often self-consciousness drives us to suppress details which are of primary importance: for we try to work out what a 'difficult' poem 'really means' instead of pointing to the much more tangible way in which a complex and rare experience is unfolded for us. One major consideration in all this is that criticism is a human affair: it will of necessity be biased and incomplete. We must aim merely at avoiding the kind of distortion which results from sweeping, unsubstantiated statements. This is as far as human objectivity can go—even when a computer is available. Riffaterre's idea of the *Average Reader* is an interesting one: its function is, by consulting a number of readers, to 'transform a fundamentally subjective reaction to style into an objective, analytic tool, to find the constant beneath the variety of judgments . . .' [583, p. 162]—but knocking on neighbours' doors or pestering colleagues in a senior common room does not seem to be a very practical or feasible way of going about one's critical business. Moreover, the unique personality of the reader is central, as Poulet, Jean-Pierre Richard, Leavis, Cleanth Brooks and Sartre have shown in their widely varying ways. The last thing we should be concerned with is 'scientific' criticism. The objective facts of a text adequately described and remembered are merely an anchor which allows the individual personality to function in a critically relevant way. The cultivation of that personality is therefore very important too. Sainte-Beuve's advice is still valid: 'Constantly vary your studies, develop your intelligence in all directions, do not restrict it to any one mode or school of thought . . . launch out with a kind of friendly disquiet towards everything which is insufficiently known and which deserves to be better known and scrutinize it with precise yet warm curiosity.' [Letter to Taxile Delord, 3 February 1864.] Too little of such sensitive open-mindedness is apparent in present-day criticism.

If it were, it would perhaps help to overcome defects inherent in textual criticism: the fact that poetry seems to be a rather more appropriate subject for close 'factual', precise examination than the novel, for example, as can be seen from my early chapters. Although language is important in the novel, the emphasis lies on the more broadly based problems of structure and human behaviour. Poems often have the fortunate habit of being shorter than novels: they may be comprehensively described with much less difficulty. This is regrettable in what is still the age of the novel. It should make us just a little suspicious (even when poetry is involved) of any criticism which uses linguistics to the exclusion of less objective phenomena.

I have said a great deal about the relation between linguistics and criticism. Perhaps the main point which needs to be stressed is that whilst one is dismayed by impressionism, one is all too often bored by the linguistic scientific analysis of a *living* text. Vendler [713] explains this boredom to a large extent when he suggests that the best linguisticians are not analysing literary texts. All too often, critics or linguisticians are jumping onto a bandwagon and they show themselves either to be incompetent in another man's field [487 passim] or unable to go beyond pure description. They may be obsessed with deviation or sentence structure *as an end in themselves*. This is the defect of the volume edited by Fowler which Vendler is referring to.

One can therefore sympathize with the rather conservative strictures of Bateson [55] or Hobsbaum [309, pp. 188–207] when they stress the crude fragmentation of facts and the irrelevances which so often restrict criticism with a linguistic bias.

Linguistics has nevertheless made a considerable contribution to modern criticism as the existence of this book demonstrates. It forces us to look closely at the mechanisms of a text, in order objectively to consider what exactly happens when we read, instead of taking the reading process for granted, as had hitherto been the case [371, p. 4]. It forces our attention onto the text as the critic's central preoccupation, and this underlines the link between 'structure and texture, sound and meaning, scene and act' as the key phenomena for scrutiny [389, p. 52]. It raises the important ideas of connotation, denotation and context.

All this is good *provided linguistics is seen as a slave to criticism* and not its master. Disciplines which have non-literary functions must be kept to heel. With linguistics this is done by resisting any attempt to allow it to be separated from meaning, significance and aesthetics (to which latter terms I shall return)—otherwise the text becomes a mere document: a means whereby the general function of language may be explored. This is as disastrous a fate for criticism as if it were to be considered merely as an historical, a philosophical or a biographical document. *The form of a text must be shown to be meaningful.* Mechanisms described must be related to their specific impact.

These then are the shifts in emphasis which criticism requires of linguistics. Articulateness must take precedence over formalization [751, p. 101]. The search for specificity must lessen the value of a consensus. *La parole* is more important than *la langue*.

Such considerations would have helped Cohen, in his otherwise stimulating book, to avoid falling into the trap of turning deviation into a general notion of poeticalness—which makes Pope or even Shakespeare less of a poet than Edward Lear! Riffaterre cleverly avoids this, by linking an affective process ('surprise') to the broadly based linguistic mechanisms which cause that surprise (micro- and macro-contexts) and by refusing to see such effects as a genre device. The dangers of taking criticism as a science are similarly avoided (providing of course one discounts the Average Reader myth). *Meaning* retains its dominant position. Linguistics stays in close contact with such central non-linguistic (or not necessarily linguistic) elements as character, behaviour, irony, point of view and the like, which are of necessity flexible.

It will be seen from what I have just been saying that criticism is concerned with the kind of truth literature seeks to communicate. A truth which relates to human language, behaviour and feelings. It must therefore bear constantly in mind those two closely related key notions: *ambiguity*, the working hypothesis that any element in any work kills many birds with one stone and must not be taken purely on face value, and *construction*, the fact that, as literature is a coherent unified organization of experience, the constants and recurrent devices in a work must be carefully tracked down and their function, variation and progression described.

These two terms allow the need to describe to be taken an essential step further. Facts take on multiple significance. They cannot be compartmentalized. They must be *interrelated*. A literary work is seen as a *field* of experience. Telling the story and the 'heresy of paraphrase' are avoided. Criticism takes on the task of making literary ambiguity more evident without explaining it away.

This is how criticism, even the close textual variety, can not only bear in mind but even underline the fact that literature is centrally concerned with human experience; the 'so what?' which purely descriptive studies too often invite is avoided. Detail, whether it be sounds in Verlaine or verb/adjective ratios in Conrad, is kept clearly focused on the emotion the poem expresses or the dynamic quality of action and event.

Textual criticism may in this way be central to more broadly based studies—and, once again the personality of the critic is not removed from the scene. The twin dangers of impressionism and excessive description are avoided by the simple device of asking what experience a given set of interconnected elements is creating and communicating. Moral considerations, in the widest sense of the term, remain central. This discourages the intellectual game so many critics (especially academic ones) like to play.

The themes of a work may be shown to have human density by reference to a particular mode of expression. As I explained in the second part of the chapter on meaning, this does not exclude relevant external elements, whether they be the political and social context of the Reform Bill in *Middlemarch* or the shift from darkness to light (and vice versa) on which Mallarmé's sonnets often hinge. David Lodge has demonstrated that close textual analysis in no way implies the rejection of the outside world. George Levine has spoken vigorously against the 'myth of the "autonomy" of the work of art' [405, p. 104]. Textual criticism need not further this myth: the techniques it employs must vary according to whether it is dealing with a work which gives the texture of life (Tolstoy, Saul Bellow), the texture of a problem (Shaw or Norman Mailer) or one which is rather (but never exclusively) preoccupied with the texture of an aesthetic experience (Ruskin). Ambiguity and construction are not displaced as key terms by all this—they merely become tangibly and humanly significant, and never degenerate into an abstract pattern. This explains the greatness of a work like Auerbach's *Mimesis*—it owes much to the fact that its author, basing his statements on quite extensive texts, sought to examine the way reality was represented in them. Need it be stressed that similar considerations are of capital importance in poetry? The most esoteric verse uses words and constructions which relate it to other fields of experience.

What must be borne in mind of course is that the relationship between art and the outside world and the *kinds* of relationship involved vary enormously [v. 760]. Any differences which come to light are of especial value because they pinpoint structuration —not because they enable us to say whether the writer is in any sense right or wrong.

What we are indeed interested in, through the interaction of the text and the world which produced it, is the particular angle, the attitude, the mode of feeling which the work expresses. This allows for the approach of a critic like Poulet for whom poetry is a potential as well as a realization—although I find it rather surprising when Poe is judged to be a great poet on the strength of his potential. More generally, at the level of realization, textual criticism allows us to define those feelings in communicable terms. We have seen that the individual work in isolation, the general attitudes peculiar to one particular period, or the historical development of feeling are all accessible to us in this way. More than one of those aspects will tend to be considered at once as I have already suggested: Keats or Mme de Lafayette are unique but they also express the tradition and the age to which they belong.

Textual criticism and the categories I have studied enable us to look at another kind of development: not only from the tradition to which a text must in some degree belong, but also, when the manuscripts are available, from the form it takes when the writer starts on his first drafts and notes to the final manuscript and proof corrections: the tightening of the work's whole thematic cohesion [v. 409, p. 74; 244, pp. 414–15; 750].

What becomes apparent from everything I have said so far is the great diversity of uses to which textual criticism may be put. This would seem to indicate that it is really restrictive only inasmuch as it makes us come down to brass tacks—it makes us more likely to talk about literature in its own terms. It discourages us from using the text as an excuse to talk about irrelevances. Above all it makes the superfluous deployment of erudition rather more difficult. That such a curb should be necessary can be seen from a reading of *The Art of Criticism* [505]. Repeatedly the individual studies in this book seek to remind us, at least by implication, that literature is virtually incomprehensible without wide historical, sociological, philosophical and aesthetic knowledge. This turns literature (especially that of the past) into an academic closed shop. It is wrong and stultifying to deny that history exists but it is critically unhealthy to make it all-powerful, otherwise Defoe's *Diary of the Plague Year* and the real thing become indistinguishable. What makes a text worth reading is the fact that it is *still* worth reading. And that is why literature cannot be a mere sub-branch of other subjects [v. i.a. 170]. Only after scrutiny of the text should we turn to other disciplines for any elucidation it may require. If literary truth, as we have already seen, is different from historical truth, Yvor Winters describes the critic's task in the following way:

> It will consist (1) of the statement of such historical or biographical knowledge as may be necessary in order to understand the mind and method of the writer; (2) of such analysis of his literary theories as we may need to understand and evaluate what he is doing; (3) of a rational critique of the paraphrasable content (roughly, the motive) of the poem; (4) of a rational critique of the feeling motivated—that is, of the details of style as seen in language and technique; (5) of the final act of judgment, a unique act, the general nature of which can be indicated, but which cannot be communicated precisely, since it consists in receiving from the poet his own final and unique judgment of his matter and in judging that judgment. It should be noted that the purpose of the first four processes is to limit as narrowly as possible the region in which the final unique act is to occur.
>
> [v. 328, pp. 23–4.]

This is an important and useful guide as far as a public and formulated statement is concerned. But the process of analysis which is a preliminary to that statement would rather set Winters's stages in the following order: (4), (3), (2), (1), (5). In this way the degree to which form and content are inseparable is worked out for each individual work and never on the basis of abstract criteria. The stylistic qualities of Alfred Cobban's account [139, vol. II, pp. 131–44] of the 1848 Revolution are thus not neglected—the historical import of Flaubert's description of the same event is also taken into consideration.

The need for this kind of flexibility is perhaps the fundamental conclusion to all the preceding chapters—it tells us what the close criticism of literary texts can and cannot do.

One question however remains and that concerns the purpose of all the effort and strain to which a book like this exhorts its readers. In other words, to what extent can textual criticism be tied into the problem of the value of the individual text? For if textual criticism cannot help us to decide whether a novel or a poem is worthwhile, its value would seem to be secondary.

This is a very thorny subject indeed and one which I should like to avoid. But it would be dishonest to do so in the sense that once again the criticism of literature might be seen as an intellectual game. The acid test of any work has always been whether it is worth reading. This means that a critical method is especially acceptable if it helps one to get nearer to the true value of a work.

The close examination and the careful description involved in textual criticism must therefore be judged in that light. Much mediocre textual criticism results from a refusal to recognize this. The following pages are not intended to be a comprehensive statement on the problem. Like the rest of the book, they are merely pointers to what is involved. It is up to the reader to develop the, at times, rather naïve ideas I put forward.

One might wonder whether, when all is said and done, described and detailed, problems of value do not centre more or less exclusively on individual taste and personal opinion. However mediocre we may be, the degree to which we like a book or a poem must play a major part in the way we talk about it, and our instinctive appreciation must come first. This is not necessarily a bad thing because it means we are involved in what we, as people, are reading. Literature is not concerned with absolute universal truths: it is rather concerned with pointing by implication to the links between particular instances and universal experience. It is meaningful only if it affects us individually. The value of a text will therefore vary from person to person.

But I do not think this means allowing private interests to dominate us completely. We should always be a little suspicious of the emotions works of art make us feel—we may be taken in by the sentimentality in much of Dickens or put off by the hard work involved in reading a poem by Hopkins. Whilst not denying our own personalities, we must accept the fact that we are perhaps mediocre and that higher experiences than we find natural do exist.

Until the nineteenth century (and even later), literature was generally evaluated according to *a priori* values. Doctrines clashed perhaps (as when the French Academy took Corneille to task for the 'defects' of *Le Cid*), but they existed independently of works and individuals. Great importance was attached to tradition and the opinions of higher (preferably long since dead) authority. Taste was universal and therefore words like style, harmony, beauty needed little or no defining. Or so it seemed.

Even in the twentieth century such attitudes survive. Much teaching of literature in France is founded on an ideology: 'this ideology does not merely insist on the objectivity which is part of any scientific research, it implies general convictions about man, history (and so forth) . . . human psychology for example . . . is essentially founded on a kind of analogical determinism which insists that the details of a work must *be like* the details of a person's life, and a character's soul must be like the author's . . .' [46, pp. 253–4].

Within this area, and yet in a totally different way, Leavis insists on tradition (and therefore influence) as a criterion of value [v. 386, opening pages]. This may not be too far from the computerized writing of poetry which has recently been experimented with [v. 443]: given certain ingredients, a certain level of achievement may be counted on.

Fenollosa, at the beginning of the century, suggested a general grammatical basis for poetic quality: verbal good, nominal bad [v. 209 and 162, pp. 33 ff.]. Similarly, Francis Berry suggests that when a poet like Pope makes especial use of the present tense and the indicative mood 'the life of *possibility* is hardly recognised' [68, pp. 119–20]. This again relates to a general theory of value.

Over the last 150 years, the *significant* shift has been towards a huge multiplication of theories of value. This is a good thing for the twentieth century because it means that criticism has kept pace with the breakdown of notions of genre. Normative criticism remains, but it is less dangerous because it is much more flexible. The value of the individual work can thus be more closely approached on its own terms. Flaubert's *Education sentimentale* may be considered great in spite of the drab monotony of its subject-matter, because it is a study of drab monotony. A work should not now be evaluated merely according to its subject-matter.

Nor should it be felt that a particular subject needs a particular treatment. George Eliot treats marriage in *Middlemarch* or *Daniel Deronda* with only very oblique reference to sex (which a twentieth-century writer would feel to be central). But this does not make her inferior to John Updike or Doris Lessing!

People today are suspicious of abstract criteria. This means that questions of value must be left to a late stage in one's critical examination of a book.

And yet relativism does not always produce satisfactory results, especially when a critic's interests are not closely textual. In this context, here, from Bateson, is one of the strangest attitudes I have come across:

> A poem . . . is not good or bad in itself but only in terms of the contexts in which it originated. For us to be able to use it, to live ourselves into it, the essential requirement is simply an understanding of those original contexts and especially the original social context. A social order, as such, is necessarily the affirmation of certain values. In the social context, therefore, the values implied in the poem become explicit, and its relative goodness or badness declares itself.
>
> [388, vol. II, p. 294.]

Subjectivism need not be tied down in that way or to that extent. We have seen that cultural background will tend to be a useful basis for *explanation*. But this does not apply to *evaluation*. Literature is admittedly produced by a particular culture, but it is at the same time a questioning, a distortion and therefore an implicit evaluation of that culture. It must also be significant for other or later societies. This is why so much polemical or ideological literature soon becomes stale and boring. A writer like Swift demonstrates the fact that something other than the subject must come into play before a work like this can survive: and this other thing is the form of expression. Conversely we tend to overvalue the works of our own times because they deal with problems which all too readily concern us. The question of literary form again arises if we are to assess such works more than superficially.

We must therefore be of our own times, but not rigidly so—we should be blinded neither by subjects nor by expression, but we should put most emphasis on the latter.

Before I stress the role of textual criticism in evaluation, the notion of great and permanent subjects might be considered: a work concerned with political power, illusion clashing with reality, communication, a young man's growth to maturity or a combination of some of these will at least be worth our attention. But such subjects are clearly not a guarantee of value although in literature greatness 'cannot be entirely dissociated from size' just 'as in basketball or football a good big man is better than a good little man' [529, p. 278].

Shifting my ground somewhat, it is clear that the idea of originality has to be considered. It enables us to criticize hackneyed subject-matter and expression. Clichés are bad in a writer unless he is describing stereotyped attitudes. If all characters in a novel speak in the same way or are grouped too schematically (as they are in most crime stories), there we might suspect that something is amiss.

But basically such approaches to value can only be given *detailed* treatment when expression is looked at very closely. The advantage of this is that our consideration of general notions of value (which fortunately we cannot get rid of) require detailed examples if they are to survive when applied to an individual text.

We are encouraged too to dispense with criteria which close textual criticism demonstrates to be clearly wrong: for example, the fact (recognized at least since I. A. Richards's early writings) that poetry is often a counterlogical affair whose *substance* is in itself not particularly interesting (see *Meaning II*). In modern literature we can say this is often true of prose.

The way is thus open for such ideas as those of Spire who relates poetic quality to the articulation of sound sequences (see *Sounds*)—acceptable providing quality is here seen (as above) to be a close integration of form and content. Laforgue's line

L'éternel fouettage des flots flasques

is successful because it is an unpleasant combination of sound and meaning. The important emotional aspect of literary experience (see *Meaning II*) is thus confirmed. Critics like Spire continue and clarify such earlier attitudes as Joubert's 'only that which transports me is poetry' [611, vol. III, p. 119]. The intensity of experience is translated into describable terms. This is indeed what a far different critic, Bachelard, is doing: the richness and the quality of the texts he reads are demonstrated by the sensitive precision with which, as a 'dreamer about words', he describes the lines of emotion and association he has been guided along.

Looking at the reader's emotive experience from a similar point of view to Bachelard's, one might even suggest that Riffaterre's notion of surprise may be considered qualitatively (in spite of Riffaterre's own refusal to bring such notions into stylistics [v. 589, p. 216]).

These are but a few examples, but it hardly needs demonstrating that a great amount of the preliminary work must be done with the help of techniques outlined in the various chapters of this book. The quality (in both senses of the term) of emotion can only be truly worked out if we are able to describe the mechanisms by which that emotion is created. Once this fact is established (and it requires considerable expansion from the points I have raised), considerations which might seem to be foreign to textual criticism can be brought in most fruitfully. William Righter has said that

> One concomitant of the obvious fact that literature is bound up with life in a multiplicity of ways . . . is that it must be equally bound up with those value systems which operate through experience as a whole, whether they are religious or derive from other metaphysical or moral claims.
>
> [594, p. 52.]

In a sense this links up with the idea of great subjects, but it also relates very closely to questions of literary expression. Morality and form are inseparable and 'when we examine the formal perfection of *Emma* we find that it can be appreciated only in terms of the moral preoccupations that characterize the novelist's peculiar interest in life'. David Lodge [411, p. 68] would prefer to put this statement by Leavis the other way round: 'when we examine the moral preoccupations that characterize Jane Austen's peculiar interest in life as manifested in *Emma* we find that they can be appreciated only in terms of the formal perfection of the novel'. This is the best way to put it, I think. Once again the emphasis on close textual criticism becomes clear. 'Morality', ultimately, is defined by form. 'Maturity' (to use another of Leavis's favourite expressions) is not in abstract attitudes—it is in the formal mechanisms through which it is expressed. (It links up closely with the idea of unity which I shall look at later on.) This fundamental fact, that the moral value of literature is formally describable, may help to explain for example why the sincerity of an author's views is unrelated to the success with which he puts them across. Sincerity is a non-problem in all art because it does not relate to technique. It relates to intention and not to realization. What we should rather be concerned with is the acceptability of the communicated experiences.

This relates very often to notions of *telling* (authorial intervention) and *showing*. One defect of H. James's *The Portrait of a Lady* is the lack of tangibility which comes from the fact that the author too readily discusses his characters and leaves them insufficient time to act. Only in a first person novel (like that of Proust) is discussion really acceptable. The poetic equivalent of this whole phenomenon is metaphor. Once again we are able to touch an experience and feel the tensions it involves rather than have it demonstrated to us. Ironic undertones result from the confrontation of elements (be they behaviour or image) and not systematic elucidation. The danger that literature may become a pamphlet is most easily avoided in this way—*Gulliver's Travels* will still be read when excessively intellectualized and pretentious works like some of Malraux's novels (whose impact for about twenty years after the time of publication was justifiably great) are long dead.

All these questions relate largely to technique. Whether one agrees with the norms I have just sketched out or not, it is possible objectively to describe the way such phenomena are set out on the page. Furthermore it is clear that there is no need to stop at mere description. The elimination of value judgements by so many modern critics (the French New Critics and semiologists offer a striking example of this) is a mistake and a distortion of what literature is about. A text should not be seen as grist for the mill—its quality must be considered. Otherwise we achieve results as aberrant as Sartre's excessive preoccupation with the degree to which literature is socially committed [v. 615]. *Emphasis must be on both form and content.* And in this, let me stress the point again, textual criticism is invaluable. If an author has something to say, the way he handles language will be very relevant.

Such facts, although true to the point of banality, only nibble at the problem. Wider *textual* criteria of value may be brought into play. I shall only deal with what I consider to be the main criterion, which all the subjects I have treated in this book will help to clarify: the idea of unity and coherence. The main function of art is to present experience as something organized. Our examination of the interrelationships of different elements in a text should therefore aim at establishing the extent to which they cohere. Butor's use of *vous* from the beginning of *La Modification* is successful because it is a mysterious and disturbing angle from which events are unfolded [see pp. 40–1 above]—in this it links up with our initial uncertainty about the details (we wonder what the *rainure de cuivre* is, and who not only *vous* is but Mathilde, Cécile etc.), and this uncertainty is further encouraged by the surprising detail in which a character is told apparently obvious facts about himself. Everything hangs together—an experience which justifies art as a kind of explanation, a *relation* of different areas of activity and emotion, is promised to us on the opening page. Neutral, separable elements are made into a whole whose significance and value are demonstrated as the important subject of the novel: a man's decision to leave his mistress and devote himself to his family is explored. Only perhaps in one aspect is the use of *vous* not really acceptable: although we realize very quickly that the *vous* involved relates to a special link between author and character (or is a voice telling the character about himself), the second person plural gives the reader the impression that he is being addressed. At the superficial level of 'participating in the character's experience', this is perhaps not a bad thing, but at a deeper level, it creates difficulties: the reader's instinctive reaction to *vous* (the feeling that he is being directly addressed) is repeatedly and confusingly thwarted by the realization that *vous* relates to someone else. The thematic structure of the novel is not furthered by this. When elements do not fit like this, they are a partial negation of art as coherent experience. The relative value of the work can thus be assessed.

In much modern literature this may mean the portrayal of what is, by definition, confused and hardly perceptible—characters' fleeting impressions in Virginia Woolf or Nathalie Saraute, surprising collocations in surrealist poetry, unexpected syntax in Mallarmé or e. e. cummings. But this kind of author does not fail because he is difficult—he fails only if his 'obscurity' is caused by the fact that he is patternless. He succeeds if fleeting impressions are shown in differing characters to group round events which concern them all; if collocations within a poem systematically bring together words from an identifiable semantic area;

or if the same kind of surprising syntactical patterns are seen to recur in a poem or to be justified, say, by the way they underline an important word, idea or form of experience.

In this and many other ways, even the most 'obscure' works may be said to clarify the experience which they embody. Like more straightforward works, they must, in a sense, function according to their own justifiable rules—they must exist in their own right—even if, like Büchner's *Woyzeck*, they are unfinished fragments. This is what Leavis means, I think, when he says that value comes from the ability to make language 'create and enact instead of merely relating' [385, p. 161].

The work takes on an inner logic in this way. The kind of logic involved is useful especially because it does not depend too heavily on notions of realism. As in Mervyn Peake, new worlds can be created which, at one and the same time, we know to be a fiction and which we accept as *coherent* inventions. Dickens's fanciful characters work because they fit. And this fitness is demonstrated by close reference to the text. Beauty which Eric Newton sees as centrally characterized by repetition and recurrence [503, pp. 24 ff.], can thus be described objectively. Nebulous notions such as authorial objectivity can be kept at arm's length.

Structuralist approaches thus once again turn out, as I suggested at the end of the last chapter, to be very useful. They lead us to see all parts as functions of a wider whole and in this they take us beyond description to question the *extent* to which everything hangs together—which is a central judgement of value.* The end of Solzhenitsyn's *First Circle* is bad (as are the last lines of *Madame Bovary*) because there is a stylistically definable shift from complexity to anecdote. This is similar to a gap between sound and sense in a poem which otherwise makes extensive use of such links.

Changes of this kind affect unity and therefore undermine quality. They do this not only for formal reasons but for a

* Note: The need to look at a work structurally shows that that work should be taken seriously.

reason which allows us to link the central qualitative considerations of coherence and humanity: when Solzhenitsyn becomes anecdotic or when the poet does not tighten links between sound and sense, they are both taking us out of a world of experience whose associations are diverse and multiple into a much simpler form of experience. The work's unity is undermined and so too is its value as human experience. A work which is poor in connotations (whatever these may be) is one which is qualitatively dubious. Unity is therefore the means whereby the complexity of experience in a work can best be exploited by the artist and therefore best evaluated by the critic.

My conclusions to this and all preceding chapters would seem therefore to be reasonably simple. The critic's task is to understand and subsequently to evaluate a work of art as the organized or unified presentation of experience. Whilst questions of the basic significance of that experience may be dependent on moral notions such as Leavis's idea of maturity, once we set about examining the way the artist has produced a coherent account, we are obliged to make systematic use of the methods I have outlined. The emphasis on sound, vocabulary, structure, sequence will vary from one work to another, but we need to possess as much objective information as possible if we are in any way to control our response to something as subjective in its appeal as a literary text. Only close textual criticism can help us to do that.

CHAPTER TEN

BIBLIOGRAPHY

This bibliography is in no sense exhaustive. It could not hope to be. It nevertheless offers a reasonable grounding in the subjects I have been examining. Where two sources for a particular work are given, the one from which I have quoted is indicated by an asterisk.

The entries are numbered. This number, and not the title, is in the main used as a means of identification in the course of the book as well as for cross references here.

1. *Actes du IVe Congrès International de Linguistes.* Copenhague, Munksgaard, 1938.
2. H. ADAMS, *The interests of criticism.* New York, Harcourt, 1969.
3. H. ADANK, *Essai sur les fondements psychologiques et linguistiques de la métaphore affective.* Genève, Editions Union, 1939.
4. B. ADRIANI, *Über das Lesen französischer lyrischer Dichtungen.* Ulm, Aegis, 1952.

4B D. AGER, *Styles and registers in contemporary French.* London, U.P., 1970.

5. J. W. ALDRIDGE, *Critiques and essays on modern fiction.* New York, Ronald Pr., 1952.
6. W. ALLEN, *The English novel.* London, Phoenix House, 1954. Harmondsworth, Penguin Books, paperback ed. 1958.
7. W. ALLEN, *Reading a novel.* Denver, Swallow, 1949.
8. M. ALLOTT (ed.), *Novelists on the novel.* New York, Columbia U.P., 1959. *London, Routledge, 1959.
9. A. ALONSO, 'The stylistic interpretation of literary texts', *Modern Language Notes*, 1942, pp. 489–96.
10. D. ALONSO, *Poesía española; ensayo de métodos y límites estilísticos.* Madrid, Gredos, 2nd ed. 1952.
11. H. ANDERSON and J. S. SHEA (eds.), *Studies in criticism and aesthetics.* Minneapolis, Minnesota U.P., 1967.

12. S. O. ANDREW, *Syntax and style in Old English*. Cambridge, U.P., 1940.

13. R. N. ANSHEN (ed.), *Language: an enquiry into its meaning and function*. New York, Harper, 1957.

14. G. ANTOINE, 'En marge d'un livre récent: stylistique et histoire de la langue à l'époque romantique', *Revue d'Histoire Littéraire de la France*, 1953, pp. 175–87.

15. F. ANTOSCH, 'The diagnosis of literary style with verb-adjective ratio'. In 172.

16. 'Approches de l'écriture poétique', *Revue des Sciences Humaines*, 1971, pp. 157–301.

16B L. ARAGON, *Les beaux quartiers*, Paris, Denoël, 1936.

17. E. A. ARMSTRONG, *Shakespeare's imagination; a study of the psychology of association and inspiration*. London, Drummond, 1946.

18. T. ARON, '*Bérénice* et *Ariane*: à la recherche de critères de littérarité'. In 409.

19. M. ARRIVÉ and J.-C. CHEVALIER (eds.), *La stylistique*. Paris, Larousse, 1969. [*Langue Française*, no. 3.]

20. E. AUERBACH, *Mimesis: the representation of reality in Western literature*. Princeton, U.P., 1968.

21. J. AUSTEN, *Sense and Sensibility. Edited by T. Tanner*. Harmondsworth, Penguin Books, 1969.

22. L. J. AUSTIN, '*L'après-midi d'un faune* de Mallarmé'. In 380.

23. L. J. AUSTIN, 'Du nouveau sur la *Prose pour des Esseintes* de Mallarmé', *Mercure de France*, no. 1,097 (1955), pp. 84–104.

24. L. J. AUSTIN, 'Mallarmé and the visual arts'. In U. FINKE (ed.), *French 19th century painting and literature*. Manchester, U.P., 1972.

25. L. J. AUSTIN, 'Mallarmé, Huysmans et la *Prose pour des Esseintes*', *Revue d'Histoire Littéraire de la France*, 1954, pp. 145–83.

26. J. R. AYER, 'Dylan Thomas in the aural dimension', *Computer Studies in the Humanities and Verbal Behaviour*, 1968, pp. 6–9.

27. H. S. BABB (ed.), *Essays in stylistic analysis*. New York, Harcourt, 1972.

28. G. BACHELARD, *L'air et les songes*. Paris, Corti, 1943.
29. G. BACHELARD, *L'eau et les rêves*. Paris, Corti, 1942.
30. G. BACHELARD, *La flamme d'une chandelle*. Paris, P.U.F., 2nd ed. 1962.
31. G. BACHELARD, *La poétique de la rêverie*, Paris, P.U.F., 2nd ed. 1968.
32. J. BAILEY, 'The stress-meter of Goethe's *Der Erlkönig*', *Language and Style*, 1969, pp. 339–51.
33. R. W. BAILEY, 'Statistics and style: a historical survey'. In 172.
34. R. W. BAILEY and D. M. BURTON, *English stylistics: a bibliography*. Cambridge, Mass., M.I.T. Press, 1968.
35. R. W. BAILEY and L. DOLEŽEL, *An annotated bibliography of statistical stylistics*. Ann Arbor, Michigan U.P., 1968. [See review in *Computer Studies in the Humanities and Verbal Behaviour*, 1970, pp. 112–5.]
36. A. BALAKIAN, 'La langue surréaliste'. In 380.
37. R. BALLY, *Le langage et la vie*. Genève, Droz, 3rd ed. 1952.
38. E. BARAT, *Le style poétique et la révolution romantique*. Paris, Hachette, 1904.
39. J. BARBIER, *Le vocabulaire, la syntaxe et le style des poèmes réguliers de Charles Péguy*. Paris, Berger-Levrault, 1957.
40. H. T. BARNWELL, 'Extract from *La Princesse de Clèves*'. In 505.
41. R. BARTHES, *Le degré zéro de l'écriture*. Paris, Seuil, 1953.
42. R. BARTHES, 'Les deux critiques'. In 46.
43. R. BARTHES, 'Drame, poème, roman'. In 214.
44. R. BARTHES, 'L'effet de réel', *Communications*, no. 11 (1968), pp. 84–9.
45. R. BARTHES, *Eléments de sémiologie*. Paris, Seuil, 1964.
46. R. BARTHES, *Essais critiques*. Paris, Seuil, 1964.
46B R. BARTHES, 'Introduction à l'analyse structurale des récits', *Communications*, no. 8 (1966), pp. 1–27.
47. R. BARTHES, 'Linguistique et littérature', *Langages*, no. 12 (1968), pp. 3–8.
48. R. BARTHES, 'Littérature et signification'. In 46.
49. R. BARTHES, *Michelet par lui-même*. Paris, Seuil, 1954.
50. R. BARTHES, *Mythologies*. Paris, Seuil, 1957.
51. R. BARTHES, 'Qu'est-ce que la critique?' In 46.

52. R. BARTHES, *Sur Racine*. Paris, Seuil, 1963.

53. R. BARTHES, *Système de la mode*. Paris, Seuil, 1967.

54. W. J. BATE, *The stylistic development of Keats*. New York, Modern Language Association of America, 1945. London, Routledge, 1958.

55. F. W. BATESON, 'The linguistic and the literary', *Times Literary Supplement*, no. 3,570 (1970), p. 854. [Letter to the Editor.]

56. F. W. BATESON, 'More on *The Fly*', *Essays in Criticism*, 1962, pp. 451–2. [Reply to 255.]

57. F. W. BATESON, 'A sort of answer', *Essays in Criticism*, 1962, pp. 347–51. [Reply to criticism of 58.]

58. F. W. BATESON and B. SHAHEVITCH, 'Katherine Mansfield's *The Fly*: a critical exercise', *Essays in Criticism*, 1962, pp. 39–53.

59. C. BAUDELAIRE, 'L'art romantique'. In *Oeuvres complètes* [Vol. 2]. Paris, Conard, 1925.

60. K. BAUMGÄRTNER, 'Formale Erklärung poetischer Texte'. In 363.

61. J. BAYLEY, *The characters of love*. London, Constable, 1960.

62. M. C. BEARDSLEY, *Aesthetics; problems in the philosophy of criticism*. New York, Harcourt, 1958.

63. J. BEATY, 'Visions and revisions: Chapter LXXXI of *Middlemarch*', *Publications of the Modern Language Association of America*, 1957, pp. 662–79.

64. E. C. van BELLEN, 'La pensée et la grammaire', *Neophilologus*, 1947, pp. 81–2.

65. T. V. BENN, 'French studies: the Twentieth Century', *Year's Work in Modern Language Studies*, 1961, pp. 121–141.

66. P. E. BENNETT, 'The statistical measurement of a stylistic trait in *Julius Caesar* and *As you like it*'. In 172.

67. E. BENVENISTE, *Problèmes de linguistique générale*. Paris, Gallimard, 1966.

68. F. BERRY, *Poets' grammar*. London, Routledge, 1958.

69. A. L. BINNS, ' "Linguistic" reading: two suggestions of the quality of literature'. In 219.

70. M. BLANCHOT, *Faux pas*. Paris, N.R.F., 1943.

71. M. BLANCHOT, *Lautréamont et Sade*. Paris, Editions de Minuit, 1963.
72. B. BLOCH, 'Linguistic structure and linguistic analysis'. In A. A. HILL (ed.), *Report of the 4th Annual Round Table Meeting on Linguistics and Language Teaching*. Washington D.C., Georgetown U.P., 1953.
73. G. BLÖCKER, *Kritisches Lesebuch*. Hamburg, Leibnitz, 1962.
74. A. M. BOASE, *The poetry of France; Vol. III: 1800–1900*. London, Methuen, 1967.
75. M. BODKIN, *Archetypal patterns in poetry*. London, Oxford U.P., paperback ed. 1963.
76. G. BONNARD (ed.), *English studies today. 2nd series*. Bern, Francke, 1961.
77. Y. BONNEFOY, 'La poésie française et le principe d'identité', *Revue d'Esthétique*, nos. 3 & 4, 1965, pp. 335–59.
78. L. BONNEROT, 'Techniques modernes en critique littéraire', *Langues Modernes*, 1951, pp. 51–62.
79. S. BOOTH, *An essay on Shakespeare's sonnets*. New Haven, Yale U.P., 1969.
80. S. BOOTH, 'On the value of *Hamlet*'. In 554.
81. W. C. BOOTH, *The rhetoric of fiction*. Chicago, U.P., 1961.
81B D. BOUVEROT, 'Comparaison et métaphore', *Français Moderne*, 1969, pp. 132–47.
82. F. BOWERS, *Textual and literary criticism*. Cambridge. U.P., 1959.
83. E. A. BOWLES (ed.), *Computers in humanistic research; readings and perspectives*. Englewood Cliffs, N.J., Prentice-Hall, 1967.
84. M. BRADBURY, *The social context of modern English literature*. Oxford, Blackwell, 1971.
85. G. BRÉE, 'Extract from *Du côté de chez Swann:* "Combray" '. In 505.
86. O. BRIK, 'Rythme et syntaxe'. In 690.
87. M. D. BRISTOL, 'Structural patterns in two Elizabethan pastorals', *Studies in English Literature 1500–1900*, 1970, pp. 33–48.
88. V. BROMBERT, 'Hugo, la prison et l'espace', *Revue des Sciences Humaines*, 1965, pp. 59–79.

89. G. L. BROOK, *The language of Dickens*. London, Deutsch, 1970.

90. C. BROOKE-ROSE, *A grammar of metaphor*. London, Secker & Warburg, 1958.

91. C. BROOKS, 'The heresy of paraphrase'. In 96.

92. C. BROOKS, 'Keats's sylvan historian'. In 96.

93. C. BROOKS, 'The language of paradox'. In 96.

94. C. BROOKS, *Modern poetry and the tradition*. London, Poetry London, 1948.

95. C. BROOKS, 'The naked babe and the cloak of manliness'. In 96.

96. C. BROOKS, *The well wrought urn*. London, Dobson, 2nd impression 1960. *London, Methuen, paperback ed. 1968.

97. C. BROOKS and R. P. WARREN, *The scope of fiction*. New York, Appleton, 1960.

98. C. BROOKS and R. P. WARREN, *Understanding fiction*. New York, Crofts, 1943.

99. H. BROWN, *Prose styles; 5 primary types*. Minneapolis, Minnesota U.P., 1966.

100. J. R. BROWN, 'Dialogue in Pinter and others', *Critical Quarterly*, 1965, pp. 225–43.

100B R. BROWN and A. GILMAN 'The pronouns of power and solidarity'. In 629.

101. F. BRUNOT, *Histoire de la langue française*. Paris, Colin, new. ed. 1966–

102. K. BÜHLER, 'L'onomatopée et la fonction représentative du langage'. In 520.

103. M. H. BULLEY, *Art and understanding*. London, Batsford, 1937.

104. K. BURKE, *A grammar of motives*. Englewood Cliffs, N.J., Prentice-Hall, 1945. *Berkeley, California U.P., 1969.

105. K. BURKE, *A rhetoric of motives*. Englewood Cliffs, N.J., Prentice-Hall, 1950. Berkeley, California U.P., 1969.

106. J. F. BURROWS, *Jane Austen's 'Emma'*. Sydney, U.P., 1969.

107. D. M. BURTON, 'Aspects of word order in two plays of Shakespeare', *Computer Studies in the Humanities and Verbal Behaviour*, 1970, pp. 34–9.

108. F. L. BURWICK, 'Stylistic continuity and change in the prose of Thomas Carlyle'. In 172.

109. J. G. CAHEN, *Le vocabulaire de Racine*. Paris, Droz, 1946.

110. *Cahiers d'Analyse Textuelle*. Paris, Les Belles Lettres, 1959–

110B *Cahiers de Lexicologie*, vols. x–xi. Paris, Didier-Larousse, 1967.

111. R. T. CARGO (ed.), *A concordance to Baudelaire's 'Les Fleurs du mal'*. Chapel Hill, North Carolina U.P., 1965.

112. W. B. CARNOCHAN, 'Johnsonian metaphor and the *Adamant of Shakespeare*', *Studies in English Literature 1500–1900*, 1970, pp. 541–9.

113. J. B. CARROLL, 'Vectors of prose style'. In 172.

114. G. A. CARVER, *Aesthetics and the problem of meaning*. New Haven, Yale U.P., 1952.

115. A. CASSAGNE, *Versification et métrique de Ch. Baudelaire*. Paris, Hachette, 1906.

116. G. CASTOR, '*Les Amours*: "Quand en songeant ma follastre j'acolle" '. In 505.

117. C. CAUDWELL, *Illusion and reality*. London, Macmillan, 1937. London, Lawrence & Wishart, 1946.

118. I. CELLINI and G. MELCHIORI (eds.), *English studies today. 4th series*. Roma, Ed. di Storia e Letteratura, 1966.

119. R. CELLY, *Répertoire des thèmes de Marcel Proust*. Paris, Gallimard, 1935.

120. A. CHANDOR, *A dictionary of computers*. Harmondsworth, Penguin Books, 1970.

121. R. de CHANTAL, *Marcel Proust critique littéraire*. Montréal, Pr. de l'Univ., 1967. Paris, Klincksieck, 1967.

121B M. CHASTAING, 'La brillance des voyelles', *Archivum Linguisticum*, 1962, pp. 1–13.

122. M. CHASTAING, 'Le symbolisme des voyelles', *Journal de Psychologie*, 1958, pp. 403–23 and 461–81.

123. S. CHATMAN, 'Comparing metrical styles'. In 128.

123B S. CHATMAN, *The later style of Henry James*. Oxford, Blackwell 1972.

124. S. CHATMAN, 'Mr. Stein on Donne', *Kenyon Review*, 1956, pp. 443–51.

125. S. CHATMAN, 'Robert Frost's *Mowing*: an inquiry into prosodic structure', *Kenyon Review*, 1956, pp. 421–38.

126. S. CHATMAN, *A theory of meter*. The Hague, Mouton, 1965.

127. S. CHATMAN (ed.), *Literary style: a symposium*. London, Oxford U.P., 1972.

128. S. CHATMAN and S. R. LEVIN (eds.), *Essays on the language of literature*. Boston, Houghton Mifflin, 1967.

129. J.-C. CHEVALIER, 'Guillaume Apollinaire. *Alcools*. Rosemonde', *Langue Française*, no. 7 (1970), pp. 36–44.

130. J.-C. CHEVALIER, '[Review of] HENRI MESCHONNIC, *Pour la poétique*', *Langue Française*, no. 7 (1970), pp. 127–8.

131. N. CHOMSKY, *Syntactic structures*. The Hague, Mouton, 1957.

132. B. CHOSEED and A. GUSS (eds.), *Report of the 11th Annual Round Table Meeting on Linguistics and Language Studies*. Washington D.C., Georgetown U.P., 1960.

133. C. D. CHRÉTIEN, '[Review of] *Who was Junius*? [and] *A statistical method for determining authorship*. By A. ELLEGÅRD', *Language*, 1964, pp. 85–90.

134. P. CLARAC, *L'enseignement du français*. Paris, P.U.F., 1963.

135. C. CLARK, '*Sir Gawain and the Green Knight*: characterisation by syntax', *Essays in Criticism*, 1966, pp. 361–74.

136. W. H. CLEMEN, *The development of Shakespeare's imagery*. London, Methuen, paperback ed. 1966.

137. W. H. CLEMEN, *Shakespeare's dramatic art*. London, Methuen, 1972.

138. D. CLOW, *The idea of revolt in 'Les chants de Maldoror'*. Unpublished M.A. thesis, University of Manchester, 1972.

139. A. COBBAN, *A history of Modern France*, 3 vols. *Harmondsworth, Penguin Books, 1957–65. London, Cape, 1963–1965.

140. J. M. COETZEE, 'Statistical indices of "difficulty"', *Language and Style*, 1969, pp. 226–32.

141. J. COHEN, *Structure du langage poétique*. Paris, Flammarion, 1966.

141A S. T. COLERIDGE, *Select poetry and prose. Edited by S. Potter*. London, The Nonesuch Pr., 1933.

141B J.-P. COLIN, 'De l'approche stylistique d'un mauvais genre littéraire: le roman policier'. In 409.

142. *Computational Linguistics*. Budapest, Hungarian Academy of Sciences Computing Centre, 1963–

143. *Computers and the Humanities*. Flushing, N.Y., Queen's College, 1966–

144. *Computers for the humanities?* New Haven, Yale U.P., 1965. [Proceedings of a conference at Yale University.]

145. *Computer Studies in the Humanities and Verbal Behaviour*. The Hague, Mouton, 1968–

146. H. COOMBES, *Literature and criticism*. London, Chatto and Windus, 1953.

147. R. A. COPLAND, 'Katherine Mansfield's *The Fly*', *Essays in Criticism*, 1962, pp. 338–41. [Comment on 58.]

148. J.-C. COQUET, 'Combinaison et transformation en poésie', *Homme*, 1969, pp. 23–41.

149. J.-C. COQUET, 'Problèmes de l'analyse structurale du récit. *L'Etranger* de Camus', *Langue Française*, no. 3 (1969), pp. 61–72.

150. E. P. CORBETT (ed.), *Rhetorical analyses of literary works*. New York, Oxford U.P., 1969.

151. P. CORTLAND, *The sentimental adventure: an examination of Flaubert's 'Education sentimentale'*. The Hague, Mouton, 1967.

152. R. G. COX, 'Statistical criticism', *Scrutiny*, 1935–6, pp. 309–311. [Review of 659.]

153. R. S. CRANE, *The language of criticism and the structure of poetry*. Toronto, U.P., 1953.

154. R. S. CRANE (ed.), *Critics and criticism*. Chicago, U.P., 1952. Cambridge, U.P., 1952.

155. M. CRESSOT, *La phrase et le vocabulaire de J.-K., Huysmans*. Paris, Droz, 1939.

155B. M. CRESSOT, *Le style et ses techniques*. Paris, P.U.F., 1969.

156. M. CRIADO DE VAL, *Análisis verbal del estílo*. Madrid, C.S.I.C., 1953.

157. 'The critical moment', *Times Literary Supplement*, no. 3,204 (1963), pp. 533–84 and no. 3,213 (1963), pp. 713–76. [Two special numbers devoted to modern criticism.]

158. M. W. CROLL, 'The baroque style in prose'. In 128.

158B D. CRYSTAL and D. DAVY, *Investigating English style*. London, Longmans, 1969.

159. J. CRUICKSHANK, 'Gide's treatment of time in *La Symphonie Pastorale*', *Essays in Criticism*, 1957, pp. 134–143.

159B J. CRUICKSHANK, 'Camus' technique in *L'Etranger*', *French Studies*, 1956, pp. 241–53.

160. C. CUÉNOT, *Le style de Paul Verlaine*. Paris, Centre de Documentation Universitaire, 1963.

160B E. R. CURTIUS, *European literature and the Latin Middle Ages*. London, Routledge, 1953.

161. D. DAICHES, *Virginia Woolf*. Norfolk, Conn., New Directions, 1942. London, Nicholson & Watson, 1945.

162. D. DAVIE, *Articulate energy. An inquiry into the syntax of English poetry*. London, Routledge, 1955.

163. H. DELACROIX, *Le langage et la pensée*. Paris, Alcan, 2nd ed. 1930.

164. G. DELATTRE, 'Le retour en arrière chez Balzac', *Romanic Review*, 1966, pp. 88–98.

165. P. DELBOUILLE, *Poésie et sonorités. La critique contemporaine devant le pouvoir suggestif des sons*. Paris, Les Belles Lettres, 1962.

166. S. DELESALLE, 'L'explication de textes. Fonctionnement et fonction', *Langue Française*, no. 7. (1970), pp. 87–95.

167. G. DEVOTO, 'Sémantique et syntaxe', *Conférences de l'Institut de Linguistique de l'Université de Paris*, 1952–3, pp. 51–62.

168. G. DI PINO, 'I generi letterari e la loro influenza nella determinazione del linguaggio poetico'. In 380.

168B 'Divided selves', *Times Literary Supplement*, no. 3,621 (1971) p. 854. [Review of 452.]

169. B. DOBREE, *Modern prose style*. London, Oxford U.P., 1934.

170. B. DOBREE, 'What is "literature" for?' In 190.

170B L. DOLEŽEL, 'A framework for the statistical analysis of style'. In 172.

171. L. DOLEŽEL, 'The Prague School and the statistical theory of poetic language', *Prague School Studies in Mathematical Linguistics*, 1967, pp. 97–104.

172. L. DOLEŽEL and R. W. BAILEY (eds.), *Statistics and style*. New York, Elsevier, 1969.

173. J. DOMERC, 'La glossématique et l'esthétique', *Langue Française*, no. 3 (1969), pp. 102–5.
174. E. DONATO, 'Of structuralism and literature', *Modern Language Notes*, 1967, pp. 549–74.
175. H. S. DONOW, *A concordance to the sonnet sequences of Daniel, Drayton, Shakespeare, Sidney and Spenser*. Carbondale, Southern Illinois U.P., 1969.
176. S. DOUBROVSKY, *Pourquoi la nouvelle critique. Critique et objectivité*. Paris, Mercure de France, 1966.
177. M. DRABBLE, *The waterfall*. London, Weidenfeld & Nicolson, 1969.
178. S. DRESDEN, 'Stylistique et science de la littérature', *Neophilologus*, 1952, pp. 193–205.
179. S. DRESDEN and others (eds.), *La notion de structure*. La Haye, Van Goor Zonen, 1961.
179B W. DRESSLER, 'Modelle und Methoden der Textsyntax', *Folia Linguistica*, 1970, pp. 64–71.
180. J. DUBOIS, 'Distribution, ensemble et marque dans le lexique', *Cahiers de Lexicologie*, no. 4 (1964), pp. 5–16.
181. J. DUBOIS, *Le vocabulaire politique et social en France de 1869 à 1872*. Paris, Larousse, 1963.
182. J. DUBOIS and others, *Rhétorique générale*. Paris, Larousse, 1970.
183. O. DUCROT and others, *Qu'est-ce que le structuralisme?* Paris, Seuil, 1968.
184. M. DUFRENNE, *Phénoménologie de l'expérience esthétique*. Paris, P.U.F., 1953.
185. M. DUFRENNE, *Le poétique*. Paris, P.U.F., 1963.
186. J. R. DUGAN, 'Flaubert's *Salammbô*, a study in immobility', *Zeitschrift für Französische Sprache und Literatur*, 1969, pp. 193–206.
187. B. DUPRIEZ, *L'étude des styles*. Paris, Didier, 1969.
188. E. DUPUY, *Victor Hugo, l'homme et le poète*. Paris, Lecène et Oudin, 1887.
189. M. DURAND, 'La spécificité du phonème. Application au cas de r/l', *Journal de Psychologie*, 1960, pp. 405–19.
190. G. I. DUTHIE (ed.), *English studies today. 3rd series*. Edinburgh, U.P., 1964.
191. A. E. DYSON, *The crazy fabric*. London, Macmillan, 1965.

191B A. E. DYSON, 'Editorial', *Critical Quarterly*, 1965, pp. 99–101.

192. T. EATON, *The semantics of literature*. The Hague, Mouton, 1966.

193. U. ECO, '[Extract from] *L'œuvre ouverte*'. In 333.

194. R. EDGLEY, 'The object of literary criticism', *Essays in Criticism*, 1964, pp. 221–36.

195. J. EHRMANN, 'Les structures de l'échange dans *Cinna*', *Temps Modernes*, 1966, pp. 929–60. Also published as: *'Structures of exchange in *Cinna*', *Yale French Studies*, 1966, pp. 169–99.

196. B. EIK-ENBAUM '[Extract from] *La théorie de la "méthode formelle"*'. In 333.

197. J. ELEMA, 'Echt oder Unecht. Zum Problem der literarischen Wertung', *Neophilologus*, 1952, pp. 33–45.

198. T. S. ELIOT, *Selected essays*. London, Faber, 1951.

199. A. ELLEGÅRD, *A statistical method for determining authorship: The Junius Letters, 1769–1772*. Stockholm, Almqvist & Wiksell, 1962.

200. A. ELLEGÅRD, *Who was Junius?* Stockholm, Almqvist & Wiksell, 1962.

201. C. EMERY, *The world of Dylan Thomas*. London, Dent, 1971.

202. W. EMPSON, *Seven types of ambiguity*. London, Chatto & Windus, 1930. *Harmondsworth, Penguin Books, paperback ed. 1961.

203. W. EMPSON, *The structure of complex words*. London, Chatto & Windus, 1951.

204. N. E. ENKVIST, 'On defining style: an essay in applied linguistics'. In 644.

205. V. ERLICH, *Russian formalism*. The Hague, Mouton, 1955.

206. S. ÉTIENNE, *Expériences d'analyse textuelle en vue de l'explication littéraire*. Liège, Faculté de Philosophie et Lettres, 1935.

207. B. EVERETT, 'The figure in Professor Knights's carpet', *Critical Quarterly*, 1960, pp. 171–6.

208. E. A. FALK, *Types of thematic structure: the nature and function of motifs in Gide, Camus and Sartre*. Chicago, U.P., 1967.

209. E. F. FENOLLOSA, *The Chinese written character as a medium for poetry; an ars poetica; with a foreword and notes by Ezra Pound.* New York, Arrow Editions, 1936. London, Nott, 1936.

210. J. R. FIRTH, 'Modes of meaning'. In 684.

211. I. FÓNAGY, 'Der Ausdruck als Inhalt'. In 363.

212. I. FÓNAGY, 'Communication in poetry', *Word*, 1961, pp. 194–218.

213. R. J. FOSTER, *The new romantics: a reappraisal of the new criticism.* Bloomington, Indiana U.P., 1962.

214. M. FOUCAULT and others, *Théorie d'ensemble.* Paris, Seuil, 1968.

215. R. FOWLER, 'Linguistics, stylistics; criticism?' *Lingua*, 1966, pp. 153–65.

216. R. FOWLER, 'Linguistic theory and the study of literature'. In 219.

217. R. FOWLER, 'Prose rhythm and metre'. In 219.

218. R. FOWLER, 'Structural metrics', *Linguistics*, 1966, pp. 49–64. Also in 128.

219. R. FOWLER (ed.), *Essays on style and language.* London, Routledge, 1966.

220. J. FOX, *The poetry of Villon*, London, Nelson, 1962.

221. P. FRAISSE, *Les structures rythmiques.* Bruxelles, Editions Erasme, 1956.

222. W. N. FRANCIS, 'Syntax and literary interpretation'. In 132.

223. J. FRANK, 'Spatial form in modern literature', *Sewanee Review*, 1945, pp. 221–40, 433–56 and 643–54.

224. E. R. FREUDEMANN, *Das Adjektiv und seine Ausdruckswerte im Stil Racines.* Berlin, Ebering, 1941.

225. J. FROGER, *La critique des textes et son automatisation.* Paris, Dunod, 1967.

225B W. M. FROHOCK (ed.), *Image and theme—studies in modern French fiction.* Harvard, U.P., 1969.

225C W. M. FROHOCK, *Style and temper.* Oxford, Blackwell, 1967.

226. J. H. FROMM, *'Les Trophées' von J. M. de Hérédia.* Greifswald, Adler, 1913.

227. N. FRYE, *The anatomy of criticism.* Princeton, U.P. 1957. Oxford, U.P., 1957.

228. N. FRYE, 'Dickens and the comedy of humors'. In 526.

229. N. FRYE (ed.), *Sound and poetry*. New York, Columbia U.P., 1957.

230. W. FUCKS, *Nach allen Regeln der Kunst*. Stuttgart, Deutsche Verlagsanstalt, 2nd ed. 1969.

231. R. FULLER, 'The filthy aunt and the anonymous seabird', *Times Literary Supplement*, no. 3,560 (1970), pp. 561–3.

232. K. FUTCH, *The syntax of C. S. Lewis's style: a statistical look at some syntactic features*. Unpublished doctoral dissertation, South California University, 1968. Résumé in *Dissertation Abstracts*, 1969, 2002 A.

233. H. G. GADAMER, *Wahrheit und Methode*. Tübingen, Mohr, 1960.

234. G. GALICHET, *Méthodologie grammaticale*. Paris, P.U.F., 1963.

235. M. GALLIOT, *Commentaires de textes français modernes. Grammaire et stylistique appliquée*. Paris, Didier, 1965.

236. T. M. GANG, 'Intention', *Essays in Criticism*, 1957, pp. 175–186.

237. P. K. GARRETT, *Scene and symbol from George Eliot to James Joyce: studies in changing fictional mode*. New Haven, Yale U.P., 1969. [See 474.]

238. G. GENETTE, *Figures*, 3 vols. Paris, Seuil, 1966–72.

239. G. GENETTE, 'Proust palimpseste'. In 238 (Vol. 1).

240. G. GENETTE, 'Raisons de la critique pure'. In 538.

241. F. GERMAIN, *L'art de commenter un texte littéraire*. Paris, Foucher, 1955.

242. F. GERMAIN, *Expliquez-moi l'art de commenter un poème lyrique*. Paris, Foucher, 1954.

243. M. C. GHYKA, *Essai sur le rythme*. Paris, Gallimard, 1938.

244. A. GILL, 'From *Quand l'ombre menaça* to *Au seul souci de voyager*: Mallarmé's debt to Chateaubriand', *Modern Language Review*, 1955, pp. 414–32.

245. R. GIRARD, 'La notion de structure en critique littéraire'. In 549.

246. L. GOLDMANN, *Le dieu caché*. Paris, Gallimard, 1955. Tr. publ. as *The hidden god*. London, Routledge, 1964.

247. L. GOLDMANN, *Pour une sociologie du roman*. Paris, Gallimard, 1964.

248. T. GOODMAN, *The techniques of fiction.* New York, Liveright, 1955.
249. C. GORDON, *How to read a novel.* New York, Viking Pr., 1957. London, Macmillan, 1957.
250. I. A. GORDON, *The movement of English prose.* London, Longmans, 1966.
251. R. de GOURMONT, *Le problème du style.* Paris, Mercure de France, new. ed. 1907.
252. M. GRAMMONT, *Le vers français, ses moyens d'expression, son harmonie.* Paris, Champion, 2nd. ed. 1913.
253. G. GRANA (ed.), *Letteratura italiana. I critici,* 5 vols. Milano, Marzorati, 1969.
254. E. B. GREENWOOD, 'Katherine Mansfield's *The Fly*', *Essays in Criticism,* 1962, pp. 341–7. [Comment on 58.]
255. E. B. GREENWOOD, 'More on *The Fly*', *Essays in Criticism,* 1962, pp. 448–50. [Reply to 57.]
256. A. L. GREIMAS, *Du sens. Essais sémiotiques.* Paris, Seuil, 1970.
257. A. L. GREIMAS, 'La linguistique structurale et la poétique'. In 256.
258. A. L. GREIMAS, 'Per una sociologia del senso commune', *Rassegna Italiana di Sociologia,* 1968, pp. 199–209.
259. A. L. GREIMAS, *Sémantique structurale.* Paris, Larousse, 1966.
260. A. L. GREIMAS, 'La structure des actants du récit'. In 256.
261. B. GROOM, *The diction of poetry from Spenser to Bridges.* Toronto, U.P., 1955.
262. A. W. de GROOT, 'Phonetics in its relation to aesthetics'. In 347.
263. F. GUENTHNER, 'Le *new criticism*', *Langue Française,* no. 7 (1970), pp. 96–101.
264. J. L. GUETTI, *The limits of metaphor.* Ithaca, Cornell U.P., 1967.
265. N. GUEUNIER, 'La pertinence de la notion d'écart', *Langue Française,* no. 3 (1969), pp. 34–45.
266. A. GUEX, *L'art baudelairien.* Lausanne, Rouge, 1936.
267. P. GUIRAUD, *Les caractères statistiques du vocabulaire.* Paris, P.U.F., 1954.

268. P. GUIRAUD, 'L'évolution statistique du style de Rimbaud et le problème des *Illuminations*', *Mercure de France*, 1954, pp. 201–34.

269. P. GUIRAUD, *Le jargon de Villon, ou Le gai savoir de la Coquille*. Paris, Gallimard, 1968.

270. P. GUIRAUD, *Langage et versification d'après l'oeuvre de Paul Valéry*. Paris, Klincksieck, 1953.

271. P. GUIRAUD, *Problèmes et méthodes de la statistique linguistique*. Paris, P.U.F., 1960.

272. P. GUIRAUD, *La sémantique*. Paris, P.U.F., 1955.

273. P. GUIRAUD, *La stylistique*. Paris, P.U.F., 1954.

274. P. GUIRAUD, 'Les tendances de la stylistique contemporaine'. In 278.

275. P. GUIRAUD, *Le testament de Villon, ou Le gai savoir de la basoche*. Paris, Gallimard, 1970.

276. P. GUIRAUD (ed.), *Index du vocabulaire du symbolisme*, 7 fasc. Paris, Klincksieck, 1953–60.

277. P. GUIRAUD and P. KUENTZ (eds.), *La stylistique*. Paris, Klincksieck, 1970.

278. P. GUIRAUD and others, *Style et littérature*. La Haye, Van Goor Zonen, 1962.

279. J.-M. GUYAU, *L'art au point de vue sociologique*. Paris, Alcan, 1889.

280. J. HAGAN, 'On the craftsmanship of *War and Peace*', *Essays in Criticism*, 1963, pp. 17–49.

281. M. A. K. HALLIDAY, 'Descriptive linguistics and literary studies'. In 428.

282. M. A. K. HALLIDAY, 'The linguistic study of literary texts'. In 128.

283. M. A. K. HALLIDAY and others, *The linguistic sciences and language teaching*. London, Longmans, 1964.

284. G. R. HAMILTON, *The tell tale article. A critical approach to modern poetry*. London, Heinemann, 1949.

285. M. L. HANLEY, *A word index to James Joyce's 'Ulysses'*. Madison, Wisconsin U.P., 1951.

286. M. HARDT, *Das Bild in der Dichtung*. München, Fink, 1966.

287. A. HARDY, 'Théorie et méthode stylistiques de Riffaterre', *Langue Française*, no. 3 (1969), pp. 90–6.

288. B. HARDY, 'Imagery in George Eliot's last novels', *Modern Language Review*, 1955, pp. 6–14.

289. B. HARDY, *The novels of George Eliot: a study in form.* London, Athlone Pr., 1959.

290. T. HARDY, *Selected shorter poems.* London, Macmillan, paperback ed. 1966.

291. Z. S. HARRIS, *Methods in structural linguistics.* Chicago, U.P., 1951. Republished as: *Structural linguistics*, 1960.

292. G. HARTMANN, 'Structuralism: the Anglo-American adventure', *Yale French Studies*, 1966, pp. 148–68.

293. W. J. HARVEY, *The art of George Eliot.* London, Chatto & Windus, 1961.

294. W. J. HARVEY, *Character and the novel.* London, Chatto & Windus, 1965.

295. H. HATZFELD, *A critical bibliography of the new stylistics applied to the Romance literatures, 1900–1952.* Chapel Hill, North Carolina U.P., 1953. (*Supplement (1953–65)*, Chapel Hill, North Carolina U.P., 1966.)

296. H. HATZFELD, *'Don Quijote' als Wortkunstwerk.* Leipzig, Teubner, 1927.

297. H. HATZFELD, 'Stylistic criticism as art-minded philology', *Yale French Studies*, 1949, pp. 1–9.

298. H. HATZFELD and Y. LE HIR, *Essai de bibliographie critique de stylistique française et romane, 1955–1960.* Paris, P.U.F., 1961.

299. R. D. HAVENS, 'Structure and prosodic pattern in Shelley's lyrics', *Publications of the Modern Language Association of America*, 1950, pp. 1076–87.

300. D. G. HAYS, 'Automatic language-data processing'. In H. BORKO (ed.), *Computer applications in the behavioral sciences.* Englewood Cliffs, N.J., Prentice-Hall, 1962.

301. D. G. HAYS, *Introduction to computational linguistics.* London, Macdonald, 1967.

302. W. O. HENDRICKS, *Linguistics and the structural analysis of literary texts.* Unpublished dissertation, University of Illinois, 1965.

303. W. O. HENDRICKS, 'Three models for the description of poetry', *Journal of Linguistics*, 1969, pp. 1–22.

303A A. HENRY, *Métonymie et métaphore*. Paris. Klincksieck, 1969.

303B G. HERDAN, *Language as choice and chance*. Groningen, Noordhoff, 1956.

304. M. B. HESTER, *The meaning of poetic metaphor*. The Hague, Mouton, 1967.

305. B. C. HEYL, *New bearings in esthetics and art criticism*. New Haven, Yale U.P., 1943.

306. E. W. HILDICK, *Thirteen types of narrative*. London, Macmillan, 1968.

307. A. A. HILL, 'An analysis of *The Windhover*: an experiment in structural method', *Publications of the Modern Language Association of America*, 1955, pp. 968–78.

308. A. A. HILL, 'Poetry and stylistics'. In 128.

309. P. HOBSBAUM, *A theory of communication*. London, Macmillan, 1970.

310. J. HOLLANDER, 'The metrical emblem'. In 128.

311. J. HOLLOWAY, *The charted mirror*. London, Routledge, 1960.

312. J. HOLLOWAY, 'The critical theory of Yvor Winters', *Critical Quarterly*, 1965, pp. 54–68.

313. J. HOLLOWAY, *The Victorian sage*. London, Macmillan, 1953.

314. P. HONAN, 'Realism, reality, and the novel', *Novel*, 1968–9, pp. 193–211. [Report on, and extracts from a symposium on the novel.]

315. L. H. HORNSTEIN, 'Analysis of imagery: a critique of literary method', *Publications of the Modern Language Association of America*, 1942, pp. 638–53.

316. J. HOSPERS, *Meaning and truth in the arts*. Chapel Hill, North Carolina U.P., 1947.

317. G. HOUGH, 'Criticism as a humanist discipline'. In 669.

318. G. HOUGH, *An essay on criticism*. London, Duckworth, 1966.

319. G. HOUGH, *Image and experience*. London, Duckworth, 1960.

320. G. HOUGH, *Style and stylistics*. London, Routledge, 1969.

321. T. H. HOWARD-HILL (ed.), *Oxford Shakespeare concordances*. Oxford, U.P., 1969–

322. W. D. HOWARTH and C. L. WALTON, *Explications: the technique of French literary appreciation*. London, Oxford U.P., 1971.

323. V. HUGO, *Oeuvres choisies*, 2 vols. Paris, Hatier, 1950.

324. E. HUGUET, *La couleur, la lumière et l'ombre dans les métaphores de Victor Hugo*. Paris, Hachette, 1905.

325. E. HUGUET, *Les métaphores et les comparaisons dans l'oeuvre de Victor Hugo*. Paris, Hachette, 1904.

326. H. M. HULME, *Explorations in Shakespeare's language*. London, Longmans, 1962.

327. I. P. HUNGERLAND, *Poetic discourse*. Berkeley, California U.P., 1958.

328. S. E. HYMAN, *The armed vision; a study in the methods of modern literary criticism*. New York, Vintage Books, rev. ed. 1955.

329. D. HYMES, 'Phonological aspects of style: some English sonnets'. In 629.

330. J. HYTIER, 'La méthode de M. Leo Spitzer', *Romanic Review*, 1950, pp. 42–59.

331. J. HYTIER, *La poétique de Valéry*. Paris, Colin, 1953.

332. 'In praise of complexity', *Times Literary Supplement*, no. 3,632 (1971), p. 1205. [Reviews of F. KERMODE, *Shakespeare, Spenser, Donne* (Routledge) & *Modern Essays* (Fontana).]

333. A. JACOB (ed.), *100 points de vue sur le langage*. Paris, Klincksieck, 1969.

334. R. JAKOBSON, *Essais de linguistique générale*. Paris, Editions de Minuit, 1963.

335. R. JAKOBSON, 'Linguistics and poetics'. In *128 and 629.

336. R. JAKOBSON, 'Parts and wholes in language'. In R. JAKOBSON, *Selected writings*, [Vol. II.] The Hague, Mouton, 1971.

337. R. JAKOBSON, 'Poesie der Grammatik und Grammatik der Poesie'. In 363.

338. R. JAKOBSON and L. G. JONES, *Shakespeare's verbal art in 'Th'expence of spirit'*. The Hague, Mouton, 1970.

339. R. JAKOBSON and C. LÉVI-STRAUSS, '*Les Chats* de Charles Baudelaire', *L'Homme*, 1962, pp. 5–21.

340. H. JAMES, *Selected literary criticism*. London, Heinemann, 1963. *Harmondsworth, Penguin Books, 1968.

341. V. JANKELEVITCH, *L'ironie*. Paris, Flammarion, 1964.

342. E. D. H. JOHNSON, *Charles Dickens; an introduction to his novels*. New York, Random House, 1969.

343. L. G. JONES, 'Grammatical patterns in English and Russian verse'. In 692 (Vol. 2).

344. A. JOUSSAIN, *L'esthétique de Victor Hugo. Le pittoresque dans le lyrisme et l'épopée*. Paris, Boivin, 1920.

345. A. G. JUILLAND, '[Extract from] Review of Bruneau's *L'époque réaliste*'. In 128.

346. F. KAINZ, *Psychologie der Sprache*, 2 vols. Stuttgart, Enke, 2nd ed. 1954.

347. L. KAISER (ed.), *Manual of phonetics*. Amsterdam, North Holland, 1957.

348. W. P. KER, *Form and style in poetry*. London, Macmillan, 1928. Reissued 1966.

349. F. KERMODE, *Romantic image*. London, Routledge, 1957.

350. F. KERMODE, *The sense of an ending*. New York, Oxford U.P., 1968.

351. A. KIBÉDI VARGA, 'A la recherche d'un style baroque'. In 278.

352. A. KIBÉDI VARGA, *Les constantes du poème*. La Haye, Van Goor Zonen, 1963.

353. S. KIERKEGAARD, *The concept of dread*. London, Oxford U.P., 1944.

354. R. A. KING, *The focusing artifice. The poetry of Robert Browning*. Athens, Ohio U.P., 1969.

355. L. KIRSCHBAUM, 'Banquo and Edgar: character or function?' *Essays in Criticism*, 1957, pp. 1–21.

356. L. C. KNIGHTS, *Explorations*. London, Chatto & Windus, 1946.

357. L. C. KNIGHTS, 'How many children had Lady Macbeth?' In 356.

358. N. KNOX, *The word irony and its context 1500–1755*. Durham, N.C., Duke U.P., 1961.

359. H. KONRAD, *Etude sur la métaphore*. Paris, Vrin, 1939. Reissued 1958.

360. J.-G. KRAFFT, 'De l'unité..., ailleurs et en poésie', *Revue d'Esthétique*, 1954, pp. 288–302.

361. J.-G. KRAFFT, *La forme et l'idée en poésie*. Paris, Vrin, 2nd ed. 1951.

362. W. KRAUSS, *Grundprobleme der Literaturwissenschaft*. Reinbek, Rowohlt, 1968.

363. H. KREUZER and R. GUNZENHÄUSER (eds.), *Mathematik und Dichtung*. München, Nymphenburger Verlagshandlung, 1965.

364. M. KRIEGER, *The new apologists for poetry*. Minneapolis, Minnesota U.P., 1956.

365. M. KRIEGER, *A window to criticism*. Princeton, U.P., 1964.

366. J. KRISTEVA, 'Narration et transformation', *Semiotica*, 1969, pp. 422–48.

367. J. KRISTEVA, 'Problèmes de la structuration du texte'. In 214.

368. J. KRISTEVA, 'La sémiologie: science critique et/ou critique de la science'. In 214.

369. K. KROEBER, 'Perils of quantification: the exemplary case of Jane Austen's *Emma*'. In 172.

370. K. KROEBER, *Styles in fictional structure*. Princeton, U.P., 1971. London, Oxford U.P., 1971.

371. P. KUENTZ, 'Remarques liminaires', *Langue Française*, no. 7 (1970), pp. 3–13.

372. P. KUENTZ, 'Tendances actuelles de la stylistique anglo-américaine', *Langue Française*, no. 3 (1969), pp. 85–9.

373. P. KUENTZ (ed.), *La description linguistique des textes littéraires*. Paris, Larousse, 1970. [*Langue Française*, no. 7.]

374. C. LA DRIÈRE, 'Structure, sound and meaning'. In 229.

375. E. LÄMMERT, *Bauformen des Erzählens*. Stuttgart, Metzler, 1955.

376. R. S. LANDON, *A statistical study of the vocabulary of six poetic collections of the surrealist period*. Unpublished doctoral dissertation, Indiana University, 1969. Résumé in *Dissertation Abstracts*, 1970, 3013 A.

377. *Le Langage. Actes du 13e Congrès des Sociétés de Philosophie de Langue Française*, Vol. 1. Neuchâtel, La Baconnière, 1966.

378. S. K. LANGER, *Feeling and form*. London, Routledge, 1953.

379. S. K. LANGER, *Philosophy in a new key*. Cambridge, Mass., Harvard U.P., 1942.

380. *Langue et littérature. Actes du VIIIe Congrès de la Fédération Internationale des Langues et Littératures Modernes.* Paris, Les Belles Lettres, 1961.

380B P. LARTHOMAS, 'La notion de genre littéraire en stylistique', *Français Moderne*, 1964, pp. 185–93.

381. H. LAUSBERG, *Handbuch der literarischen Rhetorik*, 2 vols. München, Hueber, 1960.

382. J. R. LAWLER, *The language of French symbolism*. Princeton, U.P., 1969.

383. R. F. LAWRENCE, 'The formulaic theory and its application to English alliterative poetry'. In 219.

383B F. W. LEAKEY, 'Intention in metaphor', *Essays in Criticism*, 1954, pp. 191–8.

384. M. A. LEASKA, *Virginia Woolf's 'Lighthouse': a study in critical method*. New York, Columbia U.P., 1970.

385. F. R. LEAVIS, '*Anthony and Cleopatra* and *All for love*. A critical exercise', *Scrutiny*, 1936–7, pp. 158–69.

386. F. R. LEAVIS, *The great tradition*. Harmondsworth, Penguin Books, paperback ed. 1964.

387. F. R. LEAVIS, 'Revaluations. IX. Keats', *Scrutiny*, 1935–1936, pp. 376–400.

388. F. R. LEAVIS, *A selection from 'Scrutiny'*, 2 vols. Cambridge, U.P., 1968.

389. B. LEE, 'The new criticism and the language of poetry'. In 219.

390. G. N. LEECH, *A linguistic guide to English poetry*. London, Longman, 1969.

391. G. N. LEECH, 'Linguistics and the figures of rhetoric'. In 219.

392. J. LEED (ed.), *The computer and literary style*. Kent, Ohio, Kent State U.P., 1966.

393. F. LEFEVRE, *Entretiens avec Paul Valéry*. Paris, Le Livre, 1926.

393B M. LE GUERN, *Sémantique de la métaphore et de la métonymie*. Paris, Larousse, 1973.

394. Y. LE HIR, *Esthétique et structure du vers français*. Paris, P.U.F., 1956.

395. Y. LE HIR, 'Littérature et stylistique, ou des méthodes historiques dans le commentaire des textes', *Cahiers de l'Association Internationale des Etudes Françaises*, 1964, pp. 59–69.

396. R. C. I. LEHMANN, *Die Formelemente des Stils von Flaubert in den Romanen und Novellen*. Marburg, Ebel, 1911.

397. U. LEO, *Stilforschung und dichterische Einheit*. München, Hueber, 1966.

398. P. R. LÉON, 'Principes et méthodes en phonostylistique', *Langue Française*, no. 3 (1969), pp. 73–84.

399. D. LERNER (ed.), *Parts and wholes*. New York, Free Pr., 1963. London, Macmillan, 1963.

400. L. LESAGE and A. YON, *Dictionnaire des critiques littéraires: guide de la critique française du XXe siècle*. Philadelphia, Pennsylvania State U.P., 1969.

401. S. LESSER, *Fiction and the unconscious*. New York, Beacon Pr., 1957.

402. S. R. LEVIN, 'Deviation—statistical and determinate—in poetic language', *Lingua*, 1963, pp. 276–90.

403. S. R. LEVIN, *Linguistic structures in poetry*. The Hague, Mouton, 1962.

404. G. LEVINE, *The boundaries of fiction*. Princeton, U.P., 1968.

405. G. LEVINE, '*Madame Bovary* and the disappearing author', *Modern Fiction Studies*, 1963, pp. 103–19.

406. J. LEVÝ, 'Mathematical aspects of the theory of verse'. In 172.

407. C. D. LEWIS, *The poetic image*. London, Cape, 1947.

408. R. W. B. LEWIS, *The picaresque saint*. Philadelphia, Lippincott, 1959. London, Gollancz, 1960.

409. *Linguistique et littérature. Colloque de Cluny*. Paris, La Nouvelle Critique, 1968.

410. 'The literary computer', *Times Literary Supplement*, no. 3,553 (1970), p. 368. [Report on the Cambridge Symposium on the 'Uses of the Computer in Literary Research', 1970.]

411. D. LODGE, *The language of fiction*. London, Routledge, 1966.

412. J. LOOFBOUROW, *Thackeray and the form of fiction*. Princeton, U.P., 1964.

413. G. LOTE, *Etudes sur le vers français. Première partie: l'alexandrin d'après la phonétique expérimentale*, 3 parts. Paris, Crès, 2nd ed. 1919.

414. G. A. LOVE and M. PAYNE (eds.), *Contemporary essays on style*. Glenview, Ill., Scott, Foresman, 1969.

415. P. LUBBOCK, *The craft of fiction*. London, Cape, paperback ed. 1965.

416. H. P. LUHN, *Potentialities of auto-encoding of scientific literature*. Yorktown Heights, N.Y., IBM Research Center, 1959.

417. G. LUKÁCS, *Die Theorie des Romans*. Berlin, Cassirer, 1920.

418. J. LYNCH, 'The tonality of lyric poetry: an experiment in method', *Word*, 1953, pp. 211–24.

419. L. MABILLEAU, *Victor Hugo*. Paris, Hachette, 3rd ed. 1902.

420. M. McCARTHY, 'The fact in fiction', *Partisan Review*, 1960, pp. 438–58.

421. M. McCARTHY, 'Letter to a translator about *The Group*', *Encounter*, Nov. 1964, pp. 69–71 and 74–6.

422. M. M. MACDERMOTT, *Vowel sounds in poetry*. London, Routledge, 1940.

423. P. MACHEREY, 'L'analyse littéraire, tombeau des structures', *Temps Modernes*, no. 246 (1966), pp. 907–28.

424. A. McINTOSH, '*As you like it*: a grammatical clue to character'. In 428.

425. A. McINTOSH, 'Linguistics and English studies'. In 428.

426. A. McINTOSH, 'Patterns and ranges', *Language*, 1961, pp. 325–37.

427. A. McINTOSH, 'Some thoughts on style'. In 428.

428. A. McINTOSH and M. A. K. HALLIDAY, *Patterns of language*. London, Longmans, 1966.

429. T. P. H. McKELLAR, *Imagination and thinking: a psychological analysis*. London, Cohen & West, 1957.

430. S. MALLARMÉ, *Correspondance*, 3 vols. Paris, Gallimard, 1959–69.

431. S. MALLARMÉ, *Dix poèmes, Exégèses de E. Noulet*. Lille, Giard, 1948.

432. J. MALOF, *A manual of English meters*. Bloomington, Indiana U.P., 1970.

433. P. de MAN, 'Impasse de la critique formaliste', *Critique*, 1956, pp. 483–500.

434. P. de MAN, 'New criticism et nouvelle critique', *Preuves*, no. 188 (1966), pp. 29–37.

435. J. MAROUZEAU, *Précis de stylistique française.* Paris, Masson, 3rd ed. 1950.

436. J. MAROUZEAU, 'Quelques aspects de la question du style', *Conférences de l'Institut de Linguistique de l'Université de Paris,* 1939, pp. 29–42.

437. H. C. MARTIN (ed.), *Style in prose fiction.* New York, Columbia U.P., 1959.

438. A. MARTINET, 'Connotations, poésie et culture'. In 692 (Vol. 2).

439. A. MARTINET, *La linguistique synchronique.* Paris, P.U.F., 1965.

440. D. I. MASSON, 'The thematic analysis of sounds in poetry'. In 128.

441. D. I. MASSON, 'Vowel and consonant patterns in poetry', *Journal of Aesthetics and Art Criticism,* 1953, pp. 213–27. Also in *128.

442. D. I. MASSON, 'Wilfred Owen's free phonetic patterns: their style and function', **Journal of Aesthetics and Art Criticism,* 1955, pp. 360–9. Also in 128.

443. M. MASTERMAN and R. McKINNON WOOD, 'The poet and the computer', *Times Literary Supplement,* no. 3,564 (1970), pp. 667–8.

444. G. MATORÉ, *L'espace humain.* Paris, Editions du Vieux Colombier, 1962.

445. G. MATORÉ, *La méthode en lexicologie, domaine français.* Paris, Didier, 1953.

446. G. MATORÉ, *Le vocabulaire et la société sous Louis-Philippe.* Genève, Droz, 1951.

447. J. H. MATTHEWS (ed.), *An anthology of French surrealist poetry.* London, U.P., 1966.

448. C. MAURON, *Des métaphores obsédantes au mythe personnel.* Paris, Corti, 1963.

449. C. MAURON, *L'inconscient dans l'oeuvre et la vie de Racine.* Gap, Editions Ophrys, 1957.

450. C. MAURON, *Introduction à la psychanalyse de Mallarmé.* Neuchâtel, La Baconnière, 1950. *Reissued 1968.

451. C. MAURON, *Mallarmé l'obscur.* Paris. Denoël, 1941. Paris, Corti, new ed. 1968.

452. C. MAURON, *Le théâtre de Giraudoux.* Paris, Corti, 1971.

453. J. MAZALEYRAT, *Pour une étude rythmique du vers français moderne*. Paris, Minard, 1963.

454. A. A. MENDILOW, *Time and the novel*. London, Nevill, 1953.

455. H. MESCHONNIC, 'Pour la poétique', *Langue Française*, no. 3 (1969), pp. 14–31. [Extract from 456.]

456. H. MESCHONNIC, *Pour la poétique*. Paris, Gallimard, 1970.

457. G. M. MESSING, '[Review of] *Style in Language*. Edited by T. A. SEBEOK', *Language*, 1961, pp. 256–66. [Review of 629.]

458. *Méthodes de la grammaire. Tradition et nouveauté. Actes du colloque tenu à Liège*, 1964. Paris, Les Belles Lettres, 1966.

459. M. Meuraud, *L'image végétale dans la poésie d'Eluard*. Paris, Minard, 1966.

460. G. MICHAUD, *Connaissance de la littérature. L'oeuvre et ses techniques*. Paris, Nizet, 1957.

461. J. MILES, *The continuity of poetic language*. Berkeley, California U.P., 1951.

462. J. MILES, *Eras and modes in English poetry*. Berkeley, California U.P., 1957.

463. J. MILES, 'Eras in English poetry'. In 128.

464. J. MILES, *Major adjectives in English poetry*. Berkeley, California U.P., 1946.

465. J. MILES, *The pathetic fallacy in the nineteenth century*. Berkeley, California U.P., 1942.

466. J. MILES, *The primary language of poetry in the 1640's*. Berkeley, California U.P., 1948.

467. J. MILES, *Renaissance, eighteenth-century and modern language in English poetry: a tabular view*. Berkeley, California U.P., 1960.

468. J. MILES, *Wordsworth and the vocabulary of emotion*. Berkeley, California U.P., 1942.

469. L. T. MILIC, 'Against the typology of styles'. In 128.

469B L. T. MILIC, 'Choice and option in style'. In 127.

470. L. T. MILIC, *A quantitative approach to the style of Jonathan Swift*. The Hague, Mouton, 1967.

471. L. T. MILIC, *Style and stylistics; an analytical bibliography*. New York, Free Pr., 1967. London, Macmillan, 1967.

472. L. T. MILIC, 'Unconscious ordering in the prose of Swift'. In 392.

473. J. H. MILLER, *Charles Dickens: the world of his novels.* Cambridge, Mass., Harvard U.P., 1958. London, Oxford U.P., 1959.

474. J. H. MILLER, 'Recent studies in the nineteenth century Part II', *Studies in English Literature 1500–1900*, 1970, pp. 183–214.

475. J. H. MILLER, *Thomas Hardy: distance and desire.* Cambridge, Mass., Harvard U.P., 1970.

476. J. H. MILLER, 'Three problems of fictional form'. In 526.

476B J. MILLY, 'Les pastiches de Proust; structure et correspondances', *Le Français Moderne*, 1967, pp. 33–52 and 125–41.

477. H. MITTERAND, 'Corrélations lexicales du récit: le vocabulaire du visage dans *Thérèse Raquin*'. In 409.

478. A. MIZENER, 'The structure of figurative language in Shakespeare's Sonnets', *Southern Review*, 1939–40, pp. 730–747.

479. A. MOLES, *Théorie de l'information et perception esthétique.* Paris, Flammarion, 1948. Translation published as: *Information theory and esthetic perception.* Urbana, Illinois U.P., 1966.

480. H. MONDOR, *Précocité de Valéry.* Paris, Gallimard, 1957.

481. P. MOREAU, *La critique littéraire en France.* Paris, Colin, 1960.

482. C. MORHANGE-BÉGUÉ, '*Mai*: essai d'application d'une méthode stylistique', *Langue Française*, no. 7 (1970), pp. 28–35.

483. H. MORIER, *Dictionnaire de poétique et de rhétorique.* Paris, P.U.F., 1961.

484. H. MORIER, *La psychologie des styles.* Genève, Georg, 1959.

485. H. MORIER, *Le rythme du vers libre symboliste . . . et ses relations avec le sens*, 3 vols. Genève, Les Presses Académiques, 1943–44.

486. J. F. MORRIS, *Thomas Hardy's style: a syntactic approach to the poetry.* Unpublished doctoral dissertation, University of New Mexico, 1968. Résumé in *Dissertation Abstracts*, 1969, 875–6 A.

487. G. MOUNIN, *Clefs pour la linguistique*. Paris, Seghers, 1968.

488. J. MOUROT, *Le génie d'un style: Chateaubriand. Rythme et sonorité dans les 'Mémoires d'outre-tombe'*. Paris, Colin, 1960.

489. J. MOUROT, *La stylistique littéraire est-elle l'illusion?* Nancy, C.R.A.L., 1966.

490. E. MUIR, *The structure of the novel*. London, Hogarth Pr., 1928.

491. K. MUIR, 'Image and structure in *Our mutual friend*'. In 761.

492. J. MUKAŘOVSKÝ, '[Extract from] Standard language and poetic language'. In 128.

493. J. MUKAŘOVSKÝ, 'La dénomination poétique et la fonction esthétique de la langue'. In 1.

493B C. MULLER, *Essai de statistique lexicale—'L'illusion comique' de Pierre Corneille*. Paris, Klincksieck, 1965.

494. C. MULLER, 'Sur quelques scènes de Molière; essai d'un indice du style familier', *Français Moderne*, 1962, pp. 99–108.

495. J. M. MURRY, *The problem of style*. London, Oxford U.P., paperback ed. 1960.

496. 'Myth', *Symposium*, 1971, pp. 99–220.

497. V. NABOKOV, *Nikolai Gogol*. *Norfolk, Conn., New Directions, 1944. London, Editions Poetry, 1947.

498. O. NADAL, *Paul Verlaine*. Paris, Mercure de France, 1961.

499. W. NAUMANN, 'The architecture of George Eliot's novels', *Modern Language Quarterly*, 1948, pp. 37–50.

500. L. NELSON, *Baroque lyric poetry*. New Haven, Yale U.P., 1961.

501. W. NELSON, 'Syntax and literary appreciation'. In 132.

502. 'New frontiers in the theory of fiction', *Times Literary Supplement*, no. 3,627 (1971), pp. 1055–6. [Reviews.]

503. E. NEWTON, *The meaning of beauty*. Harmondsworth, Penguin Books, 1962.

503B 'The nothing new', *Times Literary Supplement*, no. 3,622 (1971), p. 893. [Review of 201.]

504. W. NOWOTTNY, *The language poets use*. London, Athlone Pr., 1962.

505. P. H. NURSE (ed.), *The art of criticism*. Edinburgh, U.P., 1969.

505B A. D. NUTTALL, 'The argument about Shakespeare's characters', *Critical Quarterly*, 1965, pp. 107–20.

506. W. V. O'CONNOR (ed.), *Forms of modern fiction*. Minneapolis, Minnesota U.P., 1948. London, Oxford U.P., 1949.

507. C. K. OGDEN and I. A. RICHARDS, *The meaning of meaning*. New York, Harcourt, 1923. *London, Kegan Paul, 1923.

508. W. O'GRADY, 'Plot in modern fiction', *Modern Fiction Studies*, 1965, pp. 107–15.

509. R. OHMANN, 'Generative grammars and the concept of literary style', *Word*, 1964, pp. 423–39.

510. R. OHMANN, 'Literature as sentences'. In 128.

511. R. OHMANN, 'Prolegomena to the analysis of style'. In 128.

512. J. ONIMUS, *La communication littéraire*. Paris, Desclée de Brouwer, 1970.

513. A. ORAS, 'Spenser and Milton: some parallels and contrasts in the handling of sound'. In 128.

514. C. E. OSGOOD and others, *The measurement of meaning*. Urbana, Illinois U.P., 1957.

514B N. PAGE, *The language of Jane Austen*. Oxford, Blackwell, 1972.

515. M. PAGNINI, *Struttura letteraria e metodo critico*. Messina, D'Anna, 1967.

516. M. PARENT, 'Cohérence et résonance stylistiques d'après un poème de Valéry', *Travaux de Linguistique et de Littérature*, 1965, pp. 93–115.

517. M. PARENT, *Francis Jammes: étude de langue et de style*. Paris, Les Belles Lettres, 1957.

518. M. PARENT, 'Les images dans *La Colline inspirée* de Barrès', *Travaux de Linguistique et de Littérature*, 1963, pp. 201–18.

519. M. PARENT, *Saint-John Perse et quelques devanciers*. Paris, Klincksieck, 1960.

520. J.-C. PARIENTE (ed.), *Essais sur le langage*. Paris, Editions de Minuit, 1969.

521. S. M. PARRISH, 'Computers and the muse of literature'. In 144.

522. R. PASCAL, 'Tense and novel', *Modern Language Review*, 1962, pp. 1–11.

523. J. PAULHAN, *Petite préface à toute critique*. Paris, Editions de Minuit, 1951.

524. N. PAXTON, *The Development of Mallarmé's prose style*. Genève, Droz, 1968.

525. T. H. PEAR, 'The place of imagery in mental processes', *Bulletin of the John Rylands Library*, 1937, pp. 193–214.

526. R. H. PEARCE (ed.), *Experience in the novel*. New York, Columbia U.P., 1968.

527. S. PEPYS, *The diary of Samuel Pepys*. London, Bell; Berkeley and Los Angeles, University of California Press, 1970–

528. W. PERCY, 'Metaphor as mistake', *Sewanee Review*, 1958, pp. 79–99.

529. L. PERRINE, *Sound and sense*. New York, Harcourt, 1969.

530. G. PICON, *L'usage de la lecture*, 3 vols. Paris, Mercure de France, 1961–3.

531. F. PORCHÉ, *Paul Valéry et la poésie pure*. Paris, Lesage, 1926.

532. 'A portrait of the artist as a midwife: Lucien Goldmann and the "transindividual" subject', *Times Literary Supplement*, no. 3,639 (1971), pp. 1465–6.

532B R. POSNER, 'The use and abuse of stylistic statistics', *Archivum Linguisticum*, 1963, pp. 111–39.

533. J. POUILLON, *Temps et roman*. Paris, Gallimard, 1946.

534. G. POULET, *Etudes sur le temps humain*, 4 vols. Edinburgh, U.P., 1949 (Vol. 1). Paris, Plon, 1952–68 (Vols. 2–4).

535. G. POULET, *Les métamorphoses du cercle*. Paris, Plon, 1961.

536. G. POULET, 'Phénoménologie de la conscience critique'. In 549.

537. G. POULET, 'Victor Hugo'. In 534.

538. G. POULET (ed.), *Les chemins actuels de la critique*. Paris, Plon, 1967.

539. D. W. PRALL, *Aesthetic analysis*. New York, Cromwell, 1936.

540. *Preprints of papers for the 9th International Congress of Linguists*. Cambridge, Mass., M.I.T. Pr., 1962.

541. J. PRÉVOST, *Baudelaire*. Paris, Mercure de France, 1953.

542. L. PRIESTLEY, 'Reprise constructions in the *Song of Roland*', *Archivum Linguisticum*, 1950, pp. 144–57.

543. M. E. PRIOR, *The language of tragedy*. New York, Columbia U.P., 1947.
544. 'Problèmes d'expression', *Revue des Sciences Humaines*, 1971, pp. 7–52.
545. *Proceedings of the Ninth International Congress of Linguists*. The Hague, Mouton, 1964.
546. V. J. PROPP, *Morphologie du conte*. Paris, Seuil, 1970. [See 670.]
547. M. PROUST, *Contre Sainte-Beuve*. *Paris, Gallimard, 1954, and Paris, Gallimard (Bibliothèque de la Pléade), 1971.
548. M. PROUST, *Pastiches et mélanges*. Paris, N.R.F., 1919.
549. *Quatre conférences sur la 'Nouvelle critique'*. Torino, Soc. Ediz. Internazionale, 1968. [Suppl. to *Studi Francesi*, no. 34 (1968).]
550. B. QUEMADA, *Matériaux pour l'histoire du vocabulaire français*. Paris, Les Belles Lettres, 1959–
551. B. QUEMADA (ed.), *Documents pour l'étude de la langue littéraire*, Vols. 1–7. Paris, Larousse, 1965–71. [1: *Les Fleurs du Mal*; 2: *Le Cid*; 3: *Phèdre*; 4: *Polyeucte*; 5: *Calligrammes*; 6: *Andromaque*; 7: *Cinna*.]
551B R. QUENEAU, *Exercices de style*. Paris, Gallimard, 1947.
552. W. V. O. QUINE, *Word and object*. Cambridge, Mass., Technology Pr., 1960.
553. J. RABAN, *The society of the poem*. London, Harrap, 1971.
554. N. RABKIN (ed.), *Reinterpretations of Elizabethan drama*. New York, Columbia U.P., 1969.
555. P. RAHV, 'Fiction and the criticism of fiction', *Kenyon Review*, 1956, pp. 276–99.
556. P. RAHV, *Image and idea*. Norfolk, Conn., New Directions, 1949.
557. J. C. RANSOM, *The new criticism*. Norfolk, Conn., New Directions, 1941.
558. J. C. RANSOM, 'The understanding of fiction'. *Kenyon Review*, 1950, pp. 189–218.
559. J. B. RATERMANIS, 'A propos de l'harmonie des vers', *Philological Quarterly*, 1951, pp. 194–205.
560. H. READ, 'The style of criticism'. In 76.
561. P. REBOUX and C. MULLER, *A la manière de* . . ., 3 vols. Paris, Grasset, definitive ed. 1942.

562. G. REES, '[Review of] G. APOLLINAIRE: *Calligrammes, Concordances, Index et Relevés statistiques*', *French Studies*, 1971, p. 483. [Review of 551 (Vol. 5).]

563. N. F. REGALADO, *Poetic patterns in Rutebeuf*. New Haven, Yale U.P., 1970.

564. M. REMACLE, 'Analyse du sonnet de Ronsard *Comme on voit sur la branche ...*', *Cahiers d'Analyse Textuelle*, 1959, pp. 15–54.

564B *Review of English Literature*, 1965, no. 2. [Essays on style.]

565. *Revue de l'Organisation Internationale pour l'Etude des Langues Anciennes par ordinateur*. Liège, l'Organisation, 1970–

566. J. RICARDOU, *Pour une théorie du nouveau roman*. Paris, Seuil, 1971.

567. J. RICARDOU, *Problèmes du nouveau roman*. Paris, Seuil, 1967.

568. J.-P. RICHARD, 'Fadeur de Verlaine'. In 570.

569. J.-P. RICHARD, *Littérature et sensation*. Paris, Seuil, 1954.

570. J.-P. RICHARD, *Poésie et profondeur*. Paris, Seuil, 1955.

571. J.-P. RICHARD, 'Quelques aspects nouveaux de la critique littéraire en France', *Français dans le Monde*, no. 15 (1963), pp. 2–9.

572. J.-P. RICHARD, 'Sainte-Beuve et l'expérience critique'. In 538.

573. J.-P. RICHARD, *L'univers imaginaire de Mallarmé*. Paris, Seuil, 1962.

574. I. A. RICHARDS, *How to read a page*. New York, Norton, 1942.

575. I. A. RICHARDS, *Interpretation in teaching*. New York, Harcourt, 1938. London, Routledge, 1938.

576. I. A. RICHARDS, 'Jakobson's Shakespeare. The subliminal structures of a sonnet', *Times Literary Supplement*, no. 3,561 (1970), pp. 589–90.

577. I. A. RICHARDS, *The philosophy of rhetoric*. London, Oxford U.P., 1937.

578. I. A. RICHARDS, 'Poetic process and literary analysis'. In 128.

579. I. A. RICHARDS, *Practical criticism*. New York, Harcourt, 1929. *London, Routledge, paperback ed. 1964.

580. I. A. RICHARDS, *Principles of literary criticism*. London, Kegan Paul, 1924. *London, Routledge, 2nd ed. reprinted, paperback 1960.

581. I. A. RICHARDS, *Speculative instruments*. London, Routledge, 1955.

582. M. RIFFATERRE, 'Comment décrire le style de Chateaubriand?' *Romanic Review*, 1962, pp. 128–38. [Reviews.]

583. M. RIFFATERRE, 'Criteria for style analysis', *Word*, 1959, pp. 154–74.

584. M. RIFFATERRE, 'Describing poetic structures: two approaches to Baudelaire's *Les Chats*', *Yale French Studies*, 1966, pp. 200–42.

585. M. RIFFATERRE, *Essais de stylistique structurale*. Paris, Flammarion, 1971.

585B M. RIFFATERRE, 'L'étude stylistique des formes littéraires conventionnelles', *French Review*, 1964, pp. 3–14.

586. M. RIFFATERRE, 'Fonctions du cliché dans la prose littéraire', *Cahiers de l'Association Internationale des Etudes Françaises*, 1964, pp. 81–95.

587. M. RIFFATERRE, 'La métaphore filée dans la poésie surréaliste', *Langue Française*, no. 3 (1969), pp. 46–60.

587B M. RIFFATERRE, 'Le poème comme représentation', *Poétique*, 1970, pp. 401–18.

588. M. RIFFATERRE, 'La poésie métaphysique de Victor Hugo', *Romanic Review*, 1960, pp. 268–76.

589. M. RIFFATERRE, 'Problèmes d'analyse du style littéraire', *Romance Philology*, 1960–61, pp. 216–27. [Review of 517.]

590. M. RIFFATERRE, 'Réponse à M. Spitzer: sur la méthode stylistique', *Modern Language Notes*, 1958, pp. 474–80.

590B M. RIFFATERRE, *Le style des 'Pléiades' de Gobineau: essais d'application d'une méthode stylistique*. New York, Columbia U.P., 1957.

591. M. RIFFATERRE, 'Stylistic context', *Word*, 1960, pp. 207–218.

592. M. RIFFATERRE, 'Sur un singulier d'André Gide', *Français Moderne*, 1955, pp. 39–43.

593. M. RIFFATERRE, 'La vision hallucinatoire chez Victor Hugo', *Modern Language Notes*, 1963, pp. 225–41.

594. W. RIGHTER, *Logic and criticism*. London, Routledge, 1963.
595. K. RINEHART, 'The structure of *Madame Bovary*', *French Review*, 1957–8, pp. 300–6.
596. M. ROBERT, *L'ancien et le nouveau*. Paris, Grasset, 1963.
597. M. E. ROBERTSON, *L'épithète dans les oeuvres lyriques de Victor Hugo publiées avant l'exil*. Paris, Jouve, 1926.
598. R. H. ROBINS, *General linguistics: an introductory survey*. London, Longmans, 1964.
599. W. W. ROBSON, *Critical essays*. London, Routledge, 1966.
600. A. ROCHETTE, *L'alexandrin chez Victor Hugo*. Paris, Hachette, 1911.
601. A. RODWAY, 'What the critics really need', *Twentieth Century*, 1962–3, pp. 153–63.
602. C. ROSEN, 'Art has its reasons', *New York Review of Books*, vol. 16, no. 11 (1971), pp. 32–8. [Reviews.]
603. D. ROSS, *The style of Thoreau's 'Walden'*. Unpublished doctoral dissertation, Michigan University, 1967. Résumé in *Dissertation Abstracts*, 1968, 5069 A.
604. J. ROUSSET, *Forme et signification*. Paris, Corti, 1962.
605. J. ROUSSET, '*Madame Bovary* ou Le livre sur rien'. In 604.
606. J. ROUSSET, 'Positions, distances, perspectives dans *Salammbô*', *Poétique*, no. 2 (1971), pp. 145–54.
607. J. ROUSSET, 'Les réalités formelles de l'oeuvre'. In 538.
608. N. RUWET, 'L'analyse structurale de la poésie', *Linguistics*, 1963, pp. 38–59.
609. N. RUWET, 'Analyse structurale d'un poème français: un sonnet de Louise Labé', *Linguistics*, no. 3 (1964), pp. 62–83.
610. N. RUWET, 'Limites de l'analyse linguistique en poétique', *Langages*, no. 12 (1968), pp. 56–70.
611. G. SAINTSBURY, *A history of criticism and literary taste in Europe*, 3 vols. Edinburgh, Blackwood, 1900–4.
612. J. SAMSON, *Paul Claudel, poète–musicien*. Genève, Editions du Milieu du Monde, 1947.
613. S. SAPORTA, 'The application of linguistics to the study of poetic language'. In 629.
614. J.-P. SARTRE, *L'imaginaire*. Paris, N.R.F., 1940.

615. J.-P. SARTRE, '*Qu'est-ce que la littérature?*' In *616. Also published separately by Gallimard, 1965.
616. J.-P. SARTRE, *Situations, II*. Paris, Gallimard, 1948.
617. J.-P. SARTRE, *Situations, IV*. Paris, Gallimard, 1964.
618. H. A. SAUERWEIN, *Agrippa d'Aubigné's 'Les Tragiques': a study in structure and poetic method*. Baltimore, Johns Hopkins Pr., 1953.
619. A. SAURO, *La lingua poetica in Francia dal Romanticismo al Simbolismo*. Bari, Adriatica, 1954.
619B F. de SAUSSURE, *Cours de linguistique générale*. Paris, Payot, 5th ed. 1955.
620. R. A. SAYCE, 'Literature and language', *Essays in Criticism*, 1957, pp. 119–33.
621. R. A. SAYCE, *Style in French prose*. London, Oxford U.P., 1953.
622. F. SCARFE, 'A stylistic interpretation of Rimbaud', *Archivum Linguisticum*, 1951, pp. 166–92.
623. M. SCHAETTEL, 'Rythme et structure, images formelles et dynamiques dans *Clair de lune* de Verlaine', *Revue des Sciences Humaines*, 1968, pp. 259–66.
624. F. SCHALK (ed.), *Ideen und Formen: Festschrift für Hugo Friedrich*. Frankfurt, Klostermann, 1965.
625. E. SCHANZER, 'Atavism and anticipation in Shakespeare's style', *Essays in Criticism*, 1957, pp. 242–56.
626. J. SCHERER, *L'expression littéraire dans l'oeuvre de Mallarmé*. Paris, Droz, 1947.
627. M. SCHORER, 'Technique as discovery', *Hudson Review*, 1948, pp. 67–87. Also in *506.
628. M. SCHORER (ed.), *Society and self in the novel*. New York, Columbia U.P., 1955.
629. T. A. SEBEOK (ed.), *Style in language*. Cambridge, Mass., Technology Pr., 1960.
630. G. G. SEDGEWICK, *Of irony*. Toronto, U.P., paperback ed. 1967.
631. *Semiotica*. The Hague, Mouton, 1969–
632. E. SEWELL, *The structure of poetry*. London, Routledge, 1951.
633. C. SHAPIRO (ed.), *Twelve original essays on great English novels*. Detroit, Wayne State U.P., 1960.

634. R. J. SHERRINGTON, 'Louise Roque and *L'Education sentimentale*', *French Studies*, 1971, pp. 427–36.

635. R. J. SHERRINGTON, *Three novels by Flaubert: a study of techniques.* Oxford, Clarendon Pr., 1970.

636. R. W. SHORT, 'The sentence structure of Henry James', *American Literature*, 1946, pp. 71–88.

637. F. SIMONE, 'Introduzione storica alla *nouvelle critique*'. In 549.

638. P. SOLLERS, 'Niveaux sémantiques d'un texte moderne'. In 214.

639. P. SOLLERS, 'Programme', *Tel Quel*, no. 31 (1967), pp. 3–7.

640. H. H. SOMERS, *Analyse statistique du style.* Louvain, Neuwelaerts, 1967. [Vol. 2. of *Analyse mathémathique du langage.*]

641. E. SOURIAU, *La correspondance des arts.* Paris, Flammarion, 1947.

642. E. SOURIAU, *Pensée vivante et perfection formelle.* Paris, Hachette, 1925.

643. R. de SOUZA, 'Les origines du vers moderne; la rythmique de Ronsard', *Mercure de France*, no. 175 (1924), pp. 89–121.

643B J. H. A. SPARROW, *Sense and poetry.* London, Constable, 1934.

644. J. SPENCER (ed.), *Linguistics and style.* London, Oxford U.P., 1964.

645. A. SPIRE, *Plaisir poétique et plaisir musculaire.* Paris, Corti, 1949.

646. L. SPITZER, *Essays on English and American literature.* Princeton, U.P., 1962.

647. L. SPITZER, 'Etude ahistorique d'un texte: *Ballade des dames du temps jadis*', *Modern Language Quarterly*, 1940, pp. 7–22.

648. L. SPITZER, 'Les études de style et les différents pays'. In 380.

649. L. SPITZER, 'Explication linguistique et littéraire de deux textes français', *Français Moderne*, 1936, pp. 37–48.

650. L. SPITZER, 'Language of poetry'. In 13.

651. L. SPITZER, 'Linguistic perspectivism in the *Don Quijote*'. In 652.

652. L. SPITZER, *Linguistics and literary history: essays in stylistics*. Princeton, U.P., 1948.

653. L. SPITZER, *A method of interpreting literature*. Northampton, Mass., Smith College, 1949.

653. L. SPITZER, *A method of interpreting literature*. Northamp- "*Pléïades*" *de Gobineau*', *Modern Language Notes*, 1958, pp. 68–74. [Review of 590B.]

654. L. SPITZER, '[Review of] *Style in the French Novel*. By Stephen Ullmann', *Comparative Literature*, 1958, pp. 368–71.

655. L. SPITZER, *Romanische Literaturstudien, 1936–1956*. Tübingen, Niemeyer, 1959.

656. L. SPITZER, *Stilstudien*, 2 vols. München, Hueber, 1928.

657. L. SPITZER, 'The style of Diderot'. In 652.

658. L. SPITZER, 'Les théories de la stylistique', *Français Moderne*, 1952, pp. 165–8.

659. C. SPURGEON, *Shakespeare's imagery, and what it tells us*. Cambridge, U.P., 1935.

659B E. STANKIEWICZ, 'Linguistics and the study of poetic language'. In 629.

660. E. G. STANLEY, 'Old English poetic diction and the interpretation of *The Wanderer*, *The Seafarer*, and *The Penitent's prayer*', *Anglia*, 1955, pp. 413–66.

661. J. STAROBINSKI, *Jean-Jacques Rousseau*. Paris, Plon, 1957.

662. J. STAROBINSKI, *L'oeil vivant*. Paris, Gallimard, 1961.

663. J. STAROBINSKI, 'La relation critique'. In 549.

664. J. STAROBINSKI, 'Stendhal pseudonyme'. In 662.

665. J. STAROBINSKI, 'La stylistique et ses méthodes: Leo Spitzer', *Critique*, 1964, pp. 579–97.

666. A. STEIN, 'Donne's prosody', *Kenyon Review*, 1956, pp. 439–43.

667. A. STEIN, 'A note on meter', *Kenyon Review*, 1956, pp. 451–60.

668. A. STORR, 'The meaning of music', *Times Literary Supplement*, no. 3,586 (1970), pp. 1363–4.

669. *Stratford-upon-Avon Studies, 12: Contemporary Criticism*. London, Arnold, 1970.

670. 'The study of verbalized content', *Times Literary Supplement*, no. 3,569 (1970), pp. 807–8. [Review of 2nd Russian edition of 546.]

671. J. SVARTVIK, 'Computational linguistics comes of age', *Times Literary Supplement*, no. 3,568 (1970), pp. 821–3.

672. L. C. SYKES, 'Il y a une grandeur dans La Fontaine'. In J. C. IRESON (ed.), *Currents of thought in French literature. Essays in memory of G. T. Clapton.* Oxford, Blackwell, 1965.

673. D. R. TALLENTIRE, 'The mathematics of style', *Times Literary Supplement*, no. 3,624 (1971), p. 973–4.

674. J. A. G. TANS, 'La poétique de l'eau et de la lumière d'après l'oeuvre d'Albert Camus'. In 278.

675. A. TATE, *Collected essays.* Denver, Swallow, 1959.

676. A. TATE, 'Homage to St. John Perse', *Nine*, 1949–50, pp. 78–80.

677. A. TATE, 'Techniques of fiction', *Sewanee Review*, 1944, pp. 210–25.

678. A. TATE (ed.), *The language of poetry*. Princeton, U.P., 1942.

679. *Tel Quel*. Paris, Seuil, 1960–

680. B. TERRACINI, 'Analisi del concetto di lingua letteraria', *Cultura Neolatina*, 1956, pp. 9–31.

681. A. THIBAUDET, *Physiologie de la critique*. Paris, La Nouvelle Revue Critique, 1930.

682. A. THIBAUDET, *Réflexions sur le roman*. Paris, Gallimard, 1938.

682B J. P. THORNE, 'Generative grammar and stylistic analysis'. In J. LYONS (ed.), *New horizons in linguistics*. Harmondsworth, Penguin Books, 1970.

683. J. P. THORNE, 'Stylistics and generative grammars', *Journal of Linguistics*, 1965, pp. 49–59.

684. G. TILLOTSON (ed.), *Essays and studies, 1951*. London, Murray, 1951.

685. T. TODOROV, 'Les catégories du récit littéraire', *Communications*, no. 8 (1966), pp. 125–51.

686. T. TODOROV, 'La grammaire du récit', **Langages*, no. 12 (1968), pp. 94–102. Also in 689.

687. T. TODOROV, *Littérature et signification*. Paris, Larousse, 1967.

688. T. TODOROV, 'Poétique'. In 183.

689. T. TODOROV, *Poétique de la prose*. Paris, Seuil, 1971.

690. T. TODOROV (ed.), *Théorie de la littérature. Textes des formalistes russes*. Paris, Seuil, 1965.

691. K. TOGEBY, 'Littérature et linguistique', *Orbis Litterarum*, 1967, pp. 45–8.

692. *To honour Roman Jakobson*, Vols. 1, 2 & 3. The Hague, Mouton, 1967.

693. G. L. TRAGER and H. L. SMITH, *An outline of English structure*. Washington, American Council of Learned Societies, 3rd printing 1957.

694. R. TUVE, *Elizabethan and metaphysical imagery*. Chicago, U.P., 1947.

695. A. UBERSFELD, 'Structures du théâtre de Dumas'. In 409.

696. K. D. UITTI, *Linguistics and literary theory*. New York, Prentice-Hall, 1969.

697. S. ULLMANN, 'The concept of meaning in linguistics', *Archivum Linguisticum*, 1956, pp. 12–20.

698. S. ULLMANN, *The image in the modern French novel*. Cambridge, U.P., 1960.

698B S. ULLMANN, *Language and style*. Oxford, Blackwell, 1964.

699. S. ULLMANN, *Précis de sémantique française*. Bern, Francke, 1952.

700. S. ULLMANN, *The principles of semantics*. Glasgow, Jackson, 2nd ed. 1957.

701. S. ULLMANN, 'Psychologie et stylistique', *Journal de Psychologie*, 1953, pp. 133–56.

702. S. ULLMAN, '[Review of] *Cahiers de lexicologie*, Vols. x–xi (1967)', *French Studies*, 1970, pp. 425–7.

703. S. ULLMANN, *Semantics, an introduction to the science of meaning*. Oxford, Blackwell, 1962.

704. S. ULLMANN, *Style in the French novel*. Cambridge, U.P., 1957.

705. W. M. URBAN, *Language and reality*. London, Allen & Unwin, 1939.

706. P. VALÉRY, 'Au sujet d'Adonis'. In 707 (Vol. 1).

707. P. VALÉRY, *Oeuvres*, 2 vols. Paris, Gallimard, 1957–60.

708. P. VALÉRY, 'Poésie et pensée abstraite'. In 710.

709. P. VALÉRY, *Variété III*. Paris, N.R.F., 1936.

710. P. VALÉRY, *Variété V*. Paris, Gallimard, 1944.

710B B. P. VALESIO, *Strutture dell'allitterazione*. Bologna, Zanichelli, 1967.

711. E. VANCE, 'Spatial structure in the *Chanson de Roland*', *Modern Language Notes*, 1967, pp. 604–23.

712. D. VAN GHENT, *The English novel; form and function*. New York, Rinehart, 1953.

713. H. VENDLER '[Review of] *Essays on style and language*. Edited by R. FOWLER', *Essays in Criticism*, 1966, pp. 457–463. [Review of 219.]

714. J. VENDRYES, *Le langage*. Paris, La Renaissance du Livre, 1921.

715. G. VICAIRE and H. BEAUCAIRE, *Les déliquescences, poèmes décadents d'Adoré Floupette*. Paris, Vanier, 1885.

716. B. VICKERS, *Classical rhetoric in English poetry*. London, Macmillan, 1970.

717. A. VIGUIER, 'Etudes lexicologiques et études littéraires', *Revue des Sciences Humaines*, 1971, pp. 7–22.

718. J. P. VINAY and J. DARBELNET, *Stylistique comparée du français et de l'anglais*. London, Harrap, 1958.

719. 'Les visages de la critique depuis 1920', *Cahiers de l'Association Internationale des Etudes Françaises*, 1964, pp. 111–79.

720. R. S. WACHAL, 'On using a computer'. In 392.

721. R.-L. WAGNER, 'Analyse des énoncés et des textes'. In 724.

722. R.-L. WAGNER, '*Langue poétique* (du quantitatif au qualificatif)'. In C. BRUNEAU (ed.), *Studia romanica: Gedenkschrift für E. Lerch*. Stuttgart, Port, 1955.

723. R.-L. WAGNER, *Supplément bibliographique à l'introduction à la linguistique française, 1947–1953*. Genève, Droz, 1955.

724. R.-L. WAGNER, *Les vocabulaires français*, Vol. 2. Paris, Didier, 1970.

725. K. WAIS, 'Valeur de l'oeuvre, mesure de l'homme'. In 549.

726. R. P. WARREN, 'Pure and impure poetry', *Kenyon Review*, 1943, pp. 228–54.

727. E. R. WASSERMAN, *The finer tone: Keats' major poems*. Baltimore, Johns Hopkins Pr., 1953.

728. I. WATT, 'The comic syntax of *Tristram Shandy*'. In 11.

729. I. WATT, 'The first paragraph of *The Ambassadors*: an explication', *Essays in Criticism*, 1960, pp. 250–74.

730. J. WEBBER, *Contrary music: the prose style of John Donne.* Madison, Wisconsin U.P., 1963.

731. H. WEBER, *La création poétique au XVIe siècle en France*, 2 vols. Paris, Nizet, 1956.

732. J.-P. WEBER, *Domaines thématiques.* Paris, Gallimard, 1963.

733. J.-P. WEBER, *Genèse de l'oeuvre poétique.* Paris, Gallimard, 1961.

734. J.-P. WEBER, *Néo-critique et paléo-critique.* Paris, Pauvert, 1966.

735. H. WEINRICH, *Tempus*, Stuttgart, Kohlhammer, 1964.

735B H. WEINRICH, 'Tense and time', *Archivum Linguisticum*, 1970, pp. 31–42.

736. A. WELLEK, 'Der Sprachgeist als Doppelempfinder', *Zeitschrift für Ästhetik*, 1931, pp. 226–62.

737. R. WELLEK, 'Closing statement'. In 629.

738. R. WELLEK, 'The concept of evolution in literary history'. In 739.

739. R. WELLEK, *Concepts of criticism.* New Haven, Yale U.P., 1963.

740. R. WELLEK, 'Concepts of form and structure in twentieth century criticism', *Neophilologus*, 1958, pp. 2–11.

741. R. WELLEK, *A history of modern criticism*, 4 vols. London, Cape, 1955–66.

742. R. WELLEK, 'The main trends of twentieth-century criticism'. In 739.

743. R. WELLEK, 'The mode of existence of a literary work of art', *Southern Review*, 1941–2, pp. 735–54.

744. R. WELLEK and A. WARREN, *Theory of literature.* London, Cape, 1949. *Harmondsworth, Penguin Books, 3rd ed. 1963.

745. R. WELLS, 'Nominal and verbal style'. In 629.

746. P. M. WETHERILL, 'Flaubert et les distortions de la critique moderne', *Symposium*, 1971, pp. 271–9.

747. P. M. WETHERILL, '*Madame Bovary's* blind man. Symbolism in Flaubert', *Romanic Review*, 1970, pp. 35–42.

748. P. M. WETHERILL, 'Note sur la thématique de *Rouge et Noir.* Le père Sorel et Madame de Rênal', *Stendhal Club*, 1970, pp. 297–300.

749. P. M. WETHERILL, 'A reading of *Eugénie Grandet*', *Modern Languages*, 1971, pp. 166–76.

750. P. M. WETHERILL, 'Le style des thèmes. Etude sur le dernier manuscrit autographe de *l'Education Sentimentale*', *Zeitschrift für Französische Sprache und Literatur*, 1971, pp. 308–51 and 1972, pp. 1–52.

751. P. J. WEXLER, 'Distich and sentence in Corneille and Racine'. In 219.

752. P. WHEELWRIGHT, *Metaphor & reality.* Bloomington, Indiana U.P., 1962.

753. P. WHEELWRIGHT, 'On the semantics of poetry', *Kenyon Review*, 1940, pp. 263–83. Also in *128.

754. J. J. WHITE, *Mythology in the modern novel.* Princeton, U.P., 1972.

755. H. WHITEHALL, 'From linguistics to criticism', *Kenyon Review*, 1956, pp. 411–21.

756. H. WHITEHALL and others, 'English verse and what it sounds like', *Kenyon Review*, 1956, pp. 411–77. [Essays by H. WHITEHALL, S. CHATMAN, A. STEIN and J. C. RANSOM.]

757. C. B. WILLIAMS, 'A note on the statistical analysis of sentence-length as a criterion of literary style'. In 172.

758. C. B. WILLIAMS, *Style and vocabulary.* London, Griffin, 1970.

759. R. WILLIAMS, *Culture and society.* Harmondsworth, Penguin Books, paperback ed. 1971.

760. R. WILLIAMS, *The long revolution.* Harmondsworth, Penguin Books, paperback ed., 1965.

761. R. M. WILSON (ed.), *Essays and studies, 1966.* London, Murray, 1966.

762. W. K. WIMSATT, *Hateful contraries.* Lexington, Kentucky U.P., 1965.

763. W. K. WIMSATT, 'One relation of rhyme to reason: Alexander Pope', *Modern Language Quarterly*, 1944, pp. 323–38. Also in *766.

764. W. K. WIMSATT, *Philosophic words.* New Haven, Yale U.P., 1948.

765. W. K. WIMSATT, 'Style as meaning'. In 128.

766. W. K. WIMSATT, *The verbal icon.* New York, Noonday Pr., 1958. London, Methuen, 1970.

767. W. K. WIMSATT, 'Verbal style: logical and counterlogical', **Publications of the Modern Language Association of America*, 1950, pp. 5–20. Also in 766.

768. W. K. WIMSATT and M. C. BEARDSLEY, 'The affective fallacy', *Sewanee Review*, 1949, pp. 31–55.

769. W. K. WIMSATT and M. C. BEARDSLEY, 'The concept of meter: an exercise in abstraction', *Publications of the Modern Language Association of America*, 1959, pp. 585–598.

770. W. WINTER, 'Styles as dialects'. In 172.

771. Y. WINTERS, *The anatomy of nonsense*. Norfolk, Conn., New Directions, 1943. Republished in *In defence of reason*. Denver, U.P., 1947.

772. Y. WINTERS, *The function of criticism*. London, Routledge, paperback ed. 1967.

773. R. A. WISBEY, 'The computer and literary studies'. In R. REED (ed.), *Symposium on printing*. Leeds, Philosophical & Literary Society, 1971.

774. R. A. WISBEY, *Report on the first five years of the Literary and Linguistic Computing Centre in Cambridge*. Cambridge, U.P., 1969.

775. R. A. WISBEY (ed.), *The computer in literary and linguistic research*. Cambridge, U.P., 1971.

776. C. L. WRENN and G. BULLOUGH (eds.), *English studies today. 1st series*. London, Oxford. U.P., 1951.

777. A. J. WRIGHT, *Paul Verlaine and the musicians*. Unpublished thesis, Columbia University, 1950.

778. G. U. YULE, *The statistical study of literary vocabulary*. Cambridge, U.P., 1944.

779. E. M. ZIMMERMANN, 'Le rôle de Swann et de la société dans l'acte de création proustien', *Studi Francesi*, 1971, pp. 433–42.

780. G. K. ZIPF, 'The meaning-frequency relationship of words', *Journal of General Psychology*, 1945, pp. 251–6.

781. G. K. ZIPF, 'The repetition of words, time-perspective and semantic balance', *Journal of General Psychology*, 1945, pp. 127–48.

782. P. ZUMTHOR, '[Extract from] *Langue et techniques poétiques à l'époque romane (XIe–XIIIe s.)*'. In 277.

783. P. ZUMTHOR, *Langue et techniques poétiques à l'époque romane (XIe–XIIIe s.)*. Paris, Klincksieck, 1963.
784. P. ZUMTHOR, 'Le Moyen Age de Victor Hugo'. In V. HUGO, *Oeuvres complètes*, Vol. 4. Paris, Club Français du Livre, 1967.
785. P. ZUMTHOR, 'Stylistique et poétique'. In 278.
786. P. ZUMTHOR, *Victor Hugo, poète de Satan*. Paris, Laffont, 1946.

INDEX

This index contains references to selected subjects and *all* proper names in the text and bibliography. Bibliographical entry numbers and titles of literary works have been indexed as name-references to the writers concerned.